Women's Sexualities and Masculinities in a Globalizing Asia

COMPARATIVE FEMINIST STUDIES SERIES
Chandra Talpade Mohanty, Series Editor

PUBLISHED BY PALGRAVE MACMILLAN:

Sexuality, Obscenity, Community: Women, Muslims, and the Hindu Public in Colonial India
by Charu Gupta

Twenty-First-Century Feminist Classrooms: Pedagogies of Identity and Difference
edited by Amie A. Macdonald and Susan Sánchez-Casal

Reading across Borders: Storytelling and Knowledges of Resistance
by Shari Stone-Mediatore

Made in India: Decolonizations, Queer Sexualities, Trans/national Projects
by Suparna Bhaskaran

Dialogue and Difference: Feminisms Challenge Globalization
edited by Marguerite Waller and Sylvia Marcos

Engendering Human Rights: Cultural and Socio-Economic Realities in Africa
edited by Obioma Nnaemeka and Joy Ezeilo

Women's Sexualities and Masculinities in a Globalizing Asia
edited by Saskia E. Wieringa, Evelyn Blackwood, and Abha Bhaiya

Gender, Race, and Nationalism in Contemporary Black Politics
by Nikol G. Alexander-Floyd

Gender, Identity, and Imperialism: Women Development Workers in Pakistan
by Nancy Cook

Transnational Feminism in Film and Media
edited by Katarzyna Marciniak, Anikó Imre, and Áine O'Healy

Women's Sexualities and Masculinities in a Globalizing Asia

Edited by

Saskia E. Wieringa, Evelyn Blackwood, and Abha Bhaiya

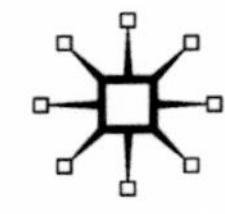

WOMEN'S SEXUALITIES AND MASCULINITIES IN A GLOBALIZING ASIA

First published in hardcover in 2007 by
PALGRAVE MACMILLAN®
in the United States—a division of St. Martin's Press LLC,
175 Fifth Avenue, New York, NY 10010.

Where this book is distributed in the UK, Europe and the rest of the world, this is by Palgrave Macmillan, a division of Macmillan Publishers Limited, registered in England, company number 785998, of Houndmills, Basingstoke, Hampshire RG21 6XS.

Palgrave Macmillan is the global academic imprint of the above companies and has companies and representatives throughout the world.

Palgrave® and Macmillan® are registered trademarks in the United States, the United Kingdom, Europe and other countries.

ISBN-13: 978–0–203–61748-3

Library of Congress Cataloging-in-Publication Data

Women's sexualities and masculinities in a globalizing Asia / edited by Saskia E. Wieringa, Evelyn Blackwood, and Abha Bhaiya.
p. cm.—(Comparative feminist studies)
Includes bibliographical references and index.
ISBN 1–4039–7768–2 (alk. paper)
1. Lesbianism—Asia. 2. Lesbians—Asia—Social conditions. I. Wieringa, Saskia, 1950– II. Blackwood, Evelyn. III. Bhaiya, Abha.

HQ75.6.A75W66 2007
306.76'63095—dc22 2006051141

A catalogue record for this book is available from the British Library.

Design by Newgen Imaging Systems (P) Ltd., Chennai, India.

First PALGRAVE MACMILLAN paperback edition: May 2009

10 9 8 7 6 5 4 3 2 1

Printed in the United States of America.

Transferred to Digital Printing in 2009.

Contents

Part III Female Masculinities

Part IV Silencing and Modes of Invisibility

List of Figures

Series Editor's Foreword

The Comparative Feminist Studies (CFS) series foregrounds writing, organizing, and reflection on feminist trajectories across the historical and cultural borders of nation-states. It takes up fundamental analytic and political issues involved in the cross-cultural production of knowledge about women and feminism, examining the politics of scholarship and knowledge in relation to feminist organizing and social movements. Drawing on feminist thinking in a number of fields, the CFS series targets innovative, comparative feminist scholarship, pedagogical and curricular strategies, and community organizing and political education. It explores and engenders a comparative feminist praxis that addresses some of the most urgent questions facing progressive, critical thinkers and activists today. *Women's Sexualities and Masculinities in a Globalizing Asia* is an original and much-needed contribution to comparative, postcolonial, and transnational feminist scholarship and praxis.

Though over the past many decades, feminists across the globe have been variously successful, we have inherited a number of the challenges our mothers and grandmothers faced. It cannot be denied that there are also new challenges to face as we attempt to make sense of a world indelibly marked by the failure of postcolonial capitalist and communist nation-states to provide for the social, economic, spiritual, and psychic needs of the majority of the world's population. In the year 2006, we are in the midst of imperial wars in Lebanon, Iraq, Afghanistan, and elsewhere. Globalization has come to represent the interests of corporations and the free market rather than self-determination and freedom from political, cultural, and economic domination for all the peoples of the world. The U.S. Empire building project alongside the dominance of corporate capitalism kills, disenfranchises, and impoverishes women everywhere. War and militarization, environmental degradation, heterosexist State practices, religious fundamentalisms, and the exploitation of women's labor by capital, all pose profound challenges for feminists at this point in time. Recovering and remembering insurgent histories have never been so important as now—at a time marked by social amnesia, global consumer culture, and the worldwide mobilization of fascist notions of "national security."

These are some of the challenges the CFS series addresses. The series takes as its fundamental premise the need for feminist engagement with global as well as local ideological, economic, and political processes, and the urgency of transnational dialogue in building an ethical culture capable of withstanding and transforming the commodified and exploitative practices of globalized culture and economics. Individual volumes in the CFS series provide systemic and challenging interventions into the (still) largely Euro-Western feminist studies knowledge base, while simultaneously highlighting the work that can and needs to be done to envision and enact cross-cultural, multiracial feminist solidarity.

Intervening in a "global queer discourse" often predicated on northern definitions of gay, lesbian, and transgender identities and movements, *Women's Sexualities and Masculinities in a Globalizing Asia* crafts a transnational feminist praxis anchored in globalizing processes and the specificities of women's same-sex experiences in Asia. The collection thus carves an epistemological space for new definitions and analyses of women's same-sex experiences in the context of colonial legacies, cultural and geopolitical particularities, national and religious state practices, and gendered and sexual subjectivities. The volume centralizes the experiences, histories and socioeconomic realities of the everyday lives and sexual subjectivities of contemporary women and transgendered females identified in Indonesia, Sri Lanka, Japan, India, Thailand, and Hong Kong. As the editors state in the Introduction, "This intervention is an attempt to integrate into global sexualities discourse not only the experiences and practices of urban, educated women, but also the experiences of working-class lesbians and transgendered females, whose voices are rarely heard" (p. 2). The collection as a whole is explicitly grounded in a critique of the homogenizing use of the term "queer" in global queer studies, choosing to focus on the production of queer sexualities in the interstices of globalizing processes in contemporary Asian countries. Arguing that "rather than constituting a 'national imprint' or a 'global subculture,' same-sex communities and relationships are a product of historical legacies, for instance, folk tales of transgendered beings and deities who join male and female in one body (Natarajan; Wieringa, this volume), and particular gender regimes that create gender binaries, as well as specific forms and processes of nationalisms, fundamentalisms, (neo)colonialisms and globalization," (Chapter 1, p. 7, this original collection is a major contribution to scholarship on the postcolonial sexual subjectivities of Asian women and transgendered females in the context of globalization, national and religious state practices, and transnational feminist movements.

Chandra Talpade Mohanty
Series Editor
Ithaca, New York

Preface

Self-styled lesbian groups are hesitantly appearing in many Asian capitals. They are only the latest form that women's same-sex communities and relationships take and they mostly belong to the educated middle classes. The history of women's sexualities and masculinities in Asia and the diversity of their communities are mostly unknown. This collection brings together a wide range of contributions from several parts of Asia to fill that gap in our knowledge of sexualities and genders.

The introduction provides the setting in which women's sexualities and masculinities appear in Asia, focusing on the present-day process of globalization and the discourses that come with it. The first section addresses historical legacies, both in Japan and in India. The two contributions provide glimpses of literary, religious, and other transgendered practices the echoes of which reverberate into present times. In the second section we present three chapters dealing with the liminal and shifting spaces between heterosexual normativity and lesbian and transgender identities in Sri Lanka, Japan, and India. The next four chapters deal with one of the most typical forms women's same-sex sexualities take in Asia, that of butch-femme relations. The focus here is on the performativity of masculinity, both historically and in contemporary settings, in Thailand, Indonesia and Hong Kong. In the final section, the silence and invisibility in which women and masculine females express their affections for each other are discussed, focusing on India and Japan. This issue takes on particular salience in view of the growing visibility of lesbian activist groups and their connection to global lesbian and gay discourse.

This collection had a long period of gestation. Two of the editors, Evelyn Blackwood and Saskia E. Wieringa, organized a session on women's same-sex practices in Asia for the third conference of the International Association for the Study of Sexuality, Culture and Society (IASSCS) in Melbourne, Australia, in 2001. Both academics and activists joined the panels; the debates were lively, as this was the first time women's same-sex sexualities and female masculinities were discussed comparatively across various Asian contexts. Together with Abha Bhaiya, who joined us at the conference, we began work toward bringing out an anthology. In the long editing process, several activists dropped out, as the demands of activism and academic writing often clashed. Some new authors joined at the next IASSCS conference that was held in Johannesburg in 2003. To complete the book, we also invited contributions from other authors. The result is an anthology that draws from various disciplines (literary theory, anthropology, and history) and combines academic work with that of scholar activists.

During the long editing process the editorial team, working in three continents, managed to meet regularly, not only in Melbourne and Johannesburg, but also in Jakarta, Delhi, New York, Lafayette, Amsterdam, Dublin, and San Francisco. We are most indebted to all contributors who stayed with us in this process and who patiently kept revising their chapters. We thank each other for the continued faith in the project and for the strong support we gave each other. We are also grateful for the helpful and supportive comments received from the anonymous reviewers, which helped us in tightening the structure and in refining our arguments. The Department of Sociology and Anthropology at Purdue University provided support for travel and assistance in the preparation of the manuscript. In addition, Evelyn Blackwood would like to thank her partner, Diana Hardy, for her patience and unfailing support during this process and for being hostess during a long weekend in which Saskia and Evelyn developed the introductory chapter. Abha Bhaiya notes that some of her work has drawn its inspiration from the Single Women's action research project that was initiated by Jagori, a feminist group. Shanti and Maya have been significant in exploring issues of sex and sexualities in multiple workshops, night meetings, and intimate conversations with many single women, including poor and marginalized women from slums and villages.

This volume will be of interest to academics working on sexuality, transgender females, and women's same-sex relations in general and on Asia in particular. Activists will find many chapters of value that address the specifically Asian context in relation to the global rights discourse. The focus on indigenous and "local" practices and discourses may help counter those voices that accuse present day lesbians of importing Western values.

Saskia E. Wieringa
Evelyn Blackwood
Abha Bhaiya

Notes on Contributors

Abha Bhaiya is one of the founding members of Jagori, a feminist resource center founded in 1984 and based in Delhi, India. She has been active in women's movements for the last 25 years as an activist, feminist trainer, researcher, and campaigner for women's dignified place in society. She has actively contributed to the strengthening of feminist consciousness by training women from the most oppressed, marginalized, and subjugated class, caste, and marital backgrounds as feminist activists to work within their communities. Her engagement with issues of women's right to dignity, bodily integrity, sexuality, and freedom from all kinds of violence, including communal and military violence, have contributed to the discourse and practices around these issues within women's movements in the South Asian subcontinent. Community mobilization and building women's grassroots leadership has been central to her work.

Evelyn Blackwood is Associate Professor in anthropology and women's studies at Purdue University. She has written extensively on topics in sexuality, gender, and kinship studies, including work on Native American female two-spirits, gender transgression in colonial and postcolonial Indonesia, gender and power, and matrilineal kinship. Her monograph on the Minangkabau of West Sumatra, Indonesia, is entitled *Webs of Power: Women, Kin and Community in a Sumatran Village* (2000). She is co-editor with Saskia Wieringa of the award-winning anthology *Female Desires: Same-sex Relations and Transgender Practices Across Cultures* (1999). She is also editor of *The Many Faces of Homosexuality: Anthropology and Homosexual Behavior* (1986). Her forthcoming book on tomboi and femme subjectivities in West Sumatra, *Falling into the Lesbi World: Desire and Difference in Indonesia*, will be available in 2010.

Sharyn Graham Davies is Senior Lecturer in the School of Social Sciences at Auckland University of Technology. Her research focuses on issues of gender and sexuality in Indonesia. Sharyn has published in the *Journal of Gender Studies, Journal of Bisexuality, Intersections: Gender, History and Culture in the Asian Context*, and has forthcoming monograph publications with RoutledgeCurzon and Wadsworth/Thompson.

Franco Lai is a lesbian from a small city, Hong Kong, China. She believes that sexuality is not just something private in bed but an important matter that reveals the power dynamics and cultures of our societies. It is also important for all of us to think about. She obtained her Master of Philosophy degree, majoring in Gender Studies/Anthropology from the Chinese University of Hong Kong in 2003.

Kanchana Natarajan teaches Indian Philosophy at Delhi University, Delhi. She is interested in Sanskritic and Tamil folk traditions where she looks at the compelling views on gender that are articulated in the two traditions.

Jennifer Robertson is Professor in the Department of Anthropology at the University of Michigan. Among her books are *Native and Newcomer: Making and Remaking a Japanese City* (University of California Press 1991); *Takarazuka: Sexual Politics and Popular Culture in Modern Japan* (University of California Press 1998). She is the editor of *Same-Sex Cultures and Sexualities: An Anthropological Reader* (Blackwell 2004) and *A Companion to the Anthropology of Japan* (Blackwell 2005). Her book-in-progress, *Blood and Beauty: Eugenic Modernity and Empire in Japan* (University of California Press), focuses on the colonial history and present circumstances of eugenics and ideologies of "blood." She is the originator and General Editor of Colonialisms, a new book series from the University of California Press.

Maya Sharma is a scholar and activist in the Indian Women's Movement. Born in the desert state of Rajasthan, where girls rarely get the opportunity to go to university, Sharma completed postgraduate work. Her life changed radically when she came in contact with the women's movement. Instead of being the staid housewife in an urban middle-class home, she chose to be an activist. Within that identity she found the space to grow and nurture her skills of listening, observing, and writing. She worked for many years with Jagori, a feminist group, and the NGO Campaign for Lesbian Rights, both located in Delhi, India. Most of her writing stems from her work as an activist. She has cowritten a book on single women's lives, women's labor rights, and several articles and reports. The chapter in this book is based on research she undertook in response to developments in the women's movement and the growing gay movement. Currently she is working with a grassroots women's organization, Vikalp in Baroda, Gujarat, India.

Megan Sinnott is Assistant Professor of Women's Studies at Georgia State University in Atlanta. Her research interests include globalization and sexuality, queer theory, and geography of sexuality. She has taught women's studies and anthropology at Yale University, University of Colorado-Boulder, and Thammasat University in Thailand. She has conducted extensive fieldwork in Thailand. Her publications include *Toms and Dees:*

Transgender Identity and Female Same-Sex Relationships in Thailand, published by University of Hawaii Press in 2004.

Shermal Wijewardene was educated in Delhi and Oxford and is Senior Lecturer at the Department of English, University of Colombo, Sri Lanka. Her main interests are in Virginia Woolf studies, gender studies, and film theory. She is a member of the Women's Support Group, a lesbian organization linked to the gay organization Companions on a Journey.

Saskia E. Wieringa holds the chair of Gender and Women's Same-sex Relations Crossculturally at the University of Amsterdam. She is also the Director of the Amsterdam Women's Library and Archives. She has done extensive research on sexual politics and women's same-sex relation in Indonesia and in other parts of the world, notably Japan and southern Africa. She is co-founder and secretariat of the Board of the Kartini Asia Network. Her recent books include *Sexual Politics in Indonesia* (2002), *Tommy Boys, Lesbian Men and Ancestral Wives* (with Ruth Morgan, 2005), *Engendering Human Security* (co-editor, 2006), and *Traveling Heritages* (editor, 2008). She is presently writing a book on heteronormativity in Asia among other projects.

Peichen Wu is Assistant Professor of the Department of Japanese Language and Culture at Soochow University, Taipei, Taiwan. She received her PhD in Modern Japanese Literature from University of Tsukuba, Japan. Some of her recent publications include "Struggles between national identity and gender: The double-bond structures in Satô Toshiko's novels on Nisei" in *The Regions of Translation: Culture, Colonialism, and Identity* (2004); "Prospects for Escape from Domestic Ideology: Tamura Toshiko's "Writing Woman" and "Performing Woman" in *Observing Japan from Within* (2004).

Chapter One

Globalization, Sexuality, and Silences: Women's Sexualities and Masculinities in an Asian Context

Evelyn Blackwood and Saskia E. Wieringa

In 1992 in Manila, Philippines, a small group of activist women who identified themselves as "lesbian" marched in the annual Women's Day celebration for the first time. In Thailand Anjaree, a national lesbian organization that has been active since 1986 campaigning for lesbian (and gay) rights, identifies its constituency as "women who love women" (*ying-rak-ying*). Caleri (Campaign for Lesbian Rights), a Delhi-based group formed in 1998, was the first Indian activist organization to consciously dedicate itself to foregrounding lesbian issues in the public domain. Equally apparent throughout Asia in both cities and rural areas are butch or masculine "lesbians" whose own identities are firmly located in local patriarchies as well as in global signifiers apparent in the proliferating forms of the English term "tomboy" with which they identify themselves. TB, tom, and *tomboi* are some of the variations used in Hong Kong, Thailand and Indonesia respectively (other terms are also used in each location). Their women partners see themselves variously as normative women, who do not fit into a marked category of sexual identity, or as different than heterosexual women because of their attraction to masculine "lesbians." These individuals, like their activist peers, are influenced by global feminist and queer processes as well as by local processes that are negotiated to construct the particular forms of sexuality and gender evident in Asia today. These seemingly divergent subjectivities—the lesbian activists and the partners in a butch/femme relationship—appear at the conjuncture of decidedly local and global processes.

In the study of the production of gendered and sexual subjectivities, a global queer perspective has gained critical importance. Through the Internet and international media, transnational "lesbian and gay" movements have become visible worldwide. Within these transnational movements Northern discourses and perspectives are often hegemonic, in many cases colonizing national discourses by setting the conditions and terms of gay and lesbian identities, strategies, and practices. We want to intervene in this global queer discourse from a transnational feminist position that attends to the specificities of women's sexualities and masculinities in particular geosocial locations. This intervention is an attempt to integrate into global sexualities discourse not only the experiences and practices of urban, educated women, but also the experiences of working-class lesbians and transgendered females, whose voices are rarely heard.[1]

Through an examination of the intersections of gender, sexuality, ethnicity, class, and religion in the emerging movements, networks, and communities of same-sex attracted women and transgendered females in Asia, we argue against the overdetermination of globalization for queer subjects. At the same time that we implicate processes of nation building, citizenship, and transnational flows of knowledge in the production of sexualities and genders, we locate the subjects of the movements and networks analyzed in the following pages within the histories and sociocultural specificities of particular places and everyday lives. In this introductory chapter we offer a feminist perspective on same-sex sexualities and transgender practices that attends to particular historical legacies and gender regimes as well as global queer discourses in theorizing the production of globalized sexual and gender subjectivities.

Elsewhere (Wieringa and Blackwood 1999) we argued against the use of the term "queer" because it ignores the specificities of women's experiences. As we noted then, the homogenizing term "queer" subsumes the marked social, economic, and sexual forms of oppression lesbians face in contradistinction to gay men. Similarly, Dorothy Smith (1990) notes the multiple ways in which women are assimilated by gender-neutral terms. Violence against women is renamed "family" violence and lesbian cultures are assimilated into "queer" cultures. "The broader term is defended on the grounds that it is more useful, inclusive, and unifying, when, in fact, it disguises the relations of the most powerful by putting them at the centre" (Smith 1990:205). When we do use the term "queer" in this introduction, we use it as a signifier of the particular discourse in which it is deployed. The term has become more popular in academic and activist circles primarily in the United States and Australia (less so in Europe), while sexual identity movements in mainland and Southeast Asia generally do not use the term, although it is becoming more visible on Asian websites.

This collection speaks to a burgeoning of "Asian" sexualities and their fertility for understanding globalization processes and the production of sexualities. By choosing "Asia" as the focus of this book, an area of highly disparate histories, polities, religions, and cultural practices, we are not making any claims to an "Asian" form of women's sexualities. Any uniform definition of "Asia" is problematic, whether based on a shared history, shared status as colonial subjects, or, in reference to this collection, shared sexual identities. Further, declaring something called "Asia" may be seen to reinforce an Orientalist definition created by European and American colonizers. "Asia" as a geographic marker is a product of colonial, postcolonial and neocolonial structures of knowledge (see Gupta and Ferguson 1997; Ong 1997). Nevertheless, "Asia" in contradistinction to the "West" has attained a certain stability in the global and academic imagination and is used both by Westerners and citizens of Asian countries, particularly in the discourse on "Asian values," as a gross marker of origin and difference.

We use the term "Asia" to refer to a contemporary geopolitical region, specifically to peoples of East, South, and Southeast Asia, exclusive of the white colonial cultures that dominated certain regions. We want to emphasize that we do not consider "Asia" as a signifier of a particular culture or identity. The chapters attend to specific nations within Asia and not generally to any pan-Asian practices. Further, as these chapters suggest, national identities within Asia, for example, Indian, Thai, or Indonesian, cannot be defined in any simplistic sense as uniform or homogeneous. This perspective reflects the importance of particular histories and social and political contexts, including the presence of strong women's movements (rather than broad national or Asian themes) to the analysis in this book of changing genders and sexualities within an Asian context.

Decolonizing Global Queer Studies

The topic of globalizing queer identities has received considerable attention since the early 1990s from both feminists and queer theorists. Plummer (1992) pointed out that same-sex experiences are increasingly fashioned through the interconnectedness of the world. He suggested that queer identity "moves in fits and starts along diverse paths to disparate becomings" (1992:16), an astute recognition of the diversity and difference that marks the lives of people in same-sex relations. He argued that lesbian and gay studies should pay close attention to the "international connectedness yet local uniqueness" of diverse practices (1992:18), thereby giving both global and local processes and practices a distinct role. In contrast, Altman (1996) initially spoke confidently about the "apparent globalization of postmodern, gay identities," arguing that new "globalized" queer identities would replace older indigenous identities, resulting in a homogeneous global gay identity. In his later work (Altman 2001), he is more attentive to cultural specificities among same-sex communities. Taking a different tack as to what constitutes the "local" in this global world, Johnson, Jackson, and Herdt (2000) suggest thinking in terms of "critical regionalities" in area studies as a way to get at specific historical circumstances and imagined communities. They argue that this perspective on regionalities "provides one means through which we can move beyond the essentialized field of the 'local' and the unspecified and unsituated field of the 'global' " (2000:373).

Feminist theorists Grewal and Kaplan (1994) move beyond the limited and simplistic dichotomy of local-global by using the term "transnational." This term points to the lines that crosscut the binary; it suggests that the "global" and "local" thoroughly infiltrate each other (1994). Carrying this definition to the discussion of sexualities, they define "transnational sexualities" as the way particular genders and sexualities are shaped by a large number of processes implicated in globalization, including capitalism, diasporic movements, political economies of state, and the disjunctive flow of meanings produced across these sites (2001). From a queer theory perspective Povinelli and Chauncey also point to the significance of transnational processes in the production of localized sexual subjectivities reflected in the "tension between increasingly powerful global discourses and institutions of homosexuality and heterosexuality and between local sexual ideologies and subjectivities . . ." (1999:446). These "local" sexual ideologies and subjectivities are the product of "multiple textual forms—speech, cyberspace, art, film, television, telephonic media" (1999:445)—in other words they are already implicated in transnational processes.

At the same time that global interconnections and emerging gay and lesbian communities and networks create new visions of and spaces for women's and men's same-sex cultures and lives, some significant oversights persist within a global queer perspective. Adam, Duyvendak, and Krouwel (1999) discuss the factors that lead to what they see as the emergence of gay and lesbian visibility worldwide. They link this emergence to the growth of a modern capitalist world system that supports greater personal autonomy in the choice of one's partner, the ascendance of romantic love ideologies and subjective feelings as a "ground for bonding," and urbanization and the growth of public space outside the control of a "traditional" community. The use of a concept such as "traditional" is itself problematic, laden with value judgments and assumptions about the isolation of past communities. If these conditions take place, they suggest, a modern rights-based gay and lesbian movement can arise that will develop a double strategy of fighting discrimination and establishing a public space of its own (Adam, Duyvendak, and Krouwel 1999). However, their analysis does not recognize that the desire for visibility itself is a "Western" construct linked to the changing perceptions of identity in the "West." Moreover, the idea that "romantic love" is linked to the spread of capitalism is seriously shortsighted (see Wieringa 2005). What is widely regarded as the world's first novel, the impressive tenth-century Japanese tale of the "Shining Prince" Genji by Murasaki Shikibu is saturated with romantic love, its codes, its trappings, its effects, and its manifestations.

Their analysis, based on a narrow historical period, cannot sustain larger conclusions beyond the "West."

The picture in Asia (and elsewhere) is more complex than Adam, Duyvendak. and Krouwel's evolutionist perspective suggests. For instance, the repression of Suharto's "New Order" regime in Indonesia entailed the growth of an aggressive form of capitalism that Adam, Duyvendak, and Krouwel discuss. Throughout this period, members of the Jakarta femme/butch community Wieringa (1999) interviewed carved out a space for themselves as couples by accepting the dominant gender ideology, living same-sex lives modeled along heterosexual parameters. They took this course without much contact with the global gay rights movement, although their exposure has increased over time. They had no desire at all to be "visible" in the "Western" sense that Adam, Duyvendak, and Krouwel (1999) define. They wanted to be as comfortable as possible within Indonesia's gender regime and not to subvert it. Attention to the implications of gender hierarchies in postcolonial nations would provide a richer canvas on which to paint the broad strokes of an emergent gay and lesbian movement worldwide.

Other characteristics attributed to the sexual regimes of the modern "Western" world echo the arguments of Adam, Duyvendak, and Krouwel (1999). Giddens (1992) speaks of the development of a "plastic sexuality" in the postmodern world, a sexuality freed from the needs of reproduction due to the wide availability of contraceptives. His view is too simplistic for Asian countries, such as India and Indonesia, and a world in general in which mostly hierarchical and multiple systems of domination are practiced. In Indonesia the drive to curb population growth never reduced state patriarchal control over women; contraceptives were made available only to married women with the consent of their husbands (Wieringa 2002). In India the state-driven agenda to limit population used coercive methods to control women's reproductive rights. It is not the availability of contraceptives as such that leads toward greater equality between heterosexual partners. For women in "Asian" countries the potentialities of what Giddens calls the "pure relationship" can be realized only in a sexuality freed from the dominant role of the phallus. Toward this end, the human and women's rights movements and in some cases the processes of democratization have played a critical role in spreading ideas of gender equality.

Another problem that arises in global queer studies is the tendency to essentialize and universalize human experiences by assuming the relevance of "Western" categories to the lives of people elsewhere (see also Plummer 1992; Jolly and Manderson 1997).[2] What is the relevance of terms such as "lesbian," "transgendered," "homosexual," "gay," or "queer" when analyzing genders and sexualities? Having developed in mainly urban, educated American, Australian, and European contexts, these terms and concepts are themselves culture-specific. Elliston's (1995) incisive critique of anthropological work on "ritualized homosexuality" makes this point quite clearly. She argues that this concept relies on Western ideas about sexuality and desire that obscure the indigenous meanings of these practices. Elsewhere we argue that the term "lesbian" is equally problematic when used cross-culturally (Blackwood 1996; Wieringa and Blackwood 1999; see also King 2002). Recent studies in South Africa on women healers who take women lovers provide another example of the problems with universalizing categories (Morgan and Reid 2003; Morgan and Wieringa 2005). Can a woman whose male ancestral spirit desires a wife be labeled "transgendered," "lesbian," or "bisexual?" Any of these terms would reduce the complexity of the person, her religious beliefs, and her desires. Many masculine females who desire women would not call themselves "lesbians," but prefer to be called "men." In some cases they use a special term marking their self-perception (see Davies; Lai; Sharma; Sinnott; this volume). Likewise, their women partners prefer to be called "women" or "girlfriends," rather than "lesbians." Bhaiya's work on women's friendships (this volume) suggests that desires and practices are so elusive that those who embody them may not want or need to explicitly label themselves. Therefore making any of the terms mentioned above a global category is problematic because it imposes a "Western" understanding of sexuality, with its reference to a fixed sexual identity, on practices and relationships that may have very different meanings and expectations in other places.

Besides obscuring other meanings, such terms prioritize sexuality as the defining aspect of these identities. Jolly and Manderson caution against reifying sexuality "as a thing unto itself" when studying non-Western sexualities (1997:24). Further, there is a danger that the imposition of "Western" categories of thought may lead to a developmental teleology that situates other sexualities as premodern, that is, not yet lesbian or gay, while placing "Western" sexualities at the pinnacle of modern, autonomous sexuality (such as the "out gay" person). In a global "queer" perspective, does emphasizing "global interactions" give dominance to the West in defining sexualities, as Jolly and Manderson query (1997:22)? Given their location in the so-called First World, the American, Australian, and European urban lesbian and gay movements have been hegemonic in creating and shaping transnational discourses about sexual identities, gay rights, and sexual freedom; these discourses are often based on simplistic dualisms of traditional and modern, as well as indigenous and foreign. In global gay discourse "butch" lesbians and transgendered or masculine females (among others) have been represented as premodern, lacking the modern same-sex identity emblematic of the lesbian and gay liberation movements of Europe, the United States, and Australia (see also Grewal and Kaplan 2001).

These problems have led some queer theorists to refuse "to provide a grammar that could make . . . cross-cultural interactions . . . transparent and universally legible" (Cruz-Malavé and Manalansan 2002:4). This stance has its appeal. By continuing to use Western terms and categories, there is a risk of ignoring the difference of other sexualities and suppressing new knowledges. Yet at the same time American, Australian, and European urban lesbian and gay categories have been appropriated and complexly intertwined with "local" meanings (see also Wieringa and Blackwood 1999). In some cases the terms "lesbian" and "gay" are used by members of national activist organizations because these are terms everyone can identify within multilingual and ethnically diverse countries. Any single solution has its particular consequences, but it is incumbent on researchers to avoid imposing meanings through the unthinking use of Western categories. We need to first examine and understand the differences that comprise sexualities and genders.

Feminist Perspective on Sexual Subjectivities

How much are women's same-sex and transgender communities and informal networks in Asia indications of a rising global culture, as some gay scholars observe? Altman, speaking particularly about Southeast Asia, suggests that "the gay world—less obviously the lesbian, largely due to marked differences in women's social and economic status, is a key example of emerging global 'subcultures' where members of particular groups have more in common across national or continental boundaries than they do with others in their own geographically defined societies" (2001:86–87). Adam, Duyvendak, and Krouwel (1999) note the significant national differences in the communities described in their anthology, yet they suggest that although one may not speak very well of a blanket global gay movement, "national imprints of a global movement" are clearly discernible.

We maintain that too much stress is put on the determining influence "from above" in the development of "queer" communities. For women's same-sex communities and relationships, with their diversity of lesbian, bisexual, transgender, and "normal" subjectivities such as those presented in this anthology, we do not see evidence of an overriding influence of a gay and lesbian global culture, particularly not of an undifferentiated queer one. Rather than constituting a "national imprint" or a "global subculture," same-sex communities and relationships are the product of historical legacies—for instance, folktales of transgendered beings and deities who join male and female in one body (see Natarajan; Wieringa; this volume)—as well as particular gender regimes and forms and processes of nationalism, fundamentalism, (neo) colonialism, and globalization.

We start with particular cultural locations to understand the plurality of lesbian, bisexual, and transgender identities and subjectivities and attend to the asymmetries and specificities of sociohistoric processes already present in these locations (see Grewal and Kaplan 1994; Hannerz 1996; Ong 1997). Global, regional, and historical flows that constitute a cultural location create specific discourses, knowledges, and ways of understanding the world. Even fluid cultural landscapes create particular histories and ideologies that individuals imbibe as part of the doxa of their world, creating a sense of place that travels with them even as it is continuously reconstructed (see Blackwood this volume). Taking into account people "in place" allows researchers to attend more precisely to gender, class, race, and ethnic relations, the differences in education and age, and to the rural/urban divide, without ignoring national, postcolonial, or global processes. Given this understanding of the relationship between cultural location and global connectedness, we argue that lesbian, gay, bisexual, or transgendered subjectivities are neither simply local nor reflective of Western discourses of queer identities, but rather reproduce and reconstitute the specific discourses, knowledges, and ways of understanding the world of their particular locations. This process of reproduction, transformation, filtration, and reconstruction of sexual cultures is not without underlying tensions or struggle.

A key aspect of our feminist perspective is the attention to the significance of gender practices and gender regimes in the production of sexual subjectivities. We maintain that the communities, groups, networks, and movements of same-sex attracted women (and men) reproduce, reflect, and sometimes explicitly resist the gender regimes in which they are located. Women have to negotiate their existence with varieties of state patriarchies and emerging fundamentalist and ethnic movements under the growing pressure of neoliberal economic policies that adversely impact the poorer groups of society (see Wieringa 2005; Robertson; Wijewardene; this volume). For example, in Indonesia an explicit construction of women's nature (*kodrat*) by the state defines the appropriate parameters of women's sexuality (Blackwood 1999; Wieringa 2000, 2002). Nationalist sentiment and growing fundamentalist fervor in India contributes to an increasing intolerance toward women's relationships (see Bhaiya, "Fire," this volume).

The consequences of these gender regimes for the formation of gender and sexual subjectivities are apparent in the differences in women's and men's same-sex communities and practices—in styles of dating, in sexual expressions, in levels of visibility, especially for transgendered communities, and in socio-psychological issues related to self-esteem and identity. Women throughout Asia have been socialized in contexts that privilege men's sexual agency and sexual gratification. Open, public expression of sexual desire is more acceptable, even encouraged for men than for women; men's search for sexual adventure has been more widely tolerated and institutionalized than women's efforts to reject patriarchal control over their sexuality. At the same time within Asian metropolises younger, middle-class, educated lesbian have taken up human and women's rights ideals. These women are often linked with the growing feminist movements in and outside their countries and are often more politically astute than gay men.

Rather than being the offspring of a global queer culture, we see women's same-sex communities and networks in the urban middle classes accessing global discourses of human, women's, and gay/lesbian rights, yet reconstituting these discourses in ways that are more meaningful and appropriate to them in their quest for socio-sexual citizenship. In most Asian countries women and transgendered females who desire women must navigate the advantages and dangers of "coming out" against the public silence about sexuality, the anti-woman discourses of rising fundamentalist movements (themselves inspired by global phenomena), and opportunistic politicians, who for reasons of building political alliances, proclaim all forms of same-sex relations decadent and "Western" (while embracing the material spoils of the West). We do agree with most authors mentioned earlier that women's same-sex communities and movements are becoming more visible, a phenomenon documented by this collection, although at great risk to the relative safety offered by their invisibility. At the same time, we place more emphasis on the political and sexual agency of these groups in the constitution of their subjectivities than other queer theorists do.

As Asian feminists struggle to attain greater rights, the tensions and differences within and across same-sex communities and networks are becoming visible as well, particularly in terms of class. For predominately working-class masculine (butch) lesbians, often their first experiences with feminists was to have their butch/femme lifestyles denounced.[3] Tomboys claim a female masculinity, while their partners claim sexual normalcy (and not bisexuality) as wives or girlfriends of their tomboy lovers (Wieringa 1999, 2005; see Blackwood; Sinnott; this volume). In Sharma's study (this volume) of working-class Indian women, she found that masculine-identified women subjects tended to take on men's behaviors "in order to create a space for themselves in a society where men are more privileged" (page 263: this volume). Many of these masculine or transgendered females conform to the dominant gender regimes in their societies. The social and sexual egalitarianism that is characteristic of Western gay or lesbian relationships (see also Weeks 1999) holds little attraction for them. In this case gender regimes produce a gendered subjectivity that does not proffer any explicit opposition to dominant ideologies; the lack of opposition preserves these identities through outward compliance with gender hierarchies.

Asian Global Processes

The pervasiveness of global processes in Asia is undeniable. Indeed the fast growing metropolises of China, Japan, India, and Indonesia are some of the most global locations in the world. With liberalization of global capital, the influence of global financial markets is felt in almost all Asian countries. Shopping malls are stuffed with goods imported from all over the world. Multilane roads in city centers as well as the potholed secondary streets in the poorer neighborhoods are constantly jammed by a deluge of luxury cars. Yet there is no uniform acceptance of global values. Rising conspicuous consumerism and a decadent capitalist lifestyle occur side by side with the rise of various fundamentalisms and ethnic identity movements.

The growth of religious fundamentalisms reflects global tendencies as well. Muslim fundamentalism itself is partly fueled by the aggressive politics of the West, particularly the U.S. abuse of its hegemonic military might, its virulent anti-Islamic rhetoric, and its invasion of Iraq. This picture is complicated by occasional eruptions of anti-Western xenophobia, when political or military leaders want to emphasize their national credentials by playing upon the simmering resentment that is the legacy of the atrocities and racism of colonialism. Religious fundamentalism in general is linked to the building of militant (nationalist) subjectivities based on the valorization of patriarchal, heterosexist family values. Aggressive attempts at creating a hegemonic religious community are inspired by images of a golden age of, for example, the "pure" Islamic *umma* (faithful) or a glorious Hindu past, in which a patriarchal family model was the major organizing principle.

The insecurities created by the breakdown of long-standing social, cultural, and economic networks through the penetration of neoliberal economic politics fuels this process. While promising progress, social justice, and development, the effects of ruthless capitalist development are realized in the growth of social injustice, the disruption of communities through urbanization, the displacement of whole communities through large scale development projects, and the neglect of agriculture. These processes lead to widespread disenchantment with modernization and its associated values such as democracy, political transparency, pluralism, diversity and social, sexual, and cultural liberalism. The hegemonic grip that fundamentalist groups have on their followers stifles the development of democratic institutions (though they may have used democratic processes to gain political power), censors discussion of cultural and sexual values, and imposes dress and behavioral codes as well as the valorization of heterosexual family values. Although women are drawn into these projects as active agents, these groups are opposed to the granting of women's rights, especially women's sexual rights. Further, to cement their political and religious cohesion, these groups often target lesbian, gay, and transgendered individuals and groups.

Economic globalization in Asia thus acquires characteristics different than those in the West. Although the process of economic liberalism associated with globalization is spreading in various Asian countries, other processes that authors such as Jameson and Miyoshi (1999) identify with globalization are either absent or take on decidedly "Asian" characteristics. The growth of bureaucracy is characterized in the West by a growing equality (within the middle classes), rationalism, as well as respect for the rule of law. In contrast, in some Asian countries such as Indonesia and Bangladesh, it is associated with favoritism, nepotism, collusion, and corruption, fostering a climate of insecurity and irrationality as well as disrespect for the rule of law. The global process of cultural standardization (dominated by Western characteristics), in which local cultures are subsumed, is reversed in many Asian countries. A steep rise in consumerism of the middle classes goes hand in hand with the fostering of so-called ethnic customs. These particular globalization processes in Asia are the ethnoscapes and ideoscapes discussed by Appadurai (1996) through which members of "Asian" butch/femme and lesbian communities have to navigate.

Invisible Love

This volume draws together the writings of both activist scholars and academics whose works focus on women's same-sex experiences and female masculinities in a globalizing Asia. The activist scholars whose writings are included here have been and continue to be active agents in the creation and development of the communities discussed here, providing a unique perspective on the social and historical changes recounted in this book. Their voices, intellectual perspectives, political passions, and unshakeable desires are crucial to this book and to a deeper understanding of the transformations and struggles faced by women and masculine females who love women in Asia. In addition to a careful rendering of particular practices in all the chapters in this volume, the inclusion of chapters by activist scholars addresses the dominance of Western definitions and understandings of sexualities by bringing a greater range of theoretical perspectives and a greater immediacy to the struggles faced by the women and masculine females whose stories they recount and share in. Further, their writings reflect the tensions in their own efforts to tread the fine line between advocacy of sexual rights and respect for female forms of sexual agency. Without their insights into, dedication to, and support of women's same-sex relationships, much of the material and analysis in this book would not be possible.

The range of disciplines included in this volume includes anthropology, sociology, history, and literary criticism. The "multiple textual forms" (Povinelli and Chauncey 1999) analyzed in this anthology include poetry, myths, and songs, as well as the coded languages women in same-sex or butch/femme relations have developed among themselves. Sculpture, graphic arts, and film are all mined to provide intriguing glimpses of these same-sex experiences.

This collection maintains the orientation of Blackwood and Wieringa's anthology *Female Desires* (1999) by including work only on women and transgendered or masculine females. In an era of proliferating "lesbian-and-gay" studies and studies of queer sexualities that do not attend to the specificities of gendered practices within and across sexualities, we feel it is critical to highlight the particular regulatory practices, state and religious ideologies, and global processes that collaborate with and reinforce each other to produce and reproduce women's sexualities and genders as different than and distinct from men's sexualities and genders. The trajectories of women's and men's sexualities are highly responsive to and reflective of the legal, economic, and political contexts within which they appear, making any statements about "queer" sexualities problematic because of structurally embedded practices and privileges attendant on gender/sexuality as well as class, caste, and ethnicity. We resist the tendency to rely on queerness as a unifying category of analysis, keeping the theoretical lens on women and those with female bodies as a more productive angle to reveal the way meanings are attached to particular bodies.

This book attends to the intersections of globalization with female sexualities and genders. As such, we take globalization broadly to incorporate processes of modernity, nation building, citizenship, religious movements, and transnational identity movements that occurred within the past 30 to 40 years. We feel that accounts of globalization processes in the production of localized sexualities are incomplete if they do not also account for the historical legacies—produced by colonization, patriarchal gender regimes, indigenous cosmologies, and other processes—that were precursors to current movements and ideologies. These legacies contribute to the production of new sexual subjectivities. In other words, any efforts to examine contemporary conditions will be strengthened by taking into account past practices.

Part I of the anthology, "Historical Legacies," draws on Grewal and Kaplan's notion of historical legacies to examine the role of historical and mythical elements in the construction and in some cases refusal of same-sex sexualities. Grewal and Kaplan (2001) point out that historical concepts of gender constitute a legacy that contributes to the production of new sexual subjectivities in the contemporary era. In this section Natarajan (Tamil Nadu, south India) and Wieringa (Japan) point to historical and mythical traces of transgenderism, transvestism, and same-sex desires in literature, philosophy, sculpture, and folktales.[4] Natarajan recounts folktales of women warriors, queens, and female deities still popular today in the south of India. This chapter provides key material to understand the covert constructions of masculinity and femininity in India as well as the possibilities and struggles women in India face today, which are further recounted in chapters by Bhaiya ("Fire") and Sharma. The folk ballad Natarajan describes subverts classical philosophical norms by ingeniously reworking them to liberate women from the prevailing constrictive models of family units. This story resonates with a pattern of women's friendships, which Bhaiya ("Spring") elaborates on; it is recouped by activist women's groups in postcolonial India as part of their historical legacy.

Wieringa's chapter addresses the historical and mythical legacies of women's same-sex practices in Japan. It explores religious, cultural, and social contexts in which women's same-sex practices have taken place and traces the changes in societal views of women's sexuality after the Meiji Restoration and the westernization of Japan. The historical legacies continue to reproduce and reinforce gendered and sexual frameworks that are deeply meaningful in people's lives today. While not suggesting that there is an unproblematic unilinear development from past practices of gender reversals to present-day categories of dual genders, such as butch/femme, Wieringa argues that the older stories provide the cultural idiom, albeit often at a subconscious level, in which women can express their desires and longings for each other. These stories are also critical elements in consciousness raising and in the growing awareness of Japanese women's own particular locations. Echoes from the past inform the cultural environment in which it is possible to imagine transgender and same-sex spaces in a globalizing era. Thus, the process of accessing historical and archeological sites of same-sex and transgender practices has a bearing on new lesbian subjectivities. Much more work needs to be done in Asian contexts more generally to document the historical traces of female bonding, transgenderism, and forms of sexual and gender liminality as well as the ways they resonate with or are strategically used in contemporary discourses.

Part II, "Conditional Subjectivities," includes three chapters that examine the contingent aspect of subjectivities—the processes of naming and renaming, fluidity and re-formation over time, and the unease with and disruption caused by unintelligible subjectivities. We recognize that all subjectivities are conditional in the sense that they are never fixed or static, but the chapters in this section reflect in particular the conditionality of subjectivities in the context of transnational queer discourses and dominant gender regimes enforced by state policies and fundamentalist religious movements. Two aspects of subjectivities are particularly clear in this section: the extreme difficulties of resisting dominant gender regimes and the pleasures of self-naming.

In the strict patriarchal Sri Lankan community discussed by Wijewardene (this volume), resistance to dominant gender regimes may entrap subjects in institutions and globalized medical discourses even as they try to claim a space for themselves. The vacillations of "trans" individuals and their efforts to locate themselves within multiple discourses—feminist, gay activist, and state—play into the dominant ideology. In India queer activist agendas create tensions for women whose own particular forms of friendship and bonding may never have been articulated as sexual—and in that way may have been tolerated, a theme that Bhaiya ("Spring") addresses. Activist and globalized definitions of sexuality may reduce the diversity of intimacies to a binary sexuality, effectively erasing the multiple expressions of women's desires and pleasures. By refusing any labels for women's friendships, Bhaiya defies the finality of categorization, claiming instead an elusive subjectivity that refuses others' categories. Wu's history of the Japanese Seitô Society explores members' efforts to resist dominant patriarchal norms and create a space for woman-centered relationships in a modernizing Japan that draws on Western theories of sexuality to marginalize nonnormative gender behavior. Ultimately, their efforts foundered on the nonnegotiable demands of societal domesticity represented in the slogan "good wives, wise mothers." Further, their attempts to create sexual relationships that relied on the masculine/feminine binary of the dominant culture derailed their efforts at intimacy. Yet their ability to change their perceptions of themselves as masculine, feminine, heterosexual, bisexual, or lesbian enabled them to reshape their subjectivities and successfully counter the dominant ideology of the state, if only temporarily.

A theme running throughout the book and highlighted in Part III, "Female Masculinities," is the connection between gender regimes and sexualities.[5] Halberstam (1998) used the term "female masculinities" as a way to separate masculinity from men, thereby usefully undermining the naturalness of men's performance of masculinity. In creating a new taxonomy she offered a way to see subjectivities beyond the binaries of Western gender categories.[6] The creation of a new taxonomy, however, often has the effect of boxing in what was meant to be loosened. In using this term we make no claims to the coherence of such a category nor do we want to place the varieties of masculine females in these chapters within a single identity framework (see also Rubin 1992). We believe that the importance of female masculinities as a topic of analysis lies in their relationship to dominant ideologies of gender. These ideologies or gender regimes are not universally patriarchal, but in the Asian context we see a range of state, fundamentalist, and global masculinities collaborating in patriarchal innovations.[7] An issue that needs to be addressed more fully in studies of transnational sexualities is the differences that masculinities and femininities encode in the practices and ideologies of sexuality. Butch/femme communities and networks offer fascinating insights into these issues. The chapters in this section tell us a great deal not only about the nonnormative desires and practices of masculine females, but also about normative heterosexuality. They reveal the way female masculinities at times participate in the excesses of hegemonic masculinities and also encode the tensions of female bodies located within masculinized gender regimes.

The four chapters presented in Part III on "Female Masculinities" are all in dialogue with both local and ethnic conditions and legacies as well as national/transnational circulations of sexual identities and state discourses on gender and sexuality. Brought out in this section is one of our key themes, namely that these masculinities are not simply a product of "premodern" sexualities, but are also reflective of broader globalizing processes, despite their appearance of being distinctly "local." These chapters purposely move away from well-documented urban centers and their burgeoning gay cultures, yet they trace the transnational dialogues taking place.

Graham (this volume) locates her subjects within the ethnic Bugis context and the sexual politics of national and transnational lesbian and gay movements. In Sulawesi, Indonesia, *calalai* who partner with women do not identify themselves as women nor do they aspire to be men. Graham argues that calalai gender both challenges and reinforces dominant Bugis and state discourses of gender. Calalai reflect ideal masculinity but, because they inhabit female bodies, they are able to move between genders in ways that men cannot. TBs (tomboys) in Hong Kong (Lai this volume) occupy a unique position, being both socially tolerated because of their masculinity and socially undesirable because their masculinity is attached to female bodies. Lai argues that TB identity is the product of negotiation with a globalized Hong Kong and the growing lesbian community. TBs' persistent display of masculinities represents their attempt to normalize and naturalize their identity within the larger society. Sinnott (this volume) examines the rapid growth and popularity of tom/ dee communities in modernized Thai society. Toms, masculine females, are paired both linguistically and romantically with feminine-identified women who are called "dees" (short for the English word "lady"). Toms and dees strategically appropriate and manipulate cultural stereotypes of Thai femininity and masculinity, creating hybrid forms that reflect the pressures of multiple gender discourses in a globalized context and their own class positions within Thai society. Blackwood (this volume) investigates the way working-class *tombois* and their girlfriends in West Sumatra, Indonesia, access and appropriate knowledge about sexualities and genders in a global world. Their identities reflect and reconstitute their cultural and class locations, as well as national and international discourses about sexuality and gender.

Although other chapters also address this theme, Part IV, "Silencing and Modes of Invisibility," provides detailed accounts of a persistent reality across Asia of the silencing and invisibility of women's genders and sexualities. One of the dilemmas facing women is the tension between the relative safety that the culture of silence surrounding their identities and desires affords them and the dangers and attractions of the new rights discourses and the strategy of "coming out." Global discourses on gay and lesbian rights are gaining some currency among urban middle-class persons with same-sex preferences. Emerging groups of formally educated middle-class lesbians are making wide use of the Internet and other forms of information technology to forge connections with lesbian groups in other parts of the world. In addition, in several major Asian cities rights-based gay and lesbian groups, who insist on full citizenship rights, have become visible in the media.

Advocacy for human and women's rights has led to a discourse of equality and individual rights and a delegitimization of various forms of discrimination. This discourse presupposes a self-ascribed gay or lesbian identity that makes visible the sexual aspects of women's same-sex relationships. Consequently, activist groups may exist side by side with communities of same-sex attracted women of different class, ethnic, or religious backgrounds, who live relatively safe lives hidden behind walls of seclusion, marginalization, and silence. These women have been able to create private spaces where they can live out their sexual lives without public scrutiny, particularly in places where there is a great segregation of sexes. Where gay men claim the public spaces of streets, parks, or bathhouses, women meet each other in the privacy of their homes or in other safe spaces. These women fear reprisals if their sexual lives come under the public scrutiny that national gay and lesbian organizations have received.

Invisibility can be both sought after as well as imposed. It comes from blending into the particular gender regime or can be imposed by the refusal (of the nation-state, dominant religious groups, or hegemonic ideology) to recognize relationships and desires outside the heterosexual paradigm. At the same time, the discourse of silence can provide a social space for building relationships and community, provided the expectations of neighbors and family members are fulfilled in respect to established gender norms (see Wieringa 2005). It also requires that the discrimination and marginalization that this position entails is accepted.

As transnational rights groups become more vocal, a backlash from religious fundamentalists and state gender regimes works to stabilize heterosexual marriage by denying the diversity of women's sexualities. The chapters in this section demonstrate that both past and present have significant impacts on contemporary expressions and repressions of sexualities. Women's friendships and all-female "husband-wife" pairs suddenly become suspect and endangered as they become imbued with sexual meaning, whether through the caring interest of researchers or the intrusion of media (see Sharma; Bhaiya, "Fire"; this volume). Bhaiya's chapter examines the responses to two films with lesbian themes released in India. These films sparked widespread violence and condemnatory statements from both state officials and religious fundamentalists, who worked to seal off perceived disruptions to the heteropatriarchal family. Robertson's chapter recounts the rise of the New Woman in Japan and state efforts to control women's gender transgressions, which led to the ultimate silencing—suicide by women who were in love with other women. In Sharma's study of working-class Indian women (this volume), she found that the more masculine-identified of her women subjects tended to consistently adopt men's behaviors in the interest of physical survival and psychological self-preservation and thereby remained invisible. The silences and coded encounters of these groups are difficult to access by formally educated researchers, as both the chapters by Sharma and Bhaiya vividly illustrate. Research into lives marked by silence and invisibility carries with it certain pitfalls and difficulties. As Sharma points out, great commitment and perseverance are necessary to find women who are willing to open their lives to outsiders.

* * *

By focusing on working-class women rather than the urban, highly educated activists who are so often the topic of global queer studies, a number of chapters in this book demonstrate the importance of class, caste, and ethnic location as well as gender regimes in producing new sexual subjectivities. Rather than a "global gay world," this book reveals a range of different subjectivities within and across regions and states, depending on their particular geosocial location.[8] Even female masculinities and butch/femme pairings, though quite prevalent within a globalizing Asia, cannot be simply explained as a product of lower-class or "premodern" environments. As revealed by Sinnott (this volume), toms and dees come from more than one social class, while tombois in West Sumatra (Blackwood this volume) draw on a range of historical and contemporary discourses to make sense of their masculinity.

This book offers fascinating insights into Asian women's same-sex sexualities and female masculinities. Same-sex attracted women are often trapped by the gender regimes and sexual codes produced by the collusion of new fundamentalist, state, and global patriarchies. Because many of the female-bodied persons involved have led or lead invisible lives, the histories of their attraction to each other are often lost and their present existence is either silenced or marginalized. Women who dare to publicly express their love for each other often face severe discrimination and hardship. At the same time, female-bodied persons, masculine or butch females, are tolerated to a degree because of the way they seem to reinforce (but ultimately challenge) the hegemonic gender order. The lesbian activists, the masculine females and their partners, and the women attracted to women who are presented here challenge the assumptions about life in the margins of heteronormative, globally oriented societies, revealing the interactions, asymmetries, and infiltrations of transnational processes.

Notes

We would like to thank Abha Bhaiya for her perceptive, thoughtful, and critical contributions to this introductory chapter.

1. We use the terms "transgendered females" as well as "masculine females" to refer to females whose gender is different than the normative gender assigned to females in their particular social context or culture. These terms cover a range of female masculinities from butches to females who identify as men. By using these terms, we do not mean to suggest that these individuals are "men" or even that they constitute a "third gender," as any such assignment of gender is extremely difficult to make and would ignore the fluidity of gender in many of these individuals' lives.
2. This problem, of course, is not just true of queer studies but has been a founding assumption in Western scholarship, as a large number of feminists and other scholars have pointed out. See for example, Collier and Yanagisako 1987; Mohanty 1991.
3. We use the term "butch/femme" as a general denominator for a masculine female and her partner. In general the persons referred to in this way use terminology derived from the heterosexual terms used in their own context. As that might create confusion among the readers, we use the Anglo-American term "butch/femme," although we are aware of its limitations.
4. See also Blackwood 2005 regarding islands in Southeast Asia.
5. See also Blackwood and Wieringa 1999; Wieringa 1999; Blackwood 2002.
6. Chapters by Graham and Wieringa in this volume use the pronouns "s/he" and "hir" to erase gender particularity. This technique is a simple method to get readers to think beyond Western gender binaries.
7. See Parker 1992; Grewal and Kaplan 1994.
8. See also Bacchetta 2002; Manalansan 2003.

References Cited

Adam, Barry D., Jan Willem Duyvendak, and Andre Krouwel. 1999. Gay and lesbian movements beyond borders: National imprints of a worldwide movement. In *The global emergence of gay and lesbian politics: National imprints of a worldwide movement*. Barry D. Adam, Jan Willem Duyvendak, and Andre Krouwel, eds. Pp. 244–373. Philadephia: Temple University Press.

Altman, Dennis. 1996. Rupture or continuity? The internationalization of gay identities. *Social Text* 48: 77–94.

———. 2001. *Global sex*. Chicago: University of Chicago Press.
Appadurai, Arjun. 1996. *Modernity at large: Cultural dimensions of globalization*. Minneapolis: University of Minneapolis Press.
Bacchetta, Paola. 2002. Rescaling transnational "queerdom": Lesbian and "lesbian" identitary-positionalities in Delhi in the 1980s. *Antipode: A Radical Journal of Geography* 34(5): 947–973.
Blackwood, Evelyn. 1996. Cross-cultural lesbian studies: Problems and possibilities. In *The new lesbian studies: Into the twenty-first century*. Bonnie Zimmerman and Toni McNaron, eds. Pp. 194–200. New York: The Feminist Press.
———. 1999. *Tombois* in West Sumatra: Constructing masculinity and erotic desire. In *Female desires: Same-sex relations and transgender practices across cultures*. Evelyn Blackwood and Saskia E. Wieringa, eds. Pp. 181–205. New York: Columbia University Press.
———. 2002. Reading sexuality across cultures: Anthropology and theories of sexuality. In *Out in theory: The emergence of lesbian and gay anthropology*. Ellen Lewin and William Leap, eds. Pp. 69–92. Urbana: University of Illinois Press.
———. 2005. Gender transgression in colonial and post-colonial Indonesia. *Journal of Asian Studies* 64(4): 849–879.
Blackwood, Evelyn and Saskia E. Wieringa, eds. 1999. *Female desires: Same-sex relations and transgender practices across cultures*. New York: Columbia University Press.
Collier, Jane Fishburne and Sylvia Junko Yanagisako, eds. 1987. *Gender and kinship: Essays toward a unified analysis*. Stanford: Stanford University Press.
Cruz-Malavé, Arnaldo and Martin F. Manalansan IV. 2002. Introduction: Dissident sexualities/alternative globalisms. In *Queer globalizations: Citizenship and the afterlife of colonialism*. Arnaldo Cruz-Malavé and Martin F. Manalansan IV, eds. Pp. 1–10. New York: New York University Press.
Elliston, Deborah. 1995. Erotic anthropology: "Ritualized homosexuality" in Melanesia and Beyond. *American Ethnologist* 22(4): 848–867.
Giddens, Anthony. 1992. *The transformation of intimacy: Sexuality, love and eroticism in modern societies*. Stanford: Stanford University Press.
Grewal, Inderpal and Caren Kaplan. 1994. Introduction: Transnational feminist practices and questions of postmodernity. In *Scattered hegemonies: Postmodernity and transnational feminist practices*. Inderpal Grewal and Caren Kaplan, eds. Pp. 1–33. Minneapolis: University of Minnesota Press.
———. 2001. Global identities: Theorizing transnational studies of sexuality. *GLQ: A Journal of Lesbian and Gay Studies* 7(4): 663–679.
Gupta, Akhil and James Ferguson, eds. 1997. *Culture, power, place: Explorations in critical anthropology*. Durham: Duke University Press.
Halberstam, Judith. 1998. *Female masculinities*. Durham: Duke University Press.
Hannerz, Ulf. 1996. *Transnational connections: Culture, people, places*. New York: Routledge.
Jameson, Fredric and Masapo Miyoshi, eds. 1998. *The cultures of globalization*. Durham and London: Duke University Press.
Johnson, Mark, Peter Jackson, and Gilbert Herdt. 2000. Critical regionalities and the study of gender and sexual diversity in South East and East Asia. *Culture, Health and Sexuality* 2(4): 361–375.

Jolly, Margaret and Lenore Manderson, eds. 1997. *Sites of desire, economies of pleasure: Sexualities in Asia and the Pacific.* Chicago: University of Chicago Press.

King, Katie. 2002. "There are no lesbians here": Lesbians, feminisms, and global gay formations. In *Queer globalizations: Citizenship and the afterlife of colonialism.* Arnaldo Cruz-Malavé and Martin F. Manalansan IV, eds. Pp. 33–45. New York: New York University Press.

Manalansan, Martin F., IV. 2003. *Global divas: Filipino gay men in the diaspora.* Durham: Duke University Press.

Mohanty, Chandra T. 1991. Cartographies of struggle: Third World women and the politics of feminism. In *Third World women and the politics of feminism.* Chandra Mohanty, Ann Russo, and Lourdes Torres, eds. Pp. 1–47. Bloomington: Indiana University Press.

Morgan, Ruth and Graeme Reid. 2003. "I've got two men and one woman": Ancestors, sexuality and identity among same-sex identified women traditional healers in South Africa. *Culture, Health and Sexuality* 5(5): 375–391.

Morgan, Ruth and Saskia E. Wieringa. 2005. *Tommy boys, lesbian men and ancestral wives: Female same-sex practices in Africa.* Johannesburg: Jacana Media.

Ong, Aihwa. 1997. Chinese modernities: Narratives of nation and of capitalism. In *Ungrounded empires: The cultural politics of modern Chinese transnationalism.* Aihwa Ong and Donald Nonini, eds. Pp. 171–202. New York: Routledge.

Parker, Andrew, Mary Russo, Doris Sommer, and Patricia Yaeger, eds. 1992. *Nationalisms and sexualities.* New York: Routledge.

Plummer, Ken. 1992. Speaking its name: Inventing a lesbian and gay studies. In *Modern homosexualities: Fragments of lesbian and gay experience.* Ken Plummer, ed. Pp. 3–25. London: Routledge.

Povinelli, Elizabeth A. and George Chauncey. 1999. Thinking sexuality transnationally. *GLQ: A Journal of Lesbian and Gay Studies* 5(4): 439–450.

Rubin, Gayle. 1992. Of catamites and kings: Reflections on butch, gender and boundaries. In *The Persistent desire: A femme-butch reader.* Joan Nestle, ed. Pp. 466–482. Boston: Alyson Publications.

Smith, Dorothy E. 1990. *The conceptual practices of power: A feminist sociology of knowledge.* Boston: Northeastern University Press.

Weeks, Jeffrey. 1999. The sexual citizen. In *Love and eroticism.* Mike Featherstone, ed. Pp. 35–52. London: Sage.

Wieringa, Saskia E. 1999. Desiring bodies or defiant cultures: Butch-femme lesbians in Jakarta and Lima. In *Female desires: Same-sex relations and transgender practices across cultures.* Evelyn Blackwood and Saskia E. Wieringa, eds. Pp. 206–230. New York: Columbia University Press.

———. 2000. Communism and women's same-sex practices in post-Suharto Indonesia. *Culture, Health and Sexuality* 2: 441–457.

———. 2002. *Sexual politics in Indonesia.* New York: PalgraveMacmillan.

———. 2005. Globalisation, love, intimacy and silence in a working class butch/fem community in Jakarta. ARRS Working paper. University of Amsterdam.

Wieringa, Saskia E. and Evelyn Blackwood. 1999. Introduction. In *Female desires: Same-sex relations and transgender practices across cultures.* Evelyn Blackwood and Saskia E. Wieringa, eds. Pp. 1–39. New York: Columbia University Press.

Part I

Historical Legacies

Chapter Two

Silence, Sin, and the System: Women's Same-Sex Practices in Japan

Saskia E. Wieringa

> Lesbian couples cannot receive the blessing of the system. The system restricts freedom and is inconvenient, but it encourages heterosexual relations to last forever . . . Even while my lover and I were embracing problems, we believed that we would continue our relationship until death do us part. Despite these feelings, a demon slipped through a crack created by our fatigue and misunderstandings. In between our accusations the crack widened. With no cover from the system, a person's heart was overwhelmed by this demon.
>
> —Itoh 1998:161

Introduction: An Earthquake-Proof Temple

In the above epigraph a heterosexually married lesbian woman reflects on the reasons why she finds it almost impossible to get a divorce from her husband, whom she does not love, while she broke up with her woman lover, whom she loves deeply even after their separation. In the collection of testimonies from which this passage is taken, lesbian women tell of the self-hate and self-destruction that follow from their realization that they do not want to lead a "normal" married life. In spite of a lesbian movement that started in Japan in the 1980s and a "gay boom" in the early 1990s, many lesbian women I spoke to during my stay in Tokyo in 1998 echoed similar feelings of isolation and despair. What then is this "system" that, with silence as one of its major tools of surveillance, and shame and sin as its major effects, encourages heterosexual marriage so strongly, while it ignores women's same-sex desires and allows "demons" to destroy lesbian relations? A prominent lesbian academic, now in her old age, said to me: "Maybe, 50 years from now sexuality will be liberated in Japan and we may enjoy it in whatever way we fancy. Some may like fishing; others may like to have sex. But present-day society is sex-obsessed. There is an enormous power game going on which controls everyone's feelings and links sexual desires to shame and guilt."[1]

In this chapter I argue that the dominant gender ideology in Japan can be regarded as a temple that is earthquake-proof. You can shake its walls but because its fundaments are multiple and its roof independently constructed, the building will always be held together by its roof. The sexual politics that form the underbelly of this system are characterized by sexual negotiations in which aggression and unprotected sex are eroticized for men, while women's pleasure is seen to lie in good motherhood.

Women's sexual autonomy is thus an anomaly to this system. Strong gender segregation in Japan, with men's dominance in sociopolitical and sexual matters, results in the difference between the relative visibility of gay men and the much deeper layers of guilt, sin, and shame surrounding lesbian sexuality. The Japanese language does not even have its own word for "lesbian," while it has several ways to denote the "male path" (Leupp 1995; Pflugfelder 1999; see also Wu, Robertson this volume). The term most commonly used nowadays, "*rezubian*" (from "lesbian"), has a connotation of pornography actress (Lunsing 1998). Yet traces of women's same-sex practices and transgender behaviors can be found in various historical and sociocultural settings in Japan.[2] I explore some of the historical material pertaining to these practices to provide building blocks that may help construct a space in which women's same-sex love can be incorporated into the temple of present-day Japanese society. Though the chapter contains references to a present-day urban lesbian culture, its dynamics and characteristics are not the focus of the present analysis.

Due to the scarcity of historical material on women's same-sex relations in Japan, this attempt is of necessity exploratory. I am aware of the dangers of building layers of meaning on quite disparate practices, yet I maintain that there is a certain value in presenting this material in a coherent context. Without further theoretical work pertaining to the different meanings the various practices discussed below may have, I shy away from linking behaviors and practices to identities and subjectivities. Thus I do not aim to uncover "premodern lesbians"; I only try to locate present-day practices in a sociohistorical context in an attempt to provide material to subvert the feelings of sin, shame, and guilt that many present-day Japanese lesbians suffer from.

The roof of this temple mostly consists of the impenetrable political, economic, and sociocultural systems in which men power holders, a veritable patriarchal gerontocracy, carefully preserve their power. An ideology based on a patriarchal, heterosexual family model pervades economic, social, and political relations. As Wolveren (1989) maintains, this ideology was carefully constructed after the abrupt ending of the "feudal" Tokugawa period when American "black ships" forcefully opened Japan to the outside world. The Meiji Restoration that started in 1868 was primarily an ideological movement in which new ties of loyalty had to be forged.[3] In this chapter I indicate how modernity was built on a particular gender construct in which nonheterosexual, in particular, "masculinized" behavior of women was condemned.

The fundaments of the temple that houses Japanese gender ideology is provided by the various religious and ideological movements that together form the syncretist spiritual landscape of Japanese society (Hardacre 1989, 1997; Davis 1992). In Japan religion and politics have strong linkages. After the Meiji Restoration, for instance, neo-Confucian, Buddhist, and Shintoist values were deployed to create a system in which sociopolitical life was modeled after a "natural" heterosexual family. In this system, even though women could have jobs, they were supposed to be domesticated, obedient wives (Bernstein 1991; Fujimura-Fanselow and Kameda 1995; Imamura 1996; Buckley 2000).

Another important element of the fundaments of this system is the separation of the social spheres in Japan. What is proper in one social setting may be highly improper in another one and vice versa. Thus people's subjectivities and identities are to a certain extent fractured along the various social settings in which they move. Subjectivity and identity, on one hand, and sexual practices and social behavior, on the other, are not as closely intertwined as in Western settings. Sexual pleasure and domestic life have been separated in such a way that the split between housewives and women who live a sexually active life parallels the division between the realm of domestic labor and the market conditions under which the commodification of sexuality is regulated.

The Meiji period introduced the ideology of "Good Wife-Wise Mother." The Japanese family system is characterized by the division between the husband as a "salaryman," who leaves home early, comes home very late, takes no part in childcare and domestic activities, and is interested only in his career and a domesticated wife. For the women in such households, *josei*, femaleness, is equated with *bosei*, maternity (Mackie 1996). The art of childbearing has been elevated to an enormous height with the propagation of the "ten commandments" for mothers, which include phrases such as "thou shall give birth in pain" and "thou shalt abandon all professional activity for (at least) five years." These dictates do not make childbearing very attractive (Jolivet 1997).

Japanese society is not so much identity-based as Western societies tend to be, but rather behavior-based. The borders between acceptable and nonacceptable behavior may vary, but they remain very real. Social ostracism is a heavily felt penalty for those whose behavior falls outside of what is accepted as proper. The different forms of proper behaviors expected from individuals are found in the distinction between the concepts of *giri* (social duty to a specific person) and *ninjo* (one's own compulsions), and of *honne* (real motives) and *tatemae* (pretext, officially given motives) (see for instance, Lebra and Lebra 1986; Garon 1997).

The focus of this chapter is two-pronged. I discuss some of the religious elements that went into the construction of this system, as it relates to gender practices. At the same time I trace the historical path of women's same-sex practices. These tracts in fact overlap, as sociohistorical practices and beliefs are intertwined with changing religious practices. It is my contention that deconstruction of the elements that went into the making of the present gender ideology may open up a space for discussing desires and practices that fall outside of the dominant heterosexual family ideology. I maintain that precisely in the area of sexuality a reflection on Japan's past practices may provoke an interesting debate on the possible linkages with present-day transgender practices.

Transgender Practices

Japan provides many different examples of transgender practices both by female-bodied and male-bodied persons. The documentation of multiple forms of transgender behavior and same-sex erotic practices between men is quite extensive, especially in the Edo period that lasted from 1602 to 1868. But historic accounts of transgendered, cross-dressing females or women engaged in same-sex erotic activities are much rarer. In Edo Japan there was a sharp distinction between male-male and female-female sexual and erotic practices. There was no single word (such as "homosexuality" in English) that might be used to denote both varieties of sexual behavior (Furukawa 1994; Pflugfelder 1999). *Nanshoku* was the word most commonly used to denote men's same-sex practices. Only after the Meiji Restoration, and in particular during the succeeding Taisho period (1912–26), did it become common to refer to both male and female same-sex practices with the term "homosexuality" (see Wu this volume). Most literature on same-sex practices focuses almost exclusively on "the male path" (for instance, Watanabe and Iwata 1989; Leupp 1995; Pflugfelder 1999). Robertson (1998, and this volume) is the only author who deals, to some historical extent, with women's same-sex practices. I review some of the historical literature, focusing on the relation between social behavior, sexual practices, and the (changing) meanings attributed to them. I use the neutral term "women's same- sex practices" to deal with the wide variety of behaviors discussed. I use the term "lesbian" only in relation to women who identify themselves as such.[4]

I distinguish three settings in which instances of female-to-male transgender practices, androgyny, cross-dressing, or women's same-sex practices were present: the religious sphere, the cultural sphere, and the social sphere, especially that of the "floating world" of Yoshiwara, Edo's pleasure quarters (Becker 2002). In presenting an account of these instances I do not want to imply that pre-Meiji Japan, and especially the Tokugawa (Edo) period, was a place in which women could lead fulfilling lives of their own choosing. Japan at that time was patriarchal, phallocentric, and stratified. Yet not all women were reduced to passive victims of this male-dominated structure; some of them tried, at times successfully, to create (or maintain) a space of their own.

Religion and Same-Sex Practices

One of the fundaments of the earthquake-proof temple can be found in the religious system. Religion and ideology help to shape and sustain gender ideologies, yet their counterdiscourses open up the possibility of subverting that system. The intermingling of various religious and ideological elements (Buddhism, Shintoism, and Confucianism) is so strong in Japan that Hori, a well-known Japanese scholar of religion, speaks of Japanese religion as one entity. The original folk religions, loosely called "Shinto," blended with ethical, magical, and other religious elements in such a way that although various religious practices can still be distinguished, many have lost their original individual identities.

> Confucianism and Shinto have borrowed Buddhist metaphysics and psychology; Buddhism and Shinto have borrowed many aspects of Confucian theory and ethics; and Confucianism and Buddhism have adapted themselves rather thoroughly to the indigenous religion of Japan instead of maintaining their particularity, though of course their manifestations are many and varied. (Hori 1968:10)

Thus many (Buddhist) temples have Shinto elements and numerous (Shinto) shrines contain images of *bodhisattvas*. In their personal lives Japanese may alternate between Buddhist and Shinto rituals and practices, although usually one particular religious practice is preferred to the other. For clarity's sake I deal with each of the major religious streams separately.

Confucianism

While Confucian teachings cannot be considered to constitute a religion in the strict sense, the weight of its ethical proscriptions was so strong in Tokugawa Japan that its influence approached that of an orthodoxy. Confucianism stresses the importance of five forms of hierarchical relations in which the subordinate partner, such as a vassal, child, wife, or younger sibling, is supposed to show obedience to its superior. Confucian morality reserves sexual pleasure to men, while admonishing women to follow the "six virtues for women": obedience, purity, goodwill, frugality, modesty, and diligence. It prescribes heterosexual marriage for women as the best way to discipline them (Robertson 1992b). These prescriptions seem to offer little space for women to express forms of behavior that deviate from these norms. Men following the "male path," however, find themselves less constricted and are able to model their relationships on the Confucian hierarchy (Pflugfelder 1999). In addition the prevalence of stratified women's same-sex relations, in so as far this can be established from the few sources available, seems supported by Confucian ethics.

Shintoism

The two other major religious streams in Japanese society, Shintoism and Buddhism, offer more scope for female sexuality and androgyny. One of the clearest allusions to women's same-sex practices occurs in the story of "The Heavenly Striptease." Ama no Uzume (the Alarming Heavenly Female) seduces the Sun Goddess Amaterasu to leave the cave near Ise in which she had hidden herself and return sunlight to the earth (Buruma 1984; Leupp 1992; Bornoff 1994). During her dance Ama no Uzume goes into a trance in which she reveals her breasts and lifts her skirt just below her genitals. In another story, Amaterasu is depicted as cross-dressing in an encounter with her fierce brother Susanoo; in male attire she starts a warrior dance, chewing her sword (Pelzel 1986). The emperor, who is believed to descend from Amaterasu, ritually incarnates himself as the Sun Goddess during the course of the *daijosai* enthronement ceremony.

Yet the potentially all-powerful Amaterasu is not usually depicted as androgynous or cross-dressing. Her tolerance toward the misconduct of her brother Susanoo is usually foregrounded in a way that turns her into the eternally forgiving mother figure, always tolerant of men's license. Haruko (1998) analyzes the symbolic meaning of the transference of Amaterasu's symbol of power, the mirror, from the sleeping quarters of the emperor to the Ise shrine, headed by the emperor's daughter, about AD third century. The separation of politics and religion from bedroom to shrine meant the demotion of Japan's principal goddess from sister to daughter and the establishment of patriarchy in the imperial family. Haruko concludes that Amaterasu actually serves as a blind to "cover sexism in Japanese society" (1998:22).

Shinto rituals, with their emphasis on fertility ceremonies, held the feminine principle in high esteem. The city of Nagoya for instance has two famous fertility shrines. The "male" one prominently displays its many phalluses, which are proudly carried around during its festival (attended by tens of thousands of worshippers and tourists). In the female temple, the enormous stone vaginas are hidden in a little shack at the back of the temple. Its festival, held on the same day, attracts far less attention and its symbols of female sexuality are far more hidden.

Shintoism had its own form of androgyny. The roadside deity Dosojin was neither male nor female, although s/he was often represented as a phallus (Leupp 1992:174). These roadside deities are found all over Japan, although the ones picturing a man and woman copulating, once quite common, have mostly disappeared (Bornoff 1994:168). The institutionalization of Shintoism through the creation of state Shintoism has done much to deny the more potentially liberating aspects of this way of living. After the Meiji Restoration many female Shinto priests who had performed at shrines as mediums and performers of sacred dances were dismissed (Hardacre 1989).

The fox-god Inari, one of the most popular Shinto deities (over one-third of Shinto shrines are dedicated to Inari), also has certain androgynous qualities (Smyers 1996, 1997, 1999). Its service was probably first connected to fertility and rice growing. In its Buddhist form, it concerns a *boddhisattva* carrying a sack of rice astride a flying white fox. Inari's gender is variable; it may be either female, male, both, or neither (Smyers 1999:8). Inari's female association derives from its function as a rice fertility deity; its male association is a later Buddhist tradition. Originally its worship was accompanied with ribald sexual orgies. As money has displaced rice as the major source of wealth, Inari has now become associated with more urban, commercial practices. Yet the fox deity is still associated with sexual symbols. Its tail is generally considered to be a phallic symbol, while often a jewel that is either balanced on the tip of its tail or held in its mouth is associated with the womb.

Smyers (1999) dwells at length on the sexual ambiguity or androgyny of the fox deity, which often occurs in paired statues. She associates this with the esoteric Buddhist Shingon sect that uses sexual symbols to configure nonduality. As she observes, "This layer of meaning may not be consciously perceived by many worshipers of Inari, but it has a powerful impact on the senses when one undertakes a circumambulation of Inari Mountain of Fushimi" (Smyers 1999:147). One of the earliest mentions of Inari, the "Record of Fox Spirits" written by Oe no Masafuna in AD 1101, presents the fox as a femme fatale, who will change into a beautiful woman to seduce innocent men (Smits 1996). The same theme is portrayed in the first novel, Murasaki Shikibu's *The Tale of Genji* (Murasaki 1976), written in the late tenth century, to which I return below.

Buddhism

The *bodhisattva* Kannon, who is widely revered in Japan, offers the major expression of sexual ambiguity in Buddhism. The present-day dominant interpretation of Kannon is masculine. However, between the age when the deity entered Japan and today s/he has gone though various transformations, remnants of which still survive. Her/his androgynous, haunting beauty is displayed in major temples all over the country. In another manifestation, as Guan Yin, her female form is more apparent. In the manifestation of the white-clad "Goddess of Mercy" she came to Japan from China (after first having entered China as the Indian male divinity Avalokiteshvara). Transformed into Kannon, she performed similar functions as she originally did in China (Paul 1985, see also Sangren 1983). In spite of her female origin and her generally androgynous appearance, she is usually referred to as male by Japan's Buddhist clergy. When a professor at one of Kyoto's universities asked a Buddhist head monk about the female origin of Kannon, he vehemently denied it: "No no no, maybe his phallus is not visible, but he has a big one tucked away under his robe!" he exclaimed.[5]

In a fourteenth-century tale, Kannon is linked to male same-sex practices. A certain Japanese Buddhist monk was a passionate worshipper of Kannon. As he was very lonely, he was rewarded for his faith by the *bodhisattva* with a young male lover, a manifestation of Kannon. S/he appeared to the monk as a beautiful young man, dressed in a lavender kimono and playing a flute. They spent three loving years together, after which Kannon returned to her/his abode in the heavens (Conner, Sparks, and Sparks 1997).

The thousand-armed Guan Yin is the protector deity of the antimarriage sisterhoods of China, which have survived in Singapore, Hong Kong, and Malaysia. The thousand arms of Kannon refer to her/his power of concentration, which is linked both to the compassion this deity is characterized by and to the balanced flow of energy within one's body. This flow of energy links the body and the sexual to the cosmos. The strict vegetarian life, to which her followers, especially the vegetarian nuns, had to adhere, prohibited both the consummation of meat and sex with men. Sexual relations among the members were not uncommon though (Sankar 1986; Wieringa 1987). How frequently these practices occurred in the numerous Buddhist nunneries in Japan is unknown, although the remarks by Sawada referred to below suggest that Japanese nuns may have engaged in same-sex practices as well. According to Leupp (1998), an ambiguous reference in "Saikaku's Miscellany, Continued" (1695) to *otoko nikumi bikuni*, has been translated as "lesbian nuns." The term "*bikunu*," literally "nun," was often used in this period to refer to a category of itinerant prostitutes, while the meaning of "*otoko nikumi*," literally "man-hating," is unclear. Saikaku uses this term to refer to Osaka's fashionable Nagachami ward, where a variety of prostitutes from elegant young women to cross-dressing young male actors were available for hire.

Another intriguing line of enquiry into androgyny, sexuality, and female desire may be found in the relation between the goddesses Benten and Kannon. Benten, who originates from the Hindu goddess of music and knowledge, Sarasvati, sailed to Japan in a boat accompanied by six shipmates. She is the only female of the so-called Gods of Luck. Her cult is connected with phallicism and fertility, as is demonstrated in the Benten shrine of Ueno's Shinobazu pond, where a statue of her looking out into the pond, seen from behind, looks like a giant phallus. As Goddess of the Sea, she is often shown riding or being escorted on a dragon. According to a popular myth, she took the form of a dragon woman and swam under the islands of Japan, mating with the white snakes that lived there (Ann and Imale 1993). The Japanese Snake God Uga, who is related to the secret fertility cult of Uga-Jin, often decorates the chignon of Benten, who is also considered to be the Japanese Love Goddess (Johnson 1988). Sometimes she is portrayed with eight arms, two of which are folded in prayer, and in that form she resembles Kannon.

In Kamakura's Hasedera Kannon temple her cult is linked with an emphatically androgynous Kannon. In the main hall of this Hasekannon temple stands an impressive Kannon of elusive beauty. On her/his right side there is a painting in which s/he is portrayed in a more or less masculine posture with a thousand arms. On her/his left side a female form is represented, that of Sarasvati/Benten with a sun in the background. The parallel locations of these panels suggest that Kannon is associated both with masculinity and with femininity, as represented by Benten. In one of the minor halls a wooden statue of a lying, nude Benten in an autoerotic pose is found in the midst of Buddhist sages and other deities and beside a huge prayer wheel. This temple on its vast terrain houses both Buddhist and Shintoist elements.

Thus Japan's major Buddhist deity, Kannon, originally arrived in a female form. The way Buddhism was introduced and interpreted in Japan increased the negative connotations of women's sexuality and in general contributed strongly to women's subordination (see for example, Minamoto Junko 1993). As Smyers (1999) writes, the original association of the popular Inari cult with femininity and fertility was rerouted into a male direction after the introduction of Buddhist teachings. Buddhist clergy masculinized Kannon, as they did in the Inari cult. Yet they cannot erase the omnipresent androgynous, beautiful statues of this god/goddess in which her/his femininity is clearly perceived. Kannon is often seen as the Madonna of East Asia, second only in popular esteem to the Amitabha Buddha (Cotterell 1979). Kannon combines both "feminine" qualities, such as mercy and compassion, as well as enormous powers that the clergy associates with masculinity. Given these associations, I contend that the religion itself offers more space for expressions of female sexual energy than is commonly thought. In spite of the negative associations with women's sexuality that Buddhism propagates (see also Paul 1985), a potentially more liberating subtext of androgyny exists in Buddhist teaching that, even if it does not subvert openly the phallocentrism of certain Buddhist sects, creates a context in which androgyny and transgenderism are sacralized, however vaguely or mutedly.

Yet in spite of the possibility of gender variance that Buddhism offers, the dominant religious practices exclude women. This exclusion is partly derived from certain teachings of Gautama Buddha himself and from other texts, such as the Mahayana Sutras in which women are seen as the sinful sex. When Buddhism spread in Japan around the tenth and eleventh centuries AD, the Buddhist clergy became almost completely masculinized. They upheld teachings that claimed women could only find salvation by either renouncing worldly life through dedicated motherhood, for instance by rearing future monks, or through rebirth as a man (Haruko 1998).

Sociohistorical Elements

Edo Period

The Japanese sexologist Sawada, trying to categorize Japanese forms of same-sex love in 1920, includes nuns and servants in the women's quarters of feudal households among the categories of people who might have "acquired" a taste for same-sex love because of the "prohibition of normal sexual relations." As other causes that might stimulate women into a same-sex relation, he refers to "man-hating" women (with an "obsessive belief that the opposite sex is unclean") and prostitutes, who might react to the "unpleasantness of forced intercourse with males" (Sawada quoted in Pflugfelder 1999:272). As I demonstrate, the few sources available do seem to suggest that female desire for other women was acknowledged in Tokugawa Japan. Certain women found ways to live their desires and thus to subvert the phallocentric ideology by which they were restricted to a life of obedience to men. Various forms of female-to-male transgender practices also existed.

Women who engaged in sex with other women in the Edo period were either wives or prostitutes; their subjectivity and identity would often have been determined by these factors rather than by the sexual pleasures they may have experienced with other women. The relationship between identity and sexual desire reflected a society in which age- and status-stratified sexual behavior among men was accepted and even approved (Leupp 1995:145). Confucianism prescribed marriage to both women and men, but women were much more restricted in their marriages than men were. In general, women lived a more subdued and dependent emotional life than men. However, a striking example of status-stratified women's same-sex desire appears in a print from Ejima Kiseki's 1717 album "Characters of Worldly Young Women." It depicts a brothel scene in which a woman, dressed in male clothing and sporting a sword, prepares to meet a courtesan. The male servant informs her that her courtesan is already waiting for her.

Among the urban cultures of Edo and Kyoto there are instances of female-to-male cross-dressing (as in "male dancing" and kabuki discussed below) or women's same-sex practices. Most references are to the "Floating World," as the pleasure quarters were called, possibly because by that time men were the major chroniclers. In contrast, in the earlier Heian period women were the major writers.[6] The author of the monumental late tenth-century novel *The Tale of Genji*, which is the story of an irresistibly attractive prince who has various love affairs with women, is Murasaki Shikibu. In her diary (Murasaki 1996) she openly speaks of her attraction to particular court ladies with whom she exchanges love poems. Dalby (2000) suggests that Murasaki discovers sexual love with a female friend from her youth and that *The Tale of Genji* is in fact begun as a game between both of them in which they took turns playing the role of the "lady killer," the "Shining Prince" Genji. Kimi Komasyaku, a well-known literary historian and one of the first Japanese lesbian feminists, states that Murasaki's same-sex love life was an inspiration to what is generally seen as the first novel in Japan.[7]

In addition to status-stratified female-to-female sexuality evidenced in Eijima Kiseki's portrayal mentioned above, there is evidence of another form in which female prostitutes were taught to cross-dress and behave like boys. In "the Life of an Amorous Man" (1682), Saikaku describes a group of female dancer-prostitutes who "are trained as dancers from early childhood, and learn to imitate the deportment and behavior of men." While from their mid-teens they sexually service men, they begin their vocation catering to female customers. "From age 11 or 12 to age 14 or 15, they are engaged by women as drinking companions, then their forelocks are shaved and they are trained to imitate men's voices" (Leupp 1998:9). They thus served both male and female patrons (Leupp 1995:172). This pattern may be seen as one of the origins of the present-day *onabe*, female-bodied, male-identified, cross-dressing hosts who cater to women clients in special bars; their services may include sexuality.

Saikaku's "Life of an Amorous Woman," which first appeared in 1686, contains the most extensive literary record of a woman's same-sex encounter in the Edo period. Using the translation Leupp (1998) provides, I quote the complete fragment below, as it is indicative of several phenomena noted in the previous section. The story relates the sexual experiences of a young woman as she moves between various jobs, including those of domestic servant and courtesan. Recently arrived in the city of Sakai she finds a job as servant to a robust widow, a woman in her seventies:

> Night began to fall and I was ordered to lay down the bedclothes. This was as I had foreseen, but the next order put me to a nonplus: "You are to sleep in the same bed as your mistress" I was told. Since this was a command, I could not gainsay it. Having joined my mistress in bed, then, I expected that she would tell me to scratch her hip, or something of the sort. But that wasn't the case. I performed the woman's [part], and my mistress assumed the male [role], and we played around all night. It was troubling to find myself [in the situation, but] the Floating World is wide. I've been employed in lots of jobs; but never before had I been used like this. "When I am reborn in the next world, I will be a man. Then I shall be free to do what really gives me pleasure!" Thus did my mistress voice her fondest wish. (Leupp 1998:11–12)

Leupp (1998) lists ten *shunga* (erotic woodblock prints) in which women's same-sex practices are depicted. These *shunga* demonstrate several issues discussed above. Often the partners are divided by social class and/or age, and often a dildo is used. These types of representations may be common because *shunga* usually depict scenes in the Floating World but they may also reflect a wider reality. After all, the practice of *nanshoku* was also age- and status-stratified. The frequent depiction of dildos may be due to the fact that most *shunga* artists were men, apart from Katsushika Oi, daughter of the great *shunga* artist Katsushika Hokusai, who was herself the creator of one of the most well-known *shunga* depicting women's same-sex activities. Men may find it easier to accept, or may even find it titillating, if women have sex using an instrument that resembles their own genitals.

There are several *shunga* in which women are portrayed making love to each other. In some cases a man is watching, raising questions about whether these *shunga* were solely produced for men and intended to titillate men's desires. The masculine presence in some of these all-female *shunga* has led the feminist sociologist Ueno Chizuko to opine that there is no evidence of Tokugawa lesbianism (Leupp 1998, and personal communication by Ueno). In a famous *shunga* painting of a woman's same-sex scene from Eiri's 1801 Album "Love-Letters, Love Consummated," the woman on the left prepares to receive a huge black *harigata* (dildo) worn by her woman lover, who holds a seashell containing lubricant. The women are alone. Leupp quotes Ueno as saying that "lesbianism in the contemporary sense, i.e. women loving women, does not exist in Tokugawa erotica" (Leupp 1998:7). While I may agree with her that the concept of lesbianism is not an appropriate term for the few examples that have survived of erotic behavior among women in Edo period, I do not agree with her contention that there is no evidence of women desiring other women and having sex with each other. The above *shunga* clearly portrays autonomous sexual desire between women (in stereotypical fashion the vagina of the woman into which the dildo will be inserted is portrayed as enlarged and dripping). Even if these *shunga* may have been primarily produced for the male gaze, they may have depicted actual life scenes. There is also a *shunga* in which two women use a double-headed dildo. This artifact is clearly intended for female pleasure only. These dildos may also signal a common sexual practice among women.

After the Meiji Restoration

It is not clear how widespread the phenomenon of women adopting men's ways was during the Edo period, but in the early Meiji period we have the record of Fukuda, who was imprisoned because of her political activities. Fukuda recounts the case of a fellow inmate, Shimazu Masa, who, convicted of theft charges, had been imprisoned in 1881. "Shimazu had lavished much of the money she stole on female geisha, attracting the attention of the police during an especially extravagant moon-viewing expedition to Kyoto, for which occasion she attired herself in virile clothing and hairstyle and adopted the masculine name of Shimazu Harusaburo" (Pflugfelder 1999:190).

The campaigns waged during the Meiji period to purge Japan of the various vices associated with the Edo period highlight the persistence of women's same-sex practices. The references to homosexuality among female students in the Meiji period are particularly striking. Furukawa Makoto quotes instances of *o-me*, which "was very popular." *O-me* was seen as "somehow feeling a somewhat abnormal attraction, similar to *nanshoku*" (1994:114). Makoto states that "intimacy between women is not infrequent and perhaps even more frequent than intimacy between men" (1994:115). However, he also notes that the borderline between a deep emotional attachment and a sexual relationship between women was difficult to draw because women were supposed to be much more emotional and friendly toward each other than men were. Initially, schoolgirl crushes, referred to as "S" relations (S from *shojo*, girl, but also from sister and sex) were not taken too seriously. Yet several double suicides drew considerable attention (see Robertson this volume). Worried policymakers decided to take measures to ensure that women's friendships would not exceed the bonds of appropriate behavior, that is, would not become sexual. Policymakers advocated sex education, introducing into Japan European sexologists, such as Ellis, Krafft-Ebing, Carpenter, Hirschfeld, and others, with their essentialist notions of sexuality. By the 1920s, the influence of sexology and its medicalization of homosexuality had spread widely. A different Eros, more than ever associated with sin and shame, was introduced.

The antisex campaign was waged on many fronts. It was, for instance, directed at sexual symbols evident in many Shinto shrines, such as those devoted to the popular fox-god Inari. Buchanan noted in 1935 that police "removed a great many of the more gross and obvious phallic symbols" from the Inari shrines (quoted in Smyers 1999:134). But the antisex campaign was primarily directed at women, who were singled out as particularly prone to sexual deviance. Meiji women were consciously directed to be "good wives, wise mothers" (Robertson 1998; Wu this volume). The "Modern Girl" phenomenon became the object of sharp criticism because the apparent masculinization of females was felt to compromise the masculinity of males. Certain same-sex practices among women were the topic of numerous critical newspaper articles.

Yet however much lesbianism was frowned upon in public discourse, records of women-loving-women exist from that period (see also Robertson this volume). The early twentieth century produced three famous women couples. Although the memory of their love for each other has almost been erased, they left enough material behind to testify to their love. Yoshiya Nobuko and her secretary Monma Chiyo lived and worked together for 50 years, until 1973, when Nobuko died. She was one of the most successful writers of her time. Their relationship was very productive, with Chiyo playing Alice B. Toklas to Nobuko's Gertrude Stein, as Izumo and Masree note (2000:79). Another relationship was formed by the founder of the Japanese women's rights movement, Hiratsuka Raicho, and the painter, Otake Kokichi, whom Raicho called "her boy" (see Wu this volume). The writer Nakajo Yuriko and Yuasa Yoshiko were another women couple the memory of whose love has survived attempts to erase it from history. Yet even among many mainstream feminists, as Izumo and Maree sadly note, the same-sex love relationships between these women is usually ignored or downplayed as "childish pastimes" (2000:87).

Sexology has had a wide-ranging influence on Japanese society, transforming a concern with proper behavior in which notions of same-sex love were integrated with notions of homosexuality to a same-sex love in which identity, desire, and guilt are closely interwoven (see also Lunsing 1995, 1998; Fruhstuck 2003) and in which one's nature is the object of investigation, rather than one's behavior (see also Bleys 1995). In the process the notion that sexuality can be a powerful source of pleasure, which can be acted out in multiple ways, lost much of its currency.

Cultural Practices

The Takarazuka Revue

The phenomenon that has presented the most obvious social space for women's erotic and same-sex fantasies and desires is the all-female Takarazuka Revue, which was established in the Meiji period in 1913. The management of the revue takes great care not to cross the boundaries imposed by the antisex campaign to discipline Japanese women. The Takaraziennes who play men's roles are portrayed by the management as cross-dressing. Yet the attraction that the all-female cast, particularly those playing the men's roles, has for their fans is widely acknowledged. The word "fan" is often taken to mean "lesbian" (see Robertson this volume). The Takaraziennes arouse same-sex (but not same-gender) erotic desire in their fans.

Robertson (1992a, 1992b, 1998), who wrote a detailed account of the history of the Takarazuka Revue, makes explicit references to the lesbian subtext underlying and subverting the dominant heterosexual gender ideology in which the shows are couched. The overt butch-femme eroticism displayed by its actresses is only barely hidden behind the patriarchally inscribed heterosexual code that its directors impose on the show. The actresses playing the male roles, the *otokoyaku*, can be compared with the *onnagata* players (male-bodied actors who play female roles) of the Kabuki theater, although they never become male in the way the *onnagata* become female. In spite of their swagger, low voices, and male attire, the *otokoyaku* always remain clearly recognizable as women. In the words of Takarazuka's founder, Kobayashi, himself: "The *otokoyaku* is not male but is more suave, more affectionate, more courageous, more charming, more handsome and more fascinating than a real male" (cited in Robertson 1992b:424). The *otokoyaku* attract most of the attention, receiving love letters in the thousands from their fans.

The most ardent Takarazuka fans form groups around a particular masculine star. They dress in similar jackets and buy the same kind of paraphernalia. Takarazuka shops sell all kinds of objects with special designs associated with the show, from videos and picture books to handkerchiefs and mugs. The buyers are mostly girls in their teens, but some of them belong to other age groups as well. After a particular show fans wait outside in orderly groups (by star). If their favorite actor/actress appears, the fans who dote on her/him cheer, squat on their hunches, and present the gifts, letters, or cards they have been busily scribbling during the long hours of their vigil. The most favorite fans are allowed to carry the bags in which the presents are collected.

Although the association of fandom with lesbianism that Robertson (this volume) describes for the fans of the early twentieth century seems to have declined, it is difficult to avoid the impression that the fantasies and aspirations of the hundreds of fans may have erotic or sexual overtones. But this is rarely spoken about in public. One fan, who had bought an apartment overlooking the Takarazuka theater and who had made every effort to invite her favorite *otokoyaku* actress to her house, answered only vaguely when I pressed her to specify the desires that underlay her invitation, "Oh, to hear her sing for me alone." She then became so frightened of this confession that she insisted she should remain anonymous.

The immense popularity of the Revue, which now gives continuous, all-year performances in two huge theaters in Takarazuka and Tokyo, clearly demonstrates that the attraction of the show is widely experienced and that the erotic message is understood. The success of Takarazuka has been explained as providing girls and women with an outlet in which they can escape from their dreary unromantic marriages that convention forces them to accept. The romantic dreams provided by the Takarazuka's *otokoyaku*, however, are not genderless, sexually ambiguous dreams only, as Buruma suggests (1984:132, see also Nakamura and Matsuo 2003). The world of Takarazuka is one of two genders and one sex in which the two stylized, opposing poles of gender provide an intensely erotic energy. It is striking that Hollywood stars such as Marilyn Monroe are unequivocally associated with erotic desire, while the sexual postures of the *otokoyaku* are portrayed as not provoking such desires.

The Takaraziennes are carefully controlled to prevent the association of the Revue with sexual licentiousness. Yet from time to time scandals erupt (see also Robertson 1992a and 1998). Some Takarazuka actresses have lesbian affairs among themselves. The brother of an older lesbian woman I interviewed (herself an ardent Takarazuka fan in her youth) was one of the chief designers of the Revue. He told her of many lesbian scandals within the group. "Once they have to retire," she added, "they are brainwashed to get married. Most of these marriages are only to disguise their lesbian relationships, just to please society. When they are out of the limelight they quickly divorce and go back to their woman lovers."[8]

An important element of the Takarazuka Revue is the eternal youth of the stars. They have to retire when they reach the age of 35 (or when they marry). In that sense a parallel can be found in men's attraction to the eternal male youth, the *bishonen*, who are also always presented as androgynous (Buruma 1984). *Bishonen* are usually portrayed as the more or less passive partners of older boys or men, while the *otokoyaku*, who exude a similar kind of youthful, androgynous beauty are presented as the "active" partners with their lovers-on-the-stage. Interestingly, male same-sex practices are also called *shudo*, the "way of youths" (Pflugfelder 1999).

Takarazuka was not created in a historical vacuum. Japanese history shows several examples of female cross-dressing actors and/or dancers. From the twelfth to the fourteenth centuries, for instance, there was a tradition of "male dancing" in Kyoto. These female dancers were called *shirabyoshi*, were dressed in men's *suikan* overshirts and high caps, and wore daggers with silver-decorated hilts and scabbards (Leupp 1995:175). Originally these dancers were associated with ritual dance dramas. *Shirabyoshi* is also the name of sometimes transgendered deities or spirits in Shinto. They are usually depicted as half-human and half-serpent. The female dancers, sometimes transgendered, were shamans or priests/priestesses linked to the Shirabyoshi spirits (Connor et al. 1997).

The kabuki theater itself was set up by a woman, Okuni, around 1603. Originally she may have been engaged as a *miko*, a shrine maiden occasionally engaged in prostitution (Bornoff 1994:253; Leupp 1995). On the banks of Kyoto's Kamo River, she started her *onna kabuki*, women's *kabuki*, the performances of which might end in sexual abandon. As the theatrical brilliance of her shows increased and her popularity rose, the *onna kabuki* changed into the Okuni *kabuki*, which enjoyed an enormous popularity among Kyoto's townspeople. Okuni is honored by a statue on the riverbank, which portrays her as a cross-dressing samurai complete with swords. Among Okuni's most popular performances is one in which, dressed as a handsome man, she trysted with a prostitute (also played by a woman) in a teahouse (Leupp 1995:90). As the Tokugawa shogunate became concerned with the urban licentiousness with which this form of *kabuki* was associated, it prohibited women from appearing on the stage in 1629. Thereafter the *wakashu kabuki*, literally youths' *kabuki* dominated the kabuki stage.

Women's Same-Sex Entertainment: Onabe Bars

The present-day *onabe* bars echo some of the themes discussed above. *Onabe* is the name of both female-bodied, male-identified (sex) workers in Japan's extensive entertainment industry and of masculine-looking women in general. According to Katsura (2001), *onabe* bars in their present form first appeared in Tokyo around 1960. Initially they had mostly male customers, as women did not have the kind of money to spend in these clubs. Only from 1985 onwards, *onabe* bars exclusively catering to women were opened.

The documentary video "Shinjuku Boys" (Longinotto and Williams 1995), named after Tokyo's major entertainment district, portrays three *onabe* who work in Club Marilyn. In the introductory comments they are described as women who decided to live like men and who are ideal men in the eyes of their clients. Gaish, one of the *onabe*, reflects on hir identity:[9] "I cannot make myself more feminine. I don't want to be a real man. If people think I'm in between, that's OK with me. I don't feel like a woman in my mind. I'm strong and straightforward. I have a girl's face but my behavior is more masculine than that of a man. I've always been like this, it is natural to me." The other *onabe* too speak of themselves in a naturalizing discourse. An *onabe* I interviewed in 1998 in another bar told me that s/he had recently arrived in Tokyo. S/he came originally from Hokkaido, in the north. At the age of 11 or 12, s/he had seen a short fragment of a documentary film on an *onabe* bar in Tokyo: "At that moment I knew that was me, that I belonged there. From that moment onwards I had only one purpose in life, go to Tokyo, find an *onabe* bar to work in."

The *onabe* play the "active" sexual role with their clients and do not want to undress in front of them: "I have heard lesbians take their clothes off, but we *onabe*, we hate that. I would never do that with a client" (Tatsu in "Shinjuku Boys"). However, Tatsu overcame this hesitation with the lover s/he was cohabiting with during the filming of the documentary. Many *onabe* bind their breasts. They wear stylish men's suits and behave in all respects like ideal gentlemen in the bars. Some of them undergo hormone treatment to grow facial hair and to lower their voices. One of the *onabe* I interviewed had undergone an operation in which the tissue from hir breasts had been sucked away. S/he proudly lifted hir shirt to display a flat chest, smooth as that of a *bishonen*.

Concluding Statements

In the early 1990s, gay groups in Japan gained much media attention. Some authors refer to this episode as a "gay boom" (Lunsing 1999). For a while gay and lesbian groups became more prominent, as the violent reactions they feared did not take place. Gay and lesbian groups sought to gain whatever advantage they could of this increased media attention. The question is whether the gay boom has broken the silence on issues of lesbianism and homosexuality in general. Lunsing is carefully positive. He maintains that although the profound changes necessary to produce such a transformation may take time, the overall effect, particularly in the enlarged possibility for open discussion, is positive (2000:316). However, the "Modern Girl" movement in the 1920s and 1930s also knew many debates on lesbianism. At that time, as discussed earlier, the visibility of particularly some masculinized women led to greater repression.

Many of the lesbian women I spoke to in Japan did not dare to come out. They spoke of discrimination at work and in their families. They were all largely ignorant of the various forms of androgyny or women's same-sex practices I have described in the foregoing section. Two young lesbian women in Kyoto I spoke to proudly showed me a bulletin they had just published that contained an article on the use of dildos. I asked them where their material came from. It turned out to be a translation of a pamphlet distributed by the New York-based lesbian sex shop, Eve's Garden. When I showed them a picture of lesbian *shunga* I had just acquired, they were very surprised. They thought they were the first ones in Japanese history who were interested in dildos. Cut off from their past and marginalized in the present, the isolation of lesbian women is increased by the social fragmentation of the different circles in which women's erotic or same-sex desires or practices are lived. Although *onabe* cater to (heterosexually identified) women's needs, they do not consider themselves lesbian. And lesbian women agree with them. They do not visit *onabe* bars, just as *onabe* will not go to lesbian activities. Neither of them can afford to be Takarazuka fans—the lesbian women, because they do not consider Takarazuka a lesbian revue, and the *onabe* precisely because they do consider it a lesbian affair.

Japanese society remains rigidly patriarchal; the pressure upon women to marry is very strong. Even if more and more women prefer to live single lives, heterosexuality remains the norm. Yet the historical presence of female-to-male cross-dressing and of transgender practices in Japan points to the possibility of the acceptance of multiple gender constructs and nonnormative sexualities. Historical inquiries such as this one may contribute to the breaking of the silence with which "the system," this earthquake-proof temple, maintains its iron grip on people's consciousness.

Most feminist and lesbian women I spoke to agreed that the dominant Buddhist teachings as yet do not allow for interpretations that might provide a more feminist perspective. Yet such a development has happened with Christianity and in Islamic regions when feminists demand the right to reinterpret certain texts and practices. Buddhism should offer scope for a similar process of reflection. After all, in comparison with the dominant representation of Christian womanhood, Mary, the *bodhisattva* Kannon appears much more powerful, more androgynous, more independent, and possibly more independent sexually. The popular Inari cult also allows for a reading in which androgyny and sexual ambiguity is stressed. While the Japanese social system stresses duality and clear separation of boundaries among various social categories and the two genders, these subtexts may, at the same time, subvert this rigidity. Cultures as well as religions are social constructs that, in the process of being created and reproduced, offer possibilities for change and re-creation. I have described the moments of change or reaffirmation in, for instance, the masculinization of Buddhism and the influence of Western sexology to identify the locations of power in which this process happens, as well as the actors involved. Such careful analyses of power structures reveal opportunities for intervention that may lead to greater acceptance of women's same-sex relations.

Potentially the presence of women's same-sex pleasure can expose the spurious stability of the family/nation nexus upon which the Japanese earthquake-proof temple is built. Although Japan's patriarchal gerontocracy will try its utmost to prevent that from happening, an awareness of the historical examples I have outlined in this chapter and an acceptance of the various present-day forms of transgender practices may help to empower women.

Notes

1. Interview held in Osaka, April 12, 1998.
2. Many historical references to women's same-sex practices pertain to transgendered females or to transgender practices. In some cases this reflects gender-stratified sexual relations, but in other cases same-sex practices are not always directly referred to. I have chosen to include discussion of both same-sex erotic practices and transgender behaviors because they both involve practices and behaviors that deviate from heterosexual normativity.
3. By the end of the fifteenth century the shogun or warlord Tokugawa Ieyasu (1542–1616) succeeded in unifying Japan. The role of the emperor was greatly restricted. He moved the center of power from Kyoto, the seat of the emperors, to Edo, present-day Tokyo. The period until the forceful opening of Japan by the American "black ships" is called the Edo or Tokugawa period (1603–1868). In 1868 the Meiji emperor was restored to power and a process of modernization started.
4. For further discussion of use of terms, see Wieringa and Blackwood 1999.
5. Personal communication, March 7, 1998.
6. The Heian period lasted from AD 794 to 1185. Its capital was present-day Kyoto, which remained the seat of the emperor's court until 1868, when it was moved to Edo, present-day Tokyo. Aristocratic men were restricted to Chinese education; women of the court, such as Murasaki Shikibu, were free to write diaries and novels in their native languages, in *kana*, a newly developed script adapted to the needs of the Japanese language.
7. Interview with Kimi Komasyaku, April 12, 1998.
8. Ibid.
9. The binary division of gendered pronouns in English does not do justice to (Japanese) forms of transgenderism. I therefore use the terms "hir" and "s/he" to refer to transgendered persons.

References Cited

Ann, Martha and Dorothy Meyers Imel. 1993. *Goddesses in world mythology*. New York: Oxford University Press.

Becker, J.E. de. 2002. *The nightless city of the Geisha: The history of the Yoshiwara*. New York: Kegan Paul.

Bernstein, Gail Lee, ed. 1991. *Recreating Japanese women, 1600–1945*. Berkeley: University of California Press.

Bleys, Rudi C. 1995. *Geography of perversion*. New York: New York University Press.

Bornoff, Nicholas. 1994. *Pink samurai: The pursuit and politics of sex in Japan*. London: HarperCollins.

Buckley, Sandra. 2000. Sexing the kitchen: Okoge and other tales of contemporary Japan. In *Queer diasporas*. Cindy Patton and Benigno Sanchez-Eppler, eds. Pp. 215–244. Durham: Duke University Press.

Buruma, Ian. 1984. *De Spiegel van de Zonnegodin* (The Mirror of the Sun Goddess). Amsterdam: Arbeiderspers.

Connor, Randy P., David Hatfield Sparks, and Mariya Sparks. 1997. *Cassell's encyclopedia of queer myth, symbol and spirit*. London: Cassell.

Cotterell, Arthur. 1979. *A dictionary of world mythology*. Leicester: Windward.

Dalby, Liza. 2000. *The tale of Murasaki*. London: Chatto and Windus.

Davis, Winston. 1992. *Japanese society and religion: Paradigms of structure and change*. Albany: State University of New York Press.

Fruhstuck, Sabina. 2003. *Colonizing sex: Sexology and social control in modern Japan*. Berkeley: University of California Press.

Fujimura-Fanselow, Kumiko and Atsuko Kameda. 1995. *Japanese women: New feminist perspectives on the past, present and future*. New York: The Feminist Press.

Furukawa Makoto. 1994. The changing nature of sexuality: The three codes framing homosexuality in modern Japan. *U.S.-Japan Women's Journal* 7: 98–127.

Garon, Sheldon. 1997. *Molding Japanese minds: The state in everyday life*. Princeton: Princeton University Press.

Hardacre, Helen. 1989. *Shinto and the state, 1868–1988*. Princeton: Princeton University Press.

———. 1997. *Marketing the menacing fetus in Japan*. Berkeley: University of California Press.

Haruko, Okano. 1998. A feminist critique of Japanese religions. In *Women and religion in Japan*. Akiko Kuda and Haruka Okano, eds. Pp. 17–45. Wiesbaden: Harassowitz Verlag.

Hori, Ichiro. 1968. *Folk religion in Japan: Continuity and change*. Chicago: University of Chicago Press.

Imamura, Anne E., ed. 1996. *Re-imaging Japanese women*. Berkeley: University of California Press.

Itoh, Etsuko. 1998. Nora. In *Queer Japan: Personal stories of Japanese lesbians, gays, bisexuals and transsexuals*. Barbara Summerhawk, Cheiron MacMahill and Darren McDonald, eds. Pp. 157–163. Norwich: New Victoria Publishers.

Izumo, Marou and Claire Maree. 2000. *Love upon the chopping board*. Melbourne: Spinifex.

Johnson, Buffie. 1988. *Lady of the beasts: Ancient images of the goddess and her sacred animals*. San Francisco: Harper & Row.

Jolivet, Muriel. 1997. *Japan: The childless society?* London: Routledge.

Katsura, Yoko. 2001. On the *onabe*: One type of female to male transgender in Japan. Paper presented at the Third International Association for the Study of Sexuality, Culture and Society Conference, Melbourne, Australia.

Krafft-Ebing, R. Von. 1912 [1902]. *Psychopathia sexualis*. Stuttgart: Enke Verlag.

Lebra, Takie Sugiyama and Willian P. Lebra, eds. 1986. *Japanese culture and behavior: Selected readings*. 2nd rev. ed. Honolulu: University of Hawaii Press.

Leupp, Gary P. 1995. *Male colors: The construction of homosexuality in Tokugawa Japan*. Berkeley: University of California Press.

———. 1998. "The Floating World is wide . . .": Some suggested approaches to researching lesbianism in Tokugawa Japan (1603–1868). *Thamyris* 5(1): 1–40.

Longinotto, Kim and Jano Williams, dirs. 1995. *Shinjuku boys*. 53 min. British Broadcasting Corporation.

Lunsing, Wim. 1997. "Gay boom" in Japan: Changing views of homosexuality? *Thamyris* (4)2: 267–293.

———. 1998. Lesbian and gay movements: Between hard and soft. In *Soziale Bewegungen in Japan* [Social movements in Japan]. Claudia Derich and Anja Osiander eds. Pp. 279–310. Hamburg: Gesellschaft fur Natur- und Volkerkunde Ostasiens.

———. 1999. Japan: Finding its way? In *The global emergence of gay and lesbian politics: National imprints of a worldwide movement*. Barry D. Adam, Jan Willem Duyvendak, and Andre Krouwel, eds. Pp. 293–326. Philadelphia: Temple University Press.

Mackie, Vera. 1996. Feminist critiques of modern Japanese politics. In *Mapping the women's movement*. Monica Threlfall, ed. Pp. 260–288. London: Verso.

Minamoto Junko. 1993. Buddhism and the historical construction of sexuality in Japan. *U.S-Japan Women's Journal* 5: 87–115.

Mishima Yukio. 1994. [1958]. *Confessions of a mask*. Tokyo: Tuttle.

Murasaki Shikibu. 1976. *The tale of Genji*. Edward G. Seidensticker, trans. Tokyo: Tuttle.

———. 1996. *The diary of Lady Murasaki*. Richard Bowring, trans. London: Penguin.

Nakamura, Karen and Hisako Matsuo. 2003. Female masculinity and fantasy spaces: Transcending genders in the Takarazuka Theatre and Japanese popular culture. In *Men and masculinities in contemporary Japan: Dislocating the salaryman doxa*. James E. Roberson and Nobue Suzuki, eds. Pp. 59–76. London: RoutledgeCurzon.

Paul, Diana Y. 1985. *Women in Buddhism: Images of the feminine in the Mahayana tradition*. Berkeley: University of California Press.

Pelzel, John C. 1986. Human nature in the Japanese myths. In *Japanese culture and behavior: Selected readings*. Takie Sugiyama Lebra and William P. Lebra, eds. Pp. 7–29. Honolulu: University of Hawaii Press.

Pflugfelder, Gregory M. 1999. *Cartographies of desire: Male-male sexuality in Japanese discourse, 1600–1950*. Berkeley: University of California Press.

Piggott, Juliet. 1969. *Japanese mythology*. London: Chancellor Press.

Robertson, Jennifer. 1992a. Doing and undoing "female" and "male" in Japan: The Takarazuka Revue. In *Japanese social organization*. Takie Sugiyama Lebra, ed. Pp. 165–193. Honolulu: University of Hawaii Press.

———. 1992b. The politics of androgyny in Japan: Sexuality and subversion in the theater and beyond. *American Ethnologist* 19(3): 419–441.

———. 1998. *Takarazuka: Sexual politics and popular culture in modern Japan*. Berkeley: University of California Press.

Sangren, P. Steven. 1983. Female gender in Chinese religious symbols: Kuan Yin, Ma Tsu and the "eternal mother." *Signs: Journal of Women in Culture and Society* 9(1): 4–25.

Sankar, Andrea. 1986. Sisters and brothers, lovers and enemies: Marriage resistance in Southern Kwangtung. In *The many faces of homosexuality: Anthropological approaches to homosexual behavior*. Evelyn Blackwood, ed. Pp. 69–81. New York: Harrington Park Press.

Smits, Ivo. 1996. An early anthropologist? Oe no Masofusa's "A Record of Fox Spirits." In *Religion in Japan: Arrows to heaven and earth*. Peter F. Kornicki and I.J. McMullen, eds. Pp. 128–147. Cambridge: Cambridge University Press.

Smyers, Karen. 1996. My own Inari: Personalization of the deity in Inari worship. *Japanese Journal of Religious Studies* 23(1/2): 85–116.

———. 1997. Inari pilgrimage: Following one's path on the mountain. *Japanese Journal of Religious Studies* 24(3/4): 429–452.

———. 1999. *The fox and the jewel: Shared and private meanings in contemporary Japanese Inari worship*. Honolulu: University of Hawai'i Press.

United Nations Development Programme. 2001. *Human development report 2001*. New York: HDRO.

Watanabe Tsunea and Iwata Jun'ichi. 1989. *The love of the samurai: A thousand years of Japanese homosexuality*. London: GMP.

Wieringa, Saskia E. 1987. *Uw toegenegen Dora D., reisbrieven* (Yours sincerely, Dora D.: Travel letters. Amsterdam: Furie.

Wieringa, Saskia E. and Evelyn Blackwood. 1999. Introduction. In *Female desires: Same-sex relations and transgender practices across cultures*. Evelyn Blackwood and Saskia E. Wieringa, eds. Pp. 1–38. New York: Columbia University Press.

Wolveren, K.G. van. 1989. *Japan: De onzichtbare drijfveren van een wereldmacht* [Japan: The invisible drives of a world power]. Amsterdam: Rainbow Pockets.

Yoshizumi, Kyoko. 1995. Marriage and family: Past and present. In *Japanese women: New feminist perspectives on the past, present and future*. Kumiko Fujimura-Fanselow and Atsuko Kameda, eds. Pp. 183–199. New York: The Feminist Press.

Chapter Three

Desire and Deviance in Classical Indian Philosophy: A Study of Female Masculinity and Male Femininity in the Tamil Folk Legend Alliyarasanimalai

Kanchana Natarajan

Conventional Indian philosophy regards desire as a mental phenomenon that has the capacity to bind human beings and cause endless physical and psychological suffering.[1] Desire arises from the mind, which is by nature perpetually fickle and restless (Bhagavad Gita 1987:34–35) and endless in its demands.[2] Desire and its related activity bring about karmic consequences that are then articulated through many lifetimes in a series of births and deaths. It is therefore crucial to understand the mind and its workings, if one is to free oneself from the mechanisms and effects of desire. Eliminating desires and thereby salvaging the self from afflictions of bondage caused by desires is unequivocally declared as liberation or the goal of human existence. True liberation is a state of absolute peace—likened to a lamp that does not flicker in a windless place (Bhagavad-Gita 1987:19). Such a state, even though "desired" by all, is sought only by few, and the foremost prerequisite for the attainment of such freedom is the annihilation of all desires (except the desire for liberation).

Desire and deviance are perennially interlocked and enmeshed with one another in a symbiotic relationship, for desire of the material world is simultaneously deviance from the spiritual goal of humankind. However inconsequential or harmless a desire appears, it inevitably is a manifestation of deviance that moves away from the path of spiritual freedom and liberation. The smallest desire can make one fall further into the trap of bondage. Hence all desires, except the intense longing for liberation, are to be scrupulously shunned.

The Brahmanical philosophies declare that all living beings are endowed with soul(s) that is/are omnipotent, omniscient, and eternal; the realization of this inviolate essence will ultimately free one from all desires.[3] By virtue of possessing self-awareness, intellect, and intuition, human beings are more capable of grasping the truth than lower forms of life, such as vegetation. Intellect is an essential faculty for cultivating dispassion and discrimination between the real and the unreal, while intuition reveals the nature of the self. But the perpetual rise and fall of desires, like waves in the ocean, distract the intellect and obstruct the intuitive faculty. Hence unless all desires are exiled from the mind, one cannot hope to know and thus realize oneself. The fundamental goal of the ascetic schools of Indian philosophy (whether orthodox or nonorthodox) is to single-mindedly focus on the mechanisms of detachment from desires and thus from suffering and bondage. Several philosophers, including Lord Buddha and Mahavira, posit various means of achieving this.

Historical, literary, and religious texts clearly articulate that dominant Indian social and familial organizations and relationships are based on the principles of hierarchy and inequality of gender and castes (Ramanujan 1999:41). Despite attaining sublime intellectual horizons, Indian philosophy has to be assessed against this backdrop of (very often brutal) hierarchy and inequality. Even though all living beings are endowed with omnipotent and omniscient souls, human beings are somewhat superior to the others by virtue of possessing intellect and intuition. According to various philosophical schemes, some human beings are superior to others by virtue of being born in a particular caste, or gender, or both. The argument is that the faculties of intellect and intuition are well developed in some, while still latent or poorly defined in others. The ability to detach from desires and thus progress on the path to spiritual liberation depends on a rational process of continual, constant discrimination between the real and the unreal, a faculty that is absent or lacking in women and low-caste men.[4]

Philosophy cannot grow in a vacuum; its matrix is the social and familial organizations that are based on gender constructions and other inequalities, validating and perpetuating existent hierarchical norms. The literature and philosophy of the orthodox Sanskritic tradition was not readily available to women and men of low castes as they were barred from learning Sanskrit, the "language of the gods," and the Vedas, the sacred texts (Leslie 1989:38).[5] The orthodox philosophy presumably derived from the Vedas and hence the knowledge of the Vedas to some extent was essential for social status and privilege. The same rule made it an imperative for men of higher castes to study the sacred texts, reflect on them, and live according to these epistemological principles. Therefore, dominant philosophers were upper-caste men; or to put it in other words, the discourse and perspectives of the upper-caste man expounded in the "language of the gods" was accorded the status of philosophy. This is true at least for the classical times. Of course, rules always create transgressors: some women, while few and far between, either acquired the language skills to debate philosophical issues with men philosophers or used simple vernacular to expound complex philosophical issues.[6]

What is of interest here are the defiant voices of the transgressors: subaltern speakers and their philosophies in vernacular discourse. Though it is not possible at this juncture to debate precisely who borrowed what from whom, it is possible to see some interesting differences in the worldviews of the two sides: the orthodox versus the folk, and upper-caste men versus women and lower-caste men. I have drawn from two sources, the canonized and sacralized philosophy of upper-caste Brahmins and the perspective of the ordinary folk, to show how the two genres differed in their metaphysics and morals. I have utilized the dominant philosophy of India called Samkhya to reveal the covert constructions of masculinity and femininity present in its texts, constructions that powerfully influenced the religious and social order. Obviously they also had a correspondingly powerful influence on social dynamics, including the perpetuation of dominant hierarchies and inequalities to the point that these culturally sanctioned constructions based on men's privilege were seen as part of the larger scheme of "nature" and therefore looked on as inviolable "truth."

The term "Samkhya" means "enumeration" or "relating to numbers."[7] This system of thought enumerates the number of realities and contends that there are 25 basic principles under which all existent phenomena can be classified and interpreted. The philosophy of Samkhya stands "at the fountainhead of systematic Indian reflection, somewhat analogous to Pythagoreanism and other pre-Socratic traditions in ancient Greece" (Larson and Bhattacharya 1987:43). Regarding the influence of Samkhya, it is said that "it is ubiquitous in South Asian cultural life, not only in philosophy, but in medicine, law, statecraft, mythology, cosmology, theology, and devotional literature" (Larson and Bhattacharya 1987:13).

The influence of Samkhya in gender constructions is equally important. This school of philosophy upholds a sharp dualism positing two independent realities—matter and consciousness. What deserves our attention here is that the characteristics attributed to matter and consciousness are identified with the physical woman and man respectively (Natarajan 2001a:1398). This trend is pervasively seen in many religiophilosophic texts that followed the growth of the Samkhya philosophy. Materiality or *prakrti* is constituted of a tripartite process of moral excellence, moral decadence, and amoral indifference (Larson and Bhattacharya 1987:65). These are transposed onto women, dividing them into three species: the best being those whose sexuality is guarded by men, the mediocre those who seek sexual pleasure, and the worst those who are totally licentious and independent (Shastri 1986:192).

In this chapter, I consider some aspects of Samkhya constructions of masculinity and femininity centering on the notion of desire and contrast them with the nonorthodox folk perceptions of the same. The Samkhya system considers desire, deviance, and lack of intellectual capabilities as feminine, and renunciation, asceticism, and intellectual capabilities and pursuits as masculine.

This chapter also analyzes the reversal of the orthodox views of masculinity and femininity as seen in the popular Tamil folk ballad *Alliyarasanimalai*. This text is radical on at least two accounts: (1) it overthrows the orthodox conception of attributing desire and deviance to women; (2) it is a woman-centered ballad with emphasis on women's desires in its description of the establishing and governance of a powerful all-women kingdom where men are rarely active agents and are presented more as intruders. The intent of this chapter is not only to unveil the rigid models for masculinity and femininity in Samkhya, but also to show how a non-Sanskritic, regional folk ballad subverts classical norms by ingeniously reworking them to liberate women from the prevailing constrictive models of family units. The text not only provides an option from the exploitative heterosexual familial archetype, but also creates an alternative by placing women in an autonomous, efficient, and self-validating homosocial, homoerotic unit. If invincible Arjuna, hero of the Mahabharata, epitomizes the masculine ideal of the Sanskritic tradition, based on the Samkhyan model of first enjoying and then renouncing the female at his own convenience and will, Alli, the indomitable empress of the folk tradition, uses her martial prowess and intellect to systematically fracture the masculinity of her powerful and privileged men opponents Neenmukan, Arjuna, Bhima, and Krishna.

Part 1

The dominant theory that the two traditions, classical/folk, great/small, often assumed as opposites, can be countered by the fact that in India these traditions are often found to be coexistent and complementary. At times folklore appears to have local and indigenous origins and other times appears to incorporate a broad theme derived from the classical epic tradition but blended with local, geographical, historical, and cultural ideologies. It is also a fact that many classical texts had their origins in the local/folk bardic traditions. The basic ideologies of the classical tradition are present in the psyche of the folk bards, but they assume new variations and genres in creative and performative arts.

It has been noted that the distinction between "high" and "low" traditions, even though often used, is not quite applicable to Indian cultural studies. There is no apparent dichotomy, but "another harmony" between the two traditions, astutely pointed out by A.K. Ramanujan and Stuart Blackburn (1986:1). During the colonial period, the scholarly philosophical and other texts in Sanskrit attracted the attention of European Indologists. Greatly impressed, they gave these works the nomenclature "the great tradition." The other indigenous local traditions, equally rich but not elevated into the canon because they were non-Sanskritic, were called the "small /little traditions." The two traditions were viewed dualistically as significant and not so significant. Much support and importance was given to the great tradition's discourse and epistemology, which was primarily Brahmanical and men-oriented. The nationalist movement revived pride in local and indigenous cultures; consequently, serious studies of the "little traditions" were undertaken by eminent scholars. Scholars of postcolonial India, who subscribed to democratic perspectives that included ethnic and religious cultural plurality, undertook regional, folk, and subaltern studies. This was the period when many folk traditions were seen with new insight.

Beginning from 1955, A.K. Ramanujan pioneered work in this field, followed by Brenda Beck (1982, 1987), Stuart Blackburn (1988) and others. Ramanujan and Blackburn (1986:14) contend that there is a shift from dualistic and hierarchical perspectives to a continuum between folk and classical traditions. Other types of shifts—psychological, stylistic, and philosophical—are also seen. Therefore classical/folk is not to be equated with the great/little. Folklore is not only a cultural system with a specific content, but is also to be seen as a permanent vehicle and repository of culture. Hence Ramanujan and Blackburn (1986) suggest that folk traditions need not be derived from a great tradition, nor be independent of each other. They can be seen as linked with one another through their own network. If this is assumed to be correct, then there are overlaps as well as departures between the folk and the classical ways of thinking. Folk and classical traditions are contextually distinct but also structurally similar and embedded with common motifs and themes (Ramanujan and Blackburn 1986).

In the ballad studied in this chapter, motifs from the well-known classical epic/myth Mahabharata have been put into local Tamil narrative contexts, with many drastic changes introduced. But prior to analysis of the ballad, it is necessary to consider in detail the classical constructions of masculinity and femininity grounded in the main tenets of the philosophical text *Samkhyakarika*.

Isvarakrsna (AD fourth century) is the author of the poetic, nonpolemical *Samkhyakarika*. The text contains 72 Sanskrit verses. Chattopadhyaya in his book *Lokayata* has evocatively suggested that the historical origins of this text can be traced to early mother worship and primitive tantra (1978:269). The text posits two independent, self-existent principles, nature and spirit or matter and consciousness. Matter is called prakrti and consciousness is called *purusa*. Matter, material cause or prakrti, is a generative force with tremendous dynamism. Just as a womb sculpts the fetus and after gestation expels it through the birth process, prakrti too with its transformative ability generates all subtle and gross evolutes, including the psyche, mind, ego, and intellect. This type of powerful cosmogony can be traced to the ancient *Rgveda* that accommodates notions of feminine engenderment as distinct from masculine creative activity.[8]

According to Samkhya, the material cause is one but constituted of three strands, often called the *trigunas*: *sattva, rajas*, and *tamas*, the principle of subtlety, activity, and production of gross evolutes (like earth, water, and air) respectively.[9] Through the principle of *rajas* a creative activity or activity that is congenial to creation begins. Prakrti is fecund but nonconscious (verse 11).[10] The text further describes prakrti as lacking in direction and motivation. In the heavily gendered Sanskrit language, prakrti is feminine.

The second Samkhyan principle, called purusa, is the principle of awareness or consciousness. It is for the sake of purusa that prakrti evolves and creates a seductive universe (verse 21). Unlike prakrti, the purusa is not constituted of *gunas*. The purusa is a mere onlooker, spectator, witness, who observes prakrti but remains detached. It, however, derives pleasure from the activities of prakrti. Purusa is nonfecund, unchanging, inactive, and immobile. Purusa is a seer, a subject, while prakrti is an object. Purusa, being the principle of intellect, offers direction for creation. Purusa brings about order in otherwise chaotic prakrti. Purusas are many, infinite in numbers (verses 19–20). Masculine gender is ascribed to the purusas.

Prakrti, though unintelligent, produces mind. The mind creates desires and through the power of desires prakrti seduces and binds purusas. Prakrti can also withdraw herself from purusas and cease tempting them, permitting freedom from bondage and suffering. Prakrti thus has a dual role of binding and liberating the purusas. Prakrti is thereby constructed to be an ambivalent power; as seductress par excellence; she is malevolent, but as one who finally unknots the knot that she has bound the purusas with, she is also benevolent (verses 56–61).

In actuality, purusas are never bound but only apparently attracted and deluded by prakrti (verse 62). This is compared to a crystal that temporarily assumes the color of the red flower kept in its proximity. Liberation for purusas is to discover that they were never trapped by prakrti, in fact they can never be. By constant remembrance—"I am not prakrti, and hence cannot be affected by her, I am I"—purusas distance themselves from prakrti (verses 64–65). This metaphorical moving away from prakrti and her bewitching creations is crucial for spiritual emancipation.

This understanding of relationship between prakrti/matter and purusas/consciousness has had tremendous influence on the constructions of masculinity and femininity in India. The most enduring cultural constructions of femininity and masculinity are indelibly branded by the influence of Samkhya philosophy. In the latter portions of *Samkhyakarika*, as well as in the larger Hindu social, cultural, and orthodox literary milieus, there occurs a remarkable fusion of semantic and social genders of prakrti and purusas (*Samkhyakarika*, verses 59–61). There is almost a direct transposition of characteristics of one to the other.

Even though every biological male or female possesses soul/consciousness/purusa, and every physical body is a product of prakrti, *Samkhyakarika* in many places blurs the philosophical principles with those of anatomy (verse 59–62). Biological females are identified with prakrti and her evolutes, while males are equated with purusas; thus, the perceptions of both are rendered almost permanent and cultural constructions are assigned the status of nature. The text feminizes prakrti by calling her a dancer who performs for the sake of her male audience (verse 59). As a dancer, she is a seductress stimulating desires in purusas/men. She is fecund, but anarchic, requiring control and order by the masculine principle. She is also a nurturing principle, benevolent like a cow that provides milk for its calf (verse 57). She is likened to a bashful virgin, who will flee if her nudity is exposed (verse 61). The overwhelmed poet comments that there is none more gentle, kind, and wonderful than she (verse 61)!

Two metaphors found in the original text that have given the commentators scope for wild speculations are the images of prakrti as a female dancer, *nartaki*, and the best amongst the existents, *sukumaratarama*. Prakrti, or matter, becomes an enchantress and a seductress or a bashful young maiden, or even a refined lady whose life centers around attracting consciousness that is gendered male. The pampered, seduced, and bewildered consciousness enjoys the pleasures offered by prakrti, but sooner or later wishes to disentangle himself, seeking the higher alternative of spiritual liberation. Matter or prakrti lures, binds, and finally releases the purusas. Unlike contemporary Smrti texts, the *Samkhyakarika* does not attempt to explicitly define norms governing gender relations. Rather, it draws on the experiences, perspectives, and attitudes developed by men in a gender-stratified society to define women as objects of pleasure and manipulation, as source of bondage from which liberation was essential, and as awesome and fearful in their reproductive role. Thus the system may be viewed as both reflecting and reinforcing men's perceptions. These perceptions in turn are woven into the growth and perpetuation of specific ideologies of gender.

What develops from this scheme—bondage by prakrti and purusa's struggle to rediscover his essential identity and subsequent liberation from her force—are the different spaces allotted to prakrti and purusas on one hand and women and men on the other. The domain of prakrti is the world, while that of a physical woman is home and its immediate surroundings. The sphere of operation for purusas is apparently twofold. One is the world created by prakrti and the other is the space away from the web created by prakrti, the renunciate's trajectory into the wilderness. This is transposed onto the activity of the biological male. Men are granted two spaces, the first within the house, where they cohabit with their wives, have control and domination over sexuality, derive sexual pleasures and have as many male children as possible. This space is only a temporary or even a fictional field of operation. For whenever interaction within the home proves to be binding and restrictive, men have the privilege to detach from it and practice ascetic spiritual disciplines in a second space far away from domestic pressures and turmoil as well as familial and conjugal responsibilities.

Masculinity, according to Samkhya and elsewhere in Indian philosophy, is to ultimately give up all desires, that is, all deviance from the spiritual path, and retire to the wilderness to practice discrimination between the self and prakrti/matter/sexual temptation. Masculinity consists in using the intellectual faculty to understand one's essential nature as consciousness that is in essence detached from matter. Disentangling from prakrti is symbolically represented as disentangling from woman and home. Woman here represents bondage, emotions, desires, lack of intellectual ability, anarchy, and seduction. Hence woman/prakrti is to be scrupulously avoided if liberation is to be sought.

In an anecdote present in the majority of the commentaries on the *Samkhyakarika*, a householder is repeatedly advised by a master to give up home and follow him to learn to the ascetic way of life (Takakusu 1933:1; Upreti 1990). The householder pays no heed to this for a long time. The master, however, does not give up, but waits for a day when the man is for some reason unhappy with the happenings at home. The master seizes the opportunity and once more asks the man to renounce that space. This time the man is happy to leave home and follows the master who gives him spiritual instruction. Thus the renunciation of wife and children is valorized. Almost all the ascetic traditions encourage men to give up desires, the chief one being woman.

If masculinity is freedom from home and household chores, femininity is confined to the walls of the house, cowsheds, marriage, male progeny, and service to the husband and his relatives. Femininity is the ability to be fecund, to nurture, and be sexually available to the husband at all times. If masculinity stands for intellectual pursuits, femininity represents subservience to men in all respects. However, in the following section we see a radical and liberating construction of femininity in the Tamil folk ballad *Alliyarasanimalai*.

Part 2

> Folklore offers another alternative, bounces off the so-called high culture in systematic ways.
>
> —A.K. Ramanujan 1999:30

The renowned folklorist and linguist A.K. Ramanujan has identified three kinds of folklore: man-centered, woman-centered, and animal-centered

(1999:413). Each has a different set of symbols, values, and priorities, offering different roles and modalities to its members. For our present purpose Ramanujan's description of woman-centered tales is crucial. He notes, ". . . by women's tales I mean two things: (1) tales told by women, and (2) tales that are centered around women" (1999:429). Ramanujan explores another significant and useful genre classification. Legends, told by women located in and around homes, describe generalized human and familial relationships (1999:488). They have a particular style and mode of communication. He calls them the domestic or interior (*akam*) genre. This may be contrasted with the exterior or public (*puram*) genre. "This is performed in public by men, and contains personal names, historical, mythological, communal events especially battles" (1989:12). For a long time in the history of village public performances, all roles were enacted by only men. Some tales centering on women may have been created by men. Quite often, ethical values of classical literature are reversed. Ramanujan's study of the folk legends also reveal that the norms and values stipulated for women by patriarchal systems—marriage, chastity, and fidelity—are overtly dismissed in women's tales; female members of the audience appreciate the conspiracy of women in sabotaging male values.

The folk legend *Alliyarasanimalai* is one such performative ballad quite popular in rural Tamil Nadu even today. It must be pointed out that this legend is not a rare and freak one. In the districts of Madurai and Kanyakumari, powerful women-centered legends have emerged; some of them are performed as bow songs. Some folk legends, such as the story of *Pennaraciyar*, depict extraordinary women who live with other women, establish an all-woman fortress, never indulge in heterosexual marriages, but give birth only to female children by allowing the erotic southerly breeze to touch their bodies; when attacked by curious neighboring kings, they fight valorously.[11] In the face of a defeat, pregnant women prefer to kill themselves in the battlefield by slashing their bellies with swords and exposing the fetuses, rather than allowing the men raiders to take them captive. Temples are dedicated to such warrior women and queens, who have been deified; festivals to commemorate their valor are annually held (Jayakumar and Boominaganathan 1996:xxvi–xxvii). That these legends might have had some historicity cannot be denied. *Alliyarasanimalai* belongs to the genre of *Madar Manjari*, a collection of woman-centered ballads portraying women who resist prevailing heterosexist norms.[12]

The expression *Allirajyam*, derived from the legendary heroine's name Alli, literally means the kingdom of Alli. The Tamil word *Allirajyam* communicates the idea of the Sanskrit *strirajyam* or the "lands of women." It involves the concept of women establishing their own kingdoms where men are made redundant. Women do not require men even for sexual pleasures or progeny. Women characters in *Pennarachiyar Katai* and *Alliyarasanimalai* have created a space for women where men are literally banned. In a paper entitled "*Strirajya*: Indian Accounts of Kingdoms of

Women" W.L. Smith (2001) delineates the accounts of Strirajya, the "lands of women" or societies ruled by women in northeast and northwest India. According to Smith, "the most common conception of a land of women" is that they are "ruled by predatory female magicians" (2001:468). These women through their sexual indulgence sap the strength of any men visitors and quite often turn them into beasts or birds by means of magic. Smith (2001) also makes a passing reference to Chinese sources that contain numerous references to women's countries and woman-dominated countries. According to Smith, there are two types of women's countries: those of mythical or fantastic character and those mentioned in historical documents. In the first kind women live in "maleless lands who mate with apes, dogs or demons, and become pregnant by bathing or drinking water from a certain river or well, or exposing to the wind" (Smith 2001:469).

The folk ballad *Alliyarasanimalai* is silent about the sexual exploits of women while definitely mentioning that men were not their partners of choice. The other ballad *Pennaraciyar Katai* has the recurring motif of royal women, who are strong and unwilling to submit to male authority. In these two ballads women are not predators. The entry of a male in any form, human or animal, is banned. According to Smith, "the fact that the Amazon theme proved to be so sterile in India indicates that it is probably not an Indian theme at all . . . . The notion of Amazon kingdom could have been taken from the Greeks, but since the Indian texts say so little about it, there is no way to tell. It could just as well have been suggested by Chinese or other Asian sources" (2001:475). Smith concludes that "they are projections of identical male presumptions and fears. Since it was presumed that women were essentially licentious, if lands were exclusively inhabited by women, they would be sexual predators since they were no longer under male control" (2001:475). Another point that Smith makes is that the narrators of the strirajyam were more interested in the erotic than the military side of the subject.

Smith's conclusions may be true with regard to Sanskrit literature of the "great tradition," but by analyzing the folk ballads, one uncovers a very different narration of the "lands ruled by women." The Tamil folk ballads are pointers to a far more emancipated understanding of the phrase in that the legends purely belong to the matrilineal Madurai and Kanyakumari districts where women have historically ruled. The legend of Alli is situated in the Pandya region with Madurai as its capital, a significant point because of the association of women with political power in Pandya kingdom, according to the historian Vijaya Ramaswamy (1998:75).[13] She draws our attention to the historian Neelakanta Shastri's remarks in his *History of South India* that according to oral tradition the Pandya kingdom was founded by a woman. The portrayal of the land of Alli is therefore indigenous and not borrowed from Greek or other Asian legends. Further, the Tamil folk ballads are unique in portraying women as strong, adept in martial arts, living in the company of women, and drawing support and sustenance from one another, not requiring men's presence, prescriptions, or domination. There are no references in the Tamil ballads to women being licentious or vampirically draining the sexual energy of men. The Tamil ballads focus on the prowess, power, and martial tactics of the heroine and her women warriors, not on their erotic life.

Alliyarasanimalai derives from the grand classical parameters of the Mahabharata. Though the legend of Alli has a Mahabharata frame story, it is deeply influenced by local motifs and local legends. Here it is useful to remember Ramanujan, according to whom we cannot talk in terms of classical and folk terms as antagonistic: "They should be seen as a continuum of forms, the endpoints of which may look like two terms in opposition" (1999:430). But in this case the classical epic and the folk legends are oppositional; the Tamil ballad becomes woman-centered, focusing on the invincible woman Alli, while the Sanksritic epic is consistently male-centered with Arjuna as the invincible hero.

It is well known that folk ballads never have a single author. They are a collective phenomenon in the social and cultural history of a population. Both women and men of other castes and communities could have contributed to the richness of folk legends. The folk legend *Alliyarasanimalai* was frozen into written ballad form in the nineteenth century along with other legends with a variety of topics, themes, diction, and styles of narratives. Even though essentially authorless, there was a literary need to ascribe authorship for the enormous range of printed matter. Interestingly, a single authorship was assigned to many ballads that were published for the first time. One Pukhazendi Pulavar, who actually belonged to the fourteenth century, was chosen as the author of a large number of Tamil folk ballads. It could have been a matter of convenience to have selected a single eminent poet from classical Tamil tradition for the authorship of the ballad. The actual poems of Pukhazendi, however, demonstrate a range of styles of writing and narration.

The focus of the legend is the all-mighty queen Alli (Lily). The story of Alli is located in the city of Madurai, South India, where goddess Meenakshi is worshipped as the supreme empress even today. As mentioned earlier, this is not just a single freak folk legend but belongs to a genre of legends that are characterized by nonconformist, unmarried, childless women, who take up well-defined masculine roles. The overemphasized quartet of feminine virtues in Tamil society—-timidity, naiveté, bashfulness, and sensitivity—are not simply ignored in these legends but relentlessly satirized. In their place, infidelity, ingenuity, astuteness, valor, courage, learning, capacity for leadership and administration, and refusal to succumb to heterosexual models of marriage are propagated in full strength. The classical and Brahmanical ideals of distinct spaces for men and women are boldly subverted.

This genre of legends promoted a different value system by applauding women characters who, by successfully practicing masculine activity, violate the exclusive and sexist Brahmanical zones of world (for men) and home (for women) and discard all the established conventions of virtuous womanhood. Women occupied both domestic and external spaces. They warred and went on elaborate hunting expeditions. They avoided heterosexual marriages and instead pursued political, social, and economic managements. Alli as a young girl went to school, learned to read and write, mastered algebra and multiplication, practiced martial arts, and wrote and read Tamil literary classics.[14] There is no way to confirm if this was a social reality for the ordinary folk, especially women. But the very presence of this utopia is stimulating and refreshing to readers.

Castes, geographical regions, and religious denominations divide Indian women into complex groupings. An important factor that creates a deep connection among all Indian women is a segregated, gender-specific and highly gender-coded way of life. Sex segregation has been integral to the functioning of modern as well as traditional India. A significant component of Indian society is the joint-family system (Karve 1953), which has promoted strong interfeminine bonding.[15] Despite rapid industrialization and urbanization, the nation continues to segregate cultural, social, religious, and familial spaces by sex. While modern nuclear families are generally organized around heterosexual relationships, the traditional joint-family system is homocentric and conducive to the existence of gender-coded spaces.[16]

Such marking and limiting of space can be interpreted either as disempowering women by controlling their movements, or empowering women by creating homosocial, eroticized spaces wherein women lend and receive mutual support. Both interpretations are historically legitimate. I subscribe to the view that sex segregation allows women to bond freely with other women. One feature of spatial sex segregation is the construction of gendered worldviews in which women and men perceive the world and utilize their spaces differently.[17] In a recent survey of village clusters outside Bangalore in southern India, researcher Seemanthini Niranjana discusses the strong spatial narrative of *olage-horage* (inside-outside) that governed people's lives (1997:111–114). These spaces are seen to be circumscribed by gender. Femininity, the female body, morality, and women's activities were embodied in the idiom "olage," often depicted as the household that represented the center of women's lives.

Niranjana's study can be extended to the neighboring Tamil state, which too makes a strong division between the female *ull/akam* (interior) and male *veli/puram* (exterior). The identification of women's interest with the household has been prevalent among the upper-class, upper-caste, nonworking women who occupy the interior space as their legitimate territory. Here, women participate in many chores together—waking, bathing, washing, cooking, eating, sleeping, and raising their children. In such family systems women experience their significant life events in the company of other women rather than the men of the clan. A strong consciousness of solidarity between women develops in this space, according to the anthropologist Margaret Egnor (1991:27). It is not improbable to conceive that within this area, women cultivate erotic relationships with one another, even while their primary function as wives of the clan is to create male progeny; hence there is tremendous silence about erotic bonding between women.

Alliyarasanimalai replicates this homosocial space for women. Though the ballad is silent about the erotic bonding between women, the reader is sensitized to the desire of the heroine Alli to bond only with her female companions. The ballad uses the metaphor "inside" and "outside" to demarcate Alli's kingdom and the male hero Arjuna's lust-provoked wanderings.[18] Alli has an all-women fort and lives "inside" while Arjuna is "outside" the fort, constantly desiring to penetrate, invade, capture, possess, and violate the kingdom as well as its queen. But Alli is not restricted to the inner space of the fort; she also accesses the "outside" when as a child she goes to school to acquire skills, when she goes on a grand hunting expedition to the forest, when she wages wars against the usurper of her father's kingdom, and when she travels from the southern peninsula to the north with her female army to battle against Arjuna, who deviously married her. Similarly, Arjuna does manage to access the inner space of both fort and queen, but only through trickery, intrigue, and supernatural assistance.

Arjuna, the valiant Pandava prince, unmatched as an archer with his victorious *gandiva* bow, is a great Mahabharata hero, but in the legend of Alli he is portrayed as selfish, compulsive, and delinquent. He cannot make a single rational or irrational move without the aid and the magic of his companion Krishna. Despite having several wives and other available women, he still lusts for women. He is not interested in male activities such as warfare or hunting; he loses in the battle with Alli. He cannot accept his failure to penetrate the all-women fortress and turns into a sexual predator when his desire is thwarted.

Having seen his eldest brother Yudhishtra and their common wife Draupadi making love on a saffron bed in the terrace of the palace, Arjuna decides to expiate this sin by undertaking a pilgrimage to all the holy places, including Madurai, where Alli reigns supreme. Yudhistra and the Pandava matriarch Kunti summon Krishna, the companion and the Lord, and beseech him to accompany Arjuna. Thus both of them set out on this long journey and finally arrive on the outskirts of Madurai, whereupon they hear from a pearl merchant all about the mighty unmarried queen

Alli. Arjuna now falls hopelessly in love with her and begins to pester Krishna for help in forcing Alli into marrying him. The pearl merchant warns Arjuna of the consequences of even proposing marriage to Alli as she will not consent to marry anyone. According to him,

> She will hit the groom with the sharp-edged weapon,
> The marital kin and kith will be whipped with a rope,
> The eyes will be pulled out of the socket if anyone utters "marriage" . . .
> Not even a male whiff can enter her palace,
> She mounts a mare and not a stallion,
> Her army is made up of female warriors . . .
>
> (Pulavar 1914:54)

The pearl merchant informs Arjuna that Alli sees marriage ruining her power and status. She has taken a vow to torture the man who seeks her hand. She has a palace in which she has exhibited all the loot that she has won in warfare. No man has the courage to gain entry into the palace. At several strategic points women warriors are deputed to guard this space from male intrusion. In that all-women city, women are administrators. Alli's friends are women; her advisers are women; her carpenter, priests, executioners, hunters, and snake charmers are all women. Even her royal elephants are all female.

Hearing this, Krishna advises Arjuna to forget about Alli. If Arjuna insists on marriage, he would arrange an alliance from his own country, caste, and clan. Unable to bear the torture of love, Arjuna plunges into its agonies. Krishna now decides to help him, but quite often renders him comic, idiotic, and almost a buffoon. When Alli goes on a hunting expedition, Arjuna follows her, disguised as her female companion, picks up arrows for her, massages her feet, and entertains her with stories while she is resting. But wanting to draw her attention to his self-proclaimed glory, he begins to give her his autobiography. Hearing a story about a man, Alli flies into a rage, looks at the face of the storyteller, and notices the thin line of hair revealing his manhood. Before Alli could gather herself, Arjuna darts like the wind into the forest.

Arjuna tries to seek entry into the palace but the women guards and companions of Alli throw him out. With the help of his magician friend Krishna, he assumes the form of a huge serpent and is carried to Allis's fort by the snake charmer, Krishna in disguise. Alli is captivated by the serpent and asks the snake charmer to leave the snake with her for a night.[19] Stealthily Arjuna enters her bedchamber and with the help of some supernatural power beckons the sleep goddess to overwhelm Alli. Arjuna rapes Alli while she is fast asleep and even manages to impregnate her. Once more Arjuna assumes the form of a woman and gains entry into the palace; in the middle of the night, while Alli is still asleep, he ties the marriage string around her neck and leaves for his hometown with Krishna.

Seeing the string around her neck Alli is furious, tries to sever it with a saw, a sword and many other devices, but is unsuccessful. Angered by this, she decides to wage a war in Hastinapur, Arjuna's home, with her army of women troopers, Tamils, Telungas, Kannadigas, and Muslims. The army and the pregnant Alli are invincible. Arjuna and his divine companion Krishna lose in the battlefield and actually run away in shame. Krishna is so hurt that his entire body is covered with blood and he too faces the fact of great failure. The indomitable Pandava brother Bheema throws down his weapons and fears for his own life. Arjuna rushes to his half brother Sahadeva and tells him to capture Alli somehow, by any means. Sahadeva connives with the gods to create a magic cage with several doors and bars, draws Alli into it during the fight, and suddenly traps her.

Alli is portrayed as a ferocious caged lion wanting to break free, but is told by Draupadi, one of the wives of Arjuna, that only if she gives up her weapons and marries Arjuna will she be released and allowed to go back to her country. Draupadi sings of the glory, valor, and chivalry of her husband to Alli, who rebuffs and ridicules every claim. However, in order to be free Alli surrenders her weapons and once more Arjuna marries her. Immediately Alli leaves for Madurai with her troop of women warriors and in due course gives birth to a son who will be taught to take revenge on his father, Arjuna (Pulavar 1912:81–86).

The folk legend of Alli is unique in reversing the almost inviolable gender norms prescribed by Brahmanical traditions. The warrior queen is born after her parents perform severe penance, in which all the citizens and animals of Madurai participate. Pleased with the collective effort, the goddess of Madurai throws a bit of flesh from her shoulder. The fragment falls into a pond of fragrant Alli, water lily, hence the child's name. The goddess picks up the child and bestows it upon the parents, saying "she is both a male and female."

Alli lived with her parents in the village, went to a school, and learned to read and write. She came home, gulped her afternoon meal and ran back to school to learn more and more. Thus when she was nine, she learned about the kingdom being usurped by her half brother, Neenmukan. She engaged him in battle, won back the kingdom, and rightfully established her all-women empire in which men were at the periphery, receiving orders and dependent for their survival on women.

This women's space is portrayed as being well-organized and self-fulfilling. It is disturbed by Arjuna, who we may identify with the Samkhyan purusa, whose function is to establish order in the chaotic world of prakrti. However, in this legend Arjuna, overpowered by lustful desire for Alli, is actually an agent of profound disorder.

In another version of the story obsessive Arjuna seeks Krishna's help. The latter, knowing of Alli's reputation as a huntress, conjures up wild and ferocious animals in forests around Alli's kingdom, metaphorically signifying Arjuna's desire and his readiness to let the blood of slaughter flow just to satiate his own desire for the few drops of the warrior queen's virgin blood. Intimidated by the prowling animals in the forest, the foresters seek Alli's help. She decides to go on a hunting expedition, a typical masculine, heroic act, in this case not to claim territory or to subjugate any beings but to fulfill the duty of a sovereign.

With a strong entourage of heavily armed women soldiers, Alli ceremoniously goes to the forest. Arjuna assumes a female form and accompanies her until he is found out. What is significant here is the reversal of masculinity and femininity. If Alli represents prakrti, she is exactly the opposite of the Samkhyan definition. Arjuna, the male principle, driven by ego, is never in control of himself. He lives in the world of fantasy and delusion, utterly abandoning the power of discrimination that is so much prized in the Brahmanical model. In the classical tradition desire, lust, delusion, or *maya*—all are identified with the feminine, but in this representation of the folk tradition it is satirically inverted. Every fantasy, every desire of Arjuna causes increasing turbulence in the well-ordered women's kingdom. His fantasy makes him assume the form of a snake to rape and impregnate Alli. His lust makes him so unstable that he quite often changes his sex, age, caste, class, and form to achieve his scheming end. Totally lacking discrimination, he is unable to see the web of delusion in which he has ensnared himself, even while he focuses obsessively on mechanisms of somehow snaring Alli in literal terms.

Deviant Arjuna's lack of discrimination and pursuit of darkness instead of light and ignorance instead of knowledge are satirized from the very beginning of the narrative. Supposedly undertaking a journey of penance and propitiation to counter the sin of accidentally witnessing his respected elder brother and their common wife Draupadi in the sexual act, Arjuna bathes in holy rivers on his pilgrimage, but is actually immersing himself further in the waters of his own desire and fantasy. Alli represents the "pearl" that he must possess at all costs, including the cost of his power of discrimination. Omniscient Krishna is by his side, yet the only advice Arjuna wants from him is how to conquer Alli, either through guile or force.

According to the Samkhyan model, woman has the power to seduce, deceive, bind, and destroy. Yet in the folk legend it is man (Arjuna) who initiates the cycle of physical violence that culminates in his raping the virgin warrior queen within her homosocial/homoerotic space. The binding is materially asserted through the symbol of the magic marriage string that he ties around her neck and which she cannot take off; the string legitimizes his claim on her body and on the body of the child he has implanted in her, his offspring now trapped, so to speak, in the interior/house of

Alli's womb. Externally, the marriage string is the perfect symbol of the household, the space that the man of discrimination is supposed to renounce in his quest for knowledge and freedom. Later in the narrative Alli is rendered captive in the interior of the magical cage erected on the battlefield by Sahadeva on Arjuna's request. Only thus can Alli's force be contained. Arjuna's act of deceiving, violating, and binding Alli expands into grotesque and blood-soaked parameters that compel others to participate in the thickening veil of pathological fantasy that now clouds the individual and collective discrimination of his family, army, and the kingdom of Hastinapuram, his homeland.

The power of the Alli legend lies in its satirical subversion of Samkhyan-influenced gender-coded worldviews, its blurring of the sociological boundaries between household and world, its radical reworking of the classical stereotypes of masculinity and femininity, and its audacious deconstruction of the principles of prakrti and purusa that have profoundly influenced Hindu culture for millennia and continue to do so.

Notes

I thank Smrti Vohra for her editorial help.

1. By "conventional" I mean the classical Brahmanical schools of philosophies like Samkhya, Yoga, and Advaita Vedanta, the early and later Buddhist philosophies and the ascetic Jainism, which lay much stress on renunciation and asceticism as means of liberation from the cycles of birth and death.
2. Indian philosophy distinguishes mind from intellect. Mind is the seat of emotions, feelings, and desires, while intellect is the rational principle. Much discussion takes place on the nature and functions of mind and intellect in Nyaya-Vaisesika schools of thought.
3. The Brahmanical schools are those that believed only in the authority and validity of the Vedas, the ancient texts of the Hindus. Non-Brahmanical schools such as Buddhism, Jainism, and others rejected the authority of the Vedas. There are at least six schools of thought that are categorized as Brahmanical or orthodox and three that are heterodox or non-Brahmanical.
4. The conceptions of real and unreal vary from school to school. For the orthodox the real is unchanging and permanent, while for the Buddhist the real is ever-changing and in flux. Jain philosophers conceived the real to be both unchanging and changing.
5. In this chapter I deliberately avoid the highly complex caste issue, but deal with some aspects of gender.
6. I would like to mention one ancient woman philosopher by name, Gargi, the daughter of Vacaknu, who challenged the imposing idealist philosopher Yajnavalkya in the royal court of Janaka thus: "As a powerful king from a warring dynasty might string his unstrung bow and appear close by, carrying in his hand two bamboo-tipped arrows highly painful to the enemy, even so, O Yajnavalkya, do I confront you with two questions, answer me those" *Brhadaranyaka Upanisad* (1965:35). There were many woman philosophers

from the vernaculars but they were localized and revered as saints. One such lesser known recent (seventeenth century) woman mystic and philosopher from Tamil Nadu is Avudaiyar Akkal. She was a prolific writer/singer, who used simple metaphorical language to communicate her philosophy and mystical experiences. See Giri 2002.

7. Some schools such as Samkhya believe that there are as many souls as bodies, while the nondualistic philosophy holds that the one and the same soul is present uniformly in all.
8. There are several types of creation myths. In some myths, the male gods create with their power by performing masculine activities, while in others cosmogony is seen as a biological activity wherein creation is akin to childbirth. See Natarajan 2001b.
9. The term "guna" in Samkhya is used in the sense of constituent strand of primordial materiality. The *gunas* can be described with reference to objectivity as well as subjectivity. From an objective standpoint the gunas are referred to as a "continuing flow of material energy that is capable of spontaneous activity (*rajas*), rational ordering (*sattva*), and determinative formulation or gross objectification (*tamas*)." From a subjective point of view, guna is a "continuing flow of experience that is prereflective, spontaneous, desiring or longing (*rajas*), reflective discernment (*sattva*), and continuing awareness of an opaque, enveloping world (*tamas*)." Guna also has a moral implication (Larson and Bhattacharya 1987:65–70).
10. All references to particular verses in the *Samkhyakarika* are taken from Pandey 1998.
11. The ballad of *Pennaraciyar* (see Jayakumar and Boominaganathan 1996) is sung to the accompaniment of the musical bow, *villu*, and the drum, *utukkai pattu*. When the bow, a weapon of war, is transformed into a musical bow, a number of jingling cymbals are strung along the string and the performer hits the string in a rhythmic beat as the ballad is sung.
12. *Alliyarasanimalai* and *Pavalakkodimalai* (Pulavar 1912, 1914) belong to the same genre. It is unfortunate that with the advent of the enticing and powerful satellite television the folk traditional performances have lost their attraction.
13. I do not subscribe to Ramaswamy's account of the ballad as "the taming and domestication of Alli into a virtuous and obedient wife of Arjuna" (1998:78). From the beginning to the end of the plot, valiant Alli resists domestication or wedlock forced upon her by Arjuna. Throughout the legend Alli rejects and fight against him.
14. Alli studied:

> ". . . The four Vedas, horse riding, elephant riding,
> Archery, administrative sciences,
> To somersault, she learnt,
> She went to school, learnt by heart the morning lessons,
> Algebra, poetry and proverbs, she learnt by rote . . ."
> *Alliyarasanimalai*
>
> (Pulavar 1914:38)

15. Karve, a noted sociologist, defines a joint-family as "a group of people who generally live under one roof, who eat food at one hearth, who hold property

in common and who participate in common family worship and are related to each other as some particular kindred" (1953:10).

16. I use the term "homocentric" in contrast to Adrienne Rich's use of the word "heterocentric" (1993:228).
17. For a compelling explanation of the concept of gendered space, see Bourdieu 1990.
18. All translations of *Alliyarasanimalai* are the author's.
19. "A snake in a male-centered tale is usually something to be killed, a rival phallus. In woman-centered tales, that is, where woman are protagonists and usually the tellers, snakes are lovers, husbands, uncles, donors and helpers" (Ramanujan 1999:413). In the ballad discussed here, the protagonist Alli seeks the help of snakes several times to kill her rivals. Alli considers snakes as her friends and hence requests the snake charmer to let her keep the snake for the night, not knowing that it is Arjuna who has changed his form to enter the fort.

References Cited

Beck, Brenda. 1982. *The three twins: The telling of a South Indian folk epic.* Bloomington: Indiana University Press.

———. 1987. *Folk tales of India.* Chicago: University of Chicago Press.

Bhagavad-Gita. 1987. Annie Besant and Bhagawan Das, trans. 2nd ed. Delhi: Anmol Publications.

Blackburn, Stuart. 1988. *Singing of birth and death: Performance as paradigm.* Phildelphia: University of Pennsylvania Press.

Blackburn, Stuart and A.K. Ramanujan, eds. 1986. *Another harmony: New essays on the folklore of India.* Berkeley: University of California Press.

Bourdieu, Pierre. 1990. *The logic of practice.* Cambridge: Polity.

Brhadaranyaka Upanishad. 1965. Swami Madhavananada, trans. Calcutta: Advaita Ashrama.

Chattopadhyaya, Debiprasad. 1978. *Lokayata: A study in ancient Indian materialism.* 4th ed. Calcutta: People's Publishing House.

Egnor, Margaret. 1991. On the meaning of *sakti* to women in Tamil Nadu. In *Powers of Tamil women.* Susan S. Wadley, ed. Pp. 1–34. New Delhi: Manohar.

Giri, Swami Nityananada, ed. 2002. *Chengottai Sri Avudai Akkal.* Thapovanam, Tamilnadu: Sri Gnanananda Niketan.

Jayakumar, K. and D. Boominaganathan, eds. 1996. *Pennaraciyar katai.* S. Mark Joseph, trans. Madras: Institute of Asian Studies.

Karve, Irawati Karmarkar. 1953. *Kinship organization in India.* Poona: Deccan College.

Larson, Gerald James and Ram Shankar Bhattacharya, eds. 1987. *Encyclopedia of Indian philosophies,* vol. 4, *Samkhya.* Delhi: Motilal Banarasidass.

Leslie, I. Julia. 1989. *The perfect wife: The orthodox Hindu woman according to the Stridharmapaddhati of Trayambakayajvan.* New Delhi: Penguin Classics.

Natarajan, Kanchana. 2001a. Gendering of early Indian philosophy: A study of "Samkhyakarika." *Economic and Political Weekly* 35(17) (April 28): 1398–1404.

Natarajan, Kanchana. 2001b. Primordial waters: Some remarks on Rig Vedic creation hymns. *Journal of Indian Council of Philosophical Research* 17(2): 147–168.

Niranjana, Seemanthini. 1997. Femininity, space, and the female body: An anthropological perspective. In *Embodiment: Essays on gender and identity*. Meenakshi Thapan, ed. Pp. 107–123. Delhi: Oxford University Press.

Pandeya, Baijnath, ed. 1998. *Isvarakrsnaviracita Samkhyakarika*. Bharatiya Vidya Prakashan.

Pulavar, Pukhazendi. 1912. *Pavalakkodimalai*. Madras: Albinton Press.

———. 1914. *Alliyarasanimalai*. Madras: Longman's Green and Co.

Ramanujan, A.K. 1999. *The collected essays of A.K. Ramanujan*. Vinay Dharwadker, ed. New Delhi: Oxford University Press.

Ramaswamy, Vijaya. 1998. The taming of Alli: Mythic images and Tamil women. *Journal of the Inter-university Center of Humanities and Social Sciences*, 5(2): 71–84.

Rich, Adrienne. 1993. Compulsory heterosexuality and the lesbian existence. In *The lesbian and gay studies reader*. Henry Abelove, Michèle Aina Barale, and David M. Halperin, eds. Pp. 227–254. New York: Routledge.

Shastri, J.L. ed. 1986. *Brahmavaivartapurana of Krishnadvaipayana Vyasa*, Part II. Delhi: Motilal Banarasidass.

Smith, W.L. 2001. *Strirajya*: Indian accounts of kingdoms of women. In *Vidyarnavavandanam: Essays in honour of Asko Parpola*. Kalus Karttunam and Pettri Koskikallio, eds. Pp. 465–477. Helsinki: Finnish Oriental Society.

Takakusu, Junjiro, ed. 1933. *The Samkhyakarika studied in the light of its Chinese version*. S.S. Suryanarayana Sastri, trans. Chennai.

Thapan, Meenakshi, ed. 1997. *Embodiment: Essays on gender and identity*. Delhi: Oxford University Press.

Upreti, Thanesh Chandra, ed. 1990. *Samkhyakarika: Mataravrtti*. Delhi: Chaukhambha Orientalia.

Vacaspatimishra. 1965. *The Tattva Kaumudi, Vacaspati Mishra's commentary on the Samkhya Karikas*. Har M.M. Pattkar, ed. Ganganath Jha, trans. Poona: Oriental Book Agency.

Part II

Conditional Subjectivities

Chapter Four

The Spring That Flowers between Women

Abha Bhaiya

It is not without certain trepidation that I write what has been difficult to withhold. I have known the tyranny of heteronormativity, yet a compulsion pushes me to defend a space that refutes labeling—a universal naming. This chapter alludes to two equally pertinent positions. The first part foregrounds simultaneously contesting and competing, age-old sociocultural practices of female bonding existent in parts of the northern region of the subcontinent of south Asia. The second part of the chapter engages with the entire discourse on labeling and naming, the universalization of conceptual and practiced categories of women's relationships with women.

This chapter is not an academic exercise or a conceptual brief on female bonding. At most, it is a narrative, an attempt to excavate buried sites where, parallel to the mainstream, histories of female bonding flourished.

> Leaving behind the silt
> Brought from the mountainous footpaths
> I flow like a river
> Adding new shores to my unknown journey.
>
> I recognize your footprints
> As you gush silently
> from the source of your origin.
> Similar flow, the same current
> With such deep reflection and
> Echo of my cascading whispers in your heart.
>
> As your and my shores hold their hands
> The earth expands suddenly
> Our waters turn azure.
>
> As you peep into my depth
> Your reflection echoes
> A million meanings!
>
> (Jagori notebook, 1989)

The meandering flow of water under the deep layers of rocks, through the veins of hard mountains, continues its hazardous journey to the other end of the earth. Who can install milestones on that hidden tunnel, full of wet flow? And who can dare to name the places of mysterious pilgrims on that journey of the spirit and the body?

Female Friendships

Women's relationships to women, wrapped in similar force and mystery, remain explicitly hidden in emotions of love, affection, hope, fear, denial, yearning, and trust. Flowing under the burden of patriarchal institutions, they chart their own path because the origin of female bonding predates the patriarchal construct of male-female consorting. The bonding between women and the décor of their intense attraction and intimacy with each other is as old as the formation of the first rock.

Saheli, sakhi, sathin, bhayeli, sangini, hamjoli, and *hamsheeran*—these are some of the numerous names that exist as part of the linguistic and cultural code of female friendships in the northern region of the South Asian subcontinent. Women bonded together exist in myriad forms of relationships. They inhabit the silent dark caves of each other's minds and bodies, swinging on the folklore of varied cultural and social ropes of relationships.

This folklore and folk music yearns for the site of the female friend during different seasons (*ritu*) of the moon and the sun. In Rajasthan, one of the desert states in the northern part of India, during monsoon months, girls celebrate a cultural festival linked to the coming of the rains. The arrival of the rains is particularly auspicious in the desert of Rajasthan. Within an exclusive female space, girls come together in gardens and mango groves to play and celebrate. Special rope swings are tied onto big branches of old trees. One of the rituals is to sing while swinging together. During this season girls put henna on each other's palms.

There are innumerable folk songs about coming home, meeting friends, and sharing each other's pain and pleasure. These songs are passed on from mothers to daughters through a very lively oral tradition. Folk music is a much evolved tradition in the region. Through these songs women express a range of emotions and feelings. As part of this tradition, there exist forms of ritualistic practices that acknowledge the presence of female bonding and intimacies. Whether sexuality is inscribed within this cultural code needs to be explored by feminist scholars and practitioners of women-centered relationships.

This oral tradition carries forward the mythology and practices of women bonding. In 1989 members of a feminist organization, Jagori, New Delhi, brought out a notebook on female friendships titled "From me to you." This notebook was a significant attempt to bring into public space the celebratory aspects of female bonding and friendship. It trod carefully on the sensual and the sexual content of female intimacies.

> You are the water of my roots
> Veins of my leaves
> The fragrance of my flowers
> The courtyard of my autumn.
> (Jagori notebook, 1989)

During an interview with two of my friends who share their lives together, I happened to meet the mother of one of them. In the course of our conversation, she mentioned the ritual of exchanging saris between two women. With some persuasion she recalled her childhood memory:

> I was hardly 12 years old. Many of us girls from our village got together to go to the river for the ceremony. We all wore new saris and carried betel leaf and flowers. We chose our own friend and as couples we stood in the shallow waters of the river and exchanged our saris. We also put betel leaves into each other's mouth [this is considered an intimate gesture] and put flowers in each other's hair. This is to mark and to seal the commitment to the friend.

On my further probing, she said, "The friend is supposed to keep all your secrets and never share it with anyone else." Of course there was no mention of any kind of sexual proximity. Little did she know that her daughter had added new meanings to the ritual. This ritual is known to many older women in villages of the two northern states of India, Uttar Pradesh, and Bihar, where I have worked extensively. In many workshops that I conducted for rural and marginalized groups of women, I heard about the practice, often from older women rather than the young ones. With the passage of time, the ritual might be getting erased.

In the desert of Rajasthan in 1986, an unforgettable incident happened. I went with friends to one of the biggest cattle fairs that takes place during the spring on the day of the full moon. The harvest festival is a time of rejoicing and celebrating. With plenty of dance and folk music, young people go around flirting with each other in search of partners. In the midst of this chaos, I came across a large group of girls laughing and giggling. In the middle of the group was a man sitting on the floor tattooing the forearm of one of the young girls. As I inquired, one of them told me that the girl was getting her girlfriend's name tattooed. I was a bit puzzled and asked, "What happens when she gets married?" (within the Indian social context, it is nearly impossible for a girl to escape marriage). The girls were clear, "There is a very special place in your heart for your friend. You can never forget her."

Later during Jagori's action research work on the status of single women, we came across two women who were married to the same man. At the time of the interview (conducted by Maya Sharma), one of them was nearly 70 years old. The description she gave of her relationship with the other woman was very vivid, "In the eyes of the world outside, his name was slowly getting erased. Gradually a friendship between us started to flourish. Inside the four walls of the home, we would rub each other's back and look at each other's bodies. We slept in the same bed with our feet locked together" (Bhaiya 1996). Reflecting on this woman's relationship, I realized that although we live in a world dictated by patriarchal doctrines where we are taught to fear and deny our desires, we do not necessarily remain passive and obedient. While external norms mediate our expressions, we continue to follow our internal desires and our emotional, physical, and sensual needs.

During one of the meetings, as we were talking about female friendships, the old woman extended her wrinkled arm and stretched her skin to show the name of her friend tattooed on it. In her usual wise way, she murmured, "Your skin may get wrinkled but the memory of your friend does not." There was neither shame nor guilt in her words. These two women came from a small village and worked as daily wage earners. Extremely poor and without any literacy skills, this woman carried within her a tremendous sense of pride and wisdom. She never asked for any affirmation nor did she pass any judgment.

Similarly in Nepal, I came across a Hindu ritual between people of the same sex called *mit* (meaning friendship). Some of the women described it in great detail. In order to sanctify a relationship that two people hold sacred, a priest is called to perform the ritual. The ritual involves feeding each other with her own hands. Once a *miteri* (friendship) is established publicly through the performance of the ritual, both women pledge to maintain the intimacy of the friendship. A *mit* is not to call the other by name but addresses her as *mit jyu*, a sign of respect. This strong bond is declared to the family and can take place between two women or two men. The ritual has sociocultural sanction and wide acceptance in society (from notes taken at a South Asian women's workshop, 1996).

Iconography and Folklore of Female Sexualities and Desires

Within the Hindu tradition, there is ample evidence of iconographic inscription and folklore of female sexualities and desires. Within the ethos of the South Asian subcontinent, friendship between women is a recognized institution. As mentioned earlier, most north Indian languages have numerous names to refer to a woman friend. Naming a relationship and defining its territory is a political act. However, I would like to challenge the assumption that a lack of a clear definition or a plural, fluid naming hides the power of a relationship.

Within the dominant discourse, especially in the northern part of the world, there is an increasing tendency to universalize experiences and homogenize languages and their meanings. Similarly, there is an increasing pressure from within and outside to narrow the diverse ways in which women and men bond within same-sex practices. It is my contention that it is counterproductive to set boundaries around women's desire for women since it is difficult to assess when a woman's relationship with another woman is physical, emotional, sexual, or spiritual. The sexual and the sensual overlap, thus defying the privileged patriarchal, penile sexuality.[1]

Throughout the civilizations of the subcontinent, the pre-Aryan, Vedic, Shaktic, Puranic, Islamic, Bhakti, Sufi, and the colonial periods, the existence of women-centered practices are well-documented. The geographic territory of the South Asian subcontinent was determined by various periods of civilization influenced by multiple invasions and territorial claims. That history is divided into various periods of cultural, religious, and social movements and the development of literature and philosophical discourse as well as writings. Prior to the institutionalization of religion, the worship of the mother goddess known as Shakti—the autonomous, eternal female energy—was widely practiced and recognized.

The Vedic period saw the consolidation of Hindu religion and writing of the most valued religious scriptures. The Puranic period, as seen in the history of the development of Hindu religion, contained a rich heritage of religious literature known as Puranas. During the Islamic period of history, within the Hindu and the Muslim philosophies and religion, there have been significant parallel voices of love and surrender to god, well known as Bhakti and Sufi traditions. These traditions were not only marked by a critique of the established religious practices, but also a new conceptualization of a spiritual-sensual relationship with the creator, who is seen more as a lover than a distant god to be worshipped.

Iconographic evidence of female-centered sexuality supports the popular cultural acceptance of expressions of autonomous female sexuality. Prior to the institutionalization of the Hindu religion, evidence of unfettered, free, and autonomous female sexualities existed in Shaktic temples. Found in different parts of India and Nepal, these medieval temples comprise 64 female figures located in a circular form with a central courtyard. These temples were known as 64 Yogini, an autonomous self-determined female energy (Thadani 1996). Thus, female sexual expression was integral to the representation of sexualities in a sculptural form in various historical monuments in India and Nepal, which bear evidence of its open expression at that time in history.

The Sufi tradition occupies a large acknowledged space within the spiritual realms of the subcontinent. Sufi writings contain rich love poetry. In the Sufi tradition the creator is the lover. Different aspects of the Sufi tradition have evolved in different parts of South Asia. In fact the existence of the Sufi tradition is not confined to this region alone.

Not only sensuality and sexuality, but a large terrain of spirituality exists that is integral to the bonds between women-centered women and men-centered men. My guru, a nearly 70-year-old *sadhuni* (an ascetic) woman lives with another *sadhuni* in a small village in the Himalayan mountains. She narrated her spiritual experience of feeling mesmerized by her guru when she was hardly 12 years old. For her it was her calling. Her guru went on a pilgrimage to Mansarovar, a lake situated at a very high altitude in Tibet. This little girl decided to follow her guru, leaving the comfort of her home, and never looked back. I know of another women couple who strongly believe that their relationship is not of this lifetime. They are both practicing Buddhists, meditating, praying, loving—a continuum.

From folklore to sculptures, there is ample evidence of woman's day-to-day lived experiences of female friendships and desires. An extremely charming folk story, again from Rajasthan and written in a local dialect, explicitly elaborates on the physical, emotional, and sensual relationship between two women. The story is a magnificent piece of folk literature, published as part of a collection of folk stories. The story begins with the formation of a pact between two rich, feudal, upper caste men. As they find out their respective wives are pregnant, they decide to get their children married to each other, provided one is a boy and the other a girl. However, as luck would have it both are born girls. One of the fathers decides to hide this fact and declares that he has had a son. He insists on bringing up the daughter as a boy and makes her wear men's clothes. Once they get married and meet each other on the first night, they find that their bodies are incredibly the same. After getting over the shock, the one dressed up like a man gives up her manly attire. Both then dress as women and come into the public space. They challenge the entire village as well as their respective fathers by announcing their resolve to live and love together, thus stopping the lie perpetuated by their fathers. They then walk out of the village and reach the top of a hill. The first time they make love with abandon. The description of that lovemaking is extremely sensuous as well as vividly sexual. The story continues about their living together and how they are helped by a spirit to build a palace (Dheta 1996).

In 1987 two policewomen married by garlanding each other. The act was symbolic of their commitment to each other. They were immediately dismissed from the service. They could not understand this violent action against them, as they had not committed any crime. According to them and several other women, many women in and outside the police force perform similar ceremonies. When asked whether they were lesbians, they were utterly surprised, as they had never heard the word.[2]

Refusing Categories

Cultural and social practices and, for that matter, iconographic locations are not fixed constructs. However, we are faced with an aggressive attempt to erase some of this collective memory. For us, it is crucial to claim this history, look at its contextual relevance and build on that. Equally important is to evolve analytic tools that can grapple with this epistemological worldview that has evolved within these fluid-fixed traditions. Similarly, pluralities of sexual and sensual, spiritual and sexual, physical and emotional occupy a large continuum of experiences. The imposition of universal categories may deprive us of the access to a rich, plural, diverse, and celebratory history of social, sensual, and spiritual bonding. Forming diverse relationships is one of the most creative expressions of human aspirations. It also expands our sexual choices.

While oral traditions often stay fluid, undefined, and beyond categorization, they are also constantly transformed as new meanings are laid over the old. My challenge is to avoid the imposition of a conceptual framework that sees categorization as the most important task of the project of modernization. Why do all of us have to be "lesbians" in the way the dominant discourse can understand, label, and demarcate it? The creation of two binary opposites, in this case "closeted versus out," imposes a regime of categorization that can hardly contain multiple experiences of women or for that matter of men. Demanding that others be "out" assumes that "liberation" is not possible without public "disclosure."

For me the lines between conservative and radical, exotic and banal, romantic and mundane keep getting blurred. The truth about my identities is constantly shifting and reconfigurating. Let us not deprive our sexualities of their twilight zones. We are not the alternative but integral to what is everyday mainstream, even if we are pushed to the margins. It is my belief that in the realm of sexuality, secrecy or rather mystery holds a powerful allure. However, experiences of mystery and the mystical have been pushed to the margins and declared apolitical ingredients of relationships. I know the difficult grounds that I am treading on; silence can be a powerful tool of resistance to the project of homogenization of my experiences. What needs to be created is an enlarged reflective space that can hold an inner mirror to us and reflect the prism of our diversities. The demand for homogeneity obstructs the contingent nature of mystery and deep playful secrecy. It is true that becoming one with universal categories of identity politics offers safety, flatness, and ease. Linearity is easy to grapple with. But we accumulate a dense complexity of lived experiences.

My truth of "who I am," when not spoken, articulated or extended as "out I am," has the potential of being richer, more complex, and nuanced. At the same time it is also more problematic.

In the end, it is my contention that the process of visibilizing sensual, sexual, and emotional relationships between women must be done with tremendous care and respect for those whose lives are at stake. I say this to ensure the protection of space for women to continue their journeys together and build on traditional and contemporary practices of female bonding. The task of redefining must take account of the voices of all those women who choose to conduct their relationship along with the political understanding of the feminist vision of plural expressions of fulfillment. As these relationships are constructed around a range of emotions, desires, and needs, they cannot be trapped in a narrow definition of sex and sexuality. The strategies to unfold their power and vulnerabilities must be well thought out. Legal strategies around issues of sexuality have been cast in a particular mode. Perhaps it is time to look at them in a more creative manner. The language of expression and resistance contains hues of multiple voices whispering behind the stage of society.

Notes

1. In a conference held in 1993 on "Gender Construction and the History of Alternative Sexuality," there was a collective affirmation of the existence of plural, parallel sexualities.
2. This practice is also mentioned in another western Indian state, Maharashtra.

References Cited

Bhaiya, Abha, ed. 1996. *Kinaron Par Ugati Pehchan* (Identities growing on the margins). New Delhi: Rajkamal Prakashan.

Dheta, Vijay Dan. 1996. *Gharwas* (Inhabiting a household together). New Delhi: Manushi.

Jagori notebook. 1989. *From me to you*. New Delhi.

Thadani, Giti. 1996. *Sakhiyani: Lesbian desire in ancient and modern India*. London: Cassel.

Chapter Five

Performing Gender along the Lesbian Continuum: The Politics of Sexual Identity in the Seitô Society

Peichen Wu

Introduction

The year 1911 was a turning point in several respects for the Japanese women's liberation movement. Matsui Sumako, the best-known Japanese actress in the 1910s, performed the role of Nora, the heroine of Henrik Ibsen's *A Doll's House*. In September of the same year, the Seitô Society was established as the first women's literary society organized by women. Several of its members were later involved in the Japanese women's liberation movement. In the beginning, the purpose of the Seitô Society was to cultivate women's literature (Hiratsuka 1911). By 1913, the members were more concerned with the women's liberation movement; more articles on women's issues appear in Seitô's magazines.[1]

Soon after the Society was established, the members were involved in several sexual scandals (Yamazaki 1999). Their activities were influenced by the discourse about the "sexually degenerate female students" of the Japanese Women's College. As soon as the Women's College was established in 1901, women students were stigmatized by the media as "sexual degenerates" (*daraku jogakusei*).[2] Most members of the Seitô Society, including its founder, Hiratsuka Raichô, were graduates of the Japanese Women's College.

During this period, some of the Seitô members dared to transgress the boundary between heterosexuality and homosexuality. As I demonstrate, this transgression made their gender identity ambiguous. Their sexuality cannot be defined as either heterosexual or homosexual because documents and literary works by Seitô members at this time demonstrate that they were sexually involved not only with men but also with women. From today's viewpoint one might think that the term "bisexual" would properly represent their orientation, yet none of these three terms is an accurate description of Seitô members' sexual orientation in that these categories presuppose stable gender/sexuality identities.

This chapter examines how members of the Seitô Society challenged the emergent heterosexist ideology that forced women to accept a restrictively feminine gender identity. The nature of this ideology is suggested by the slogan *ryôsai kenbo* (good wives, wise mothers) that was used in relation to women's education at the time. The *Kôtô Jogakkô Rei* (Women's High School Law) of 1899 gave Japanese women a better chance to obtain a higher education. However, the goal of these women's schools was to create more "good wives, wise mothers" to support Japan's qualities as a modern country (Fukuya 1998). Although the Seitô members' critique of stereotypical gender roles has been deservedly well documented and investigated, less attention has been paid to their same-sex relationships and their radical questioning of the norm of heterosexuality. In other words, even though much attention has been paid to the Seitô members' gender politics, their sexual politics have been left uninvestigated.

My aim is to deepen an understanding of (1) how members of the Seitô Society demonstrated their own order of sex/gender/desire, and (2) how the Seitô Society countered contemporary Japanese patriarchy through their outrageous behavior and writings that questioned the doctrine of "good wives, wise mothers." Rather than identify Seitô members' "genuine" sexual option and gender, I examine how the discontinuity among their biological sex, gender, and sexuality conflicted with the contemporary discourse of gender/sex—a discourse in which Seitô members were often stigmatized as being proponents of *dôseiai* (same-sex love) because of their subversion of socially accepted gender roles.

Seitô members were certainly outrageous enough to assume the stigmatized "lesbian" persona in order to challenge the gender ideology of their day, but does this mean that they were indeed lesbians? As already mentioned, this chapter does not offer an essentialist answer to the question of the Seitô members' "genuine" sexual orientation. Rather, it attempts to deconstruct the hierarchical binary logic inherent in dichotomies such as homosexuality/heterosexuality and male/female. The first step is to historicize how homophobic and misogynist discourses emerged in the 1910s in Japan; the second is to examine the radical ambivalence in Seitô members' sexual/gender identities. Roden (1990) mentions that the "new women's" self-assertion on sexuality is related to their self-awakening. He points out how their behavior transgressed the boundary between men and women and made their gender ambivalent; however, the relationship between their ambivalent gender and their "same-sex love" seems to be beyond his concern. I show how the Seitô members' radical ambivalence in their gender/sexuality opened possibilities for conceptualizing nonbinary, antimisogynist, antiheterosexist, and antihomophobic ways of being feminists.

In the latter part of this chapter, I use the term "lesbian" to describe the *dôseiai* relationships of Seitô Society members. Lest there be an objection that these two terms are not equivalent, let me state that I realize that what is considered lesbianism today and what Seitô members meant by *dôseiai* cannot be simplistically regarded as the same. Adrienne Rich defines "the lesbian continuum" as that which embraces "many more forms of primary intensity between and among women, including the sharing of a rich inner life, the bonding against male tyranny, the giving and receiving of practical and political support" (Rich 1980:648–649). Rich's "lesbian continuum" embraces not only lesbian but also heterosexual women, who are conceptualized not as part of a hierarchical binary but as part of a continuum. Rich's continuum also includes female bonding against homophobic tendencies in some of the feminist movements. Though historically and culturally distinct from the Japanese context, Rich's continuum is a most fitting idea to represent the Seitô members' gender/sexual ambiguities.

Moreover, Judith Butler's gender theory is useful to interpret Seitô members' gender performance in their lesbian relationships. Butler defines gender as follows:

> If gender is drag, and if it is an imitation that regularly produces the ideal it attempts to approximate, then gender is a performance that *produces* the illusion of an inner sex or essence or psychic gender core; it *produces* on the illusion, through the gesture, the move, the gait (that array of the corporeal theatrics understood as gender presentation), the illusion of an inner depth. (Butler 1993:317)

Butler's gender theory makes sense of Seitô members' masculine role playing in both their homosexual and their heterosexual relationships.

Though keenly aware of the risk of using the term "lesbian" in my argument, I maintain that there is continuity as well as difference between the notion of *dôseiai* attached to the Seitô members and the contemporary notion of lesbianism. Hence my task is twofold: (1) to historicize the culturally specific significance of the emergent notion of *dôseiai*, and (2) to connect it with the contemporary theory of gender/sexuality.[3]

"Revolting Lesbianism" in the 1910s

The emergent Japanese discourse on female same-sex love (*dôseiai*) in the 1910s demonized it as a "revolting" pathological problem. Lesbianism came to people's attention through two cases of love-suicide by women couples. These cases are noteworthy because their coverage by the media mirrored the heterosexist, reproduction-centered logic of modern Japanese patriarchy. The two couples' love-suicides were reported in newspapers of July 30–31, 1911. The first couple, who were maids in

Tokyo, jumped into the Tamagawa River together but were rescued by local policemen.[4] The second couple, graduates of women's schools, drowned themselves in the sea near Niigata; their bodies were found on the seashore.[5]

After these successive love-suicides, there were special columns in the August 11, 1911 *Fujo Shinbun*—entitled "Dôsei no ai" (Same-sex love), "Dôsei no ai kenkyû" (Studies of same-sex love), and "Dôsei no koi to sono jitsurei" (Same-sex love and examples thereof)—discussing the love-suicides and drawing them to the attention of women's school teachers and parents. Because of their higher social status, the women's school graduates (the daughters of a professor and a bureaucrat) were of more interest to the mass media than were the two women who had worked as maids. In September 1911, articles appeared that tended to treat "same-sex love" as pathology: *Shin Kôron*'s was entitled "Senritsu subeki no josei kan no tentô seiyoku" (Revolting sexual inversion among women) and *Shin Fujin*'s was "Ôsoru beki dôsei no ai" (Revolting same-sex love), though *Fujin no tomo*'s had the heading "Hokkai ni tôshin seru karen no ni shôjo" (Two pretty girls drowned themselves in the North Sea). These and earlier headlines indicate that the discourse of "revolting lesbianism" became dominant in describing the "same-sex love" relationship between these women.[6]

This journalistic hyperbole shows mass media's rejection of female same-sex love. Yet it was only in the 1910s that lesbianism was conceived of as a category of sexuality and of sexual identity in some cases in Japan.[7] Before that, the term for same-sex love was *danshoku* (male-color), which applied exclusively to male same-sex love.[8] Given the lack of a term for female same-sex love before the 1910s, it is not an overstatement to say that discourses on it emerged with the first appearance of the term *dôseiai*.

Even though the date of the first use of the term of *dôseiai* has not been ascertained, in general the 1910s and 1920s in Japan reflect the emergence of a national discourse on female same-sex love. Prior to that time, such relations between women were invisible. Furukawa Makoto insists that "from the 1890s to 1920s, there were various terms to express the same-sex relationship, but the specific term *dôseiai* was coined in the end" (1995:206). He points out that the discourse on the love-suicide of the female couple in Niigata Prefecture was influential in making *dôseiai* a fixed term defining the same-sex love relationship (Furukawa 1995). His argument clarifies not only how the establishment of the term overlapped with the timing of the two female couples' love-suicides, but also how these suicides coincided with a shift in the epistemology of homosexuality in Japan:

> The social problematization of lesbianism by female students during the 1910s and 1920s was closely related to the fact that the term *dôseiai* (same-sex love) was first accepted in the Japanese language in the same period. Undoubtedly,

> there lurked an epistemological shift of key words from *danshoku* (male-color) between men to *dôseiai* (same-sex love), which mainly but not exclusively referred to female same-sex love. (Furukawa 1995:207)

Until the 1910s and the 1920s, when the term *dôseiai* was coined, as Furukawa suggests, female same-sex love was inconceivable. This is not to say that female same-sex behavior did not exist in Japan prior to this time, but only that it may not have been recognized as a particular form of sexuality before the term was coined. The discourse of female same-sex love as a revolting pathological illness and source of contamination emerged exactly at the moment when the term *doseiai* appeared.

The reason that women's same-sex love attracted public attention was the nation's strict control over the sexuality of female students. Within this social context, the policing of Japanese women's sexuality became more severe. Immediately after the successive love-suicides in July 1911, the mass media started paying attention to lesbianism among female students, decrying it as a "revolting phenomenon" in a patriarchal society that championed the doctrine of *ryôsai kenbo*.

Soon after the Sino-Japanese War of 1894–95, women's education was taken more seriously; many women's schools were established after the Kôtô Jogakkô Rei (Women's High School Law) was promulgated in 1899. This law made the importance of women's education clearer; it urged women to fulfill their obligation to their country by mastering household affairs and nurturing the next generation (Koyama 1993; Fukaya 1998). *Ryôsai kenbo shugi* (the doctrine of "good wives, wise mothers") not only came to be a powerful tool in the modernization of Meiji Japan, but also reinforced the foundation of patriarchy. Under the norm of *ryôsai kenbo*, the Japanese patriarchy theorized that reproduction was the ultimate end of heterosexuality—and this, in turn, created the image of the lesbian as a "revolting alien" vis-à-vis the patriarchal system, which was, of course, based on compulsory heterosexuality. Moreover, while the lesbian was theorized as abnormal, the heterosexual was constructed as a "healthy" and "natural" sexual being. Contemporary educators' comments about female students' sexuality show that the educational system was a forceful means of disciplining female students' sexuality.

Fujo shinbun, a newspaper strongly championing the doctrine of "good wives, wise mothers," provides a typical example. It invited medical doctors, educators, and graduates of women's schools to discuss the issue of same-sex love soon after the double suicides occurred. The comments by these "specialists" were published in the August 1911 issue mentioned above.[9] The reports claimed that lesbian practices among female students were caused by "perverse friendship" or "sick sexual desire."

A special September 1911 issue of *Shin Kôron* (New Opinion) featured "Seiyoku ron" (A discourse on sexuality), including an interview by

Kuwaya Sadaitsu entitled "Senritsu subeki joseikan no tentôseiyoku" (The revolting female sexual inversion) about proper discipline in women's schools. This article shows how educators began to pay much more attention to disciplining female same-sex relations.

> The homosexual is not rare anymore. This tendency is obvious among other schools' students. "Passion" (*onetsu*) is used in Ochanomizu Women's School, "newness" (*haikara*) in Gakushyuin Women's School, and "friendship" (*oshinyu*) in Atomi Women's School, while in other women's schools these kinds of words are also used. The usage of these words is extraordinary and tends to make students emotional. Women's educators should seriously consider not only this problem but a resolution to this problem. (Kuwaya 1911:35)[10]

This comment was intended to warn against "lesbian play" among female students, since women's school educators were now aware of the possibility of love-suicides among their students. The schools were supposed to educate young women according to the "good wives, wise mothers" doctrine, so they were also supposed to ensure that they grew up to be heterosexual. However, through intimate associations among the female students, this system was subverted from the inside. Because two women's school graduates had committed love-suicide, passionate friendships among female students came to be seen as a "danger." The July 1911 incident radically shook the women's school system, so that intimacy among female students was thought to be a symptom of "illness." This discourse on female students' "friendship" shows how same-sex love was discriminated against. It was also an ominous sign for Seitô members, all of them female students at this time, who were involved in lesbian scandals in the years that followed. As female same-sex love became visible, the intimacy between female students, and the lives of Seitô members, were labeled "lesbian" by the public.

Further examination of the September 1911 special issue *Shin kôron* shows how the homosexual discourse in the medical field tended to stigmatize lesbianism as illness and how this theory was gradually accepted by the Japanese populace: "For our social sanitation, the homosexual should sublimate his or her abnormal desire and must not transmit *it* to others" (*Shin Kôron*, September 1911:42). Thus lesbianism in Japan was attacked ideologically, in accordance with the women's school's doctrine of "good wives, wise mothers," labeled as contagion, and demonized by sexologists.

Sexology had been introduced to Japan from the West in the late nineteenth century (Furukawa 1995). Sexologists such as Havelock Ellis and Krafft-Ebing had immense influence on Japanese sexology; they identified the lesbian as a "sexual invert" or as "ill."[11] Though the discourses of homosexuality and lesbianism in Japan before 1911 were mainly a product of medical studies, they came to the attention of various domains, including education, as soon as lesbianism was represented as a disturbing symptom to Japanese society. In "Seiyoku kenkyû no hitsuyô o ronzu" (The discourse of sexology studies), also part of the September 1911 special issue of *Shin Kôrôn*, Uchida Roan marked female couple love-suicides as a turning point for the study of sexology in Japan. "In Germany, sexual education has turned out to be the problem in education recently. This problem has also gradually become manifest in Japan's education. Since degenerate homosexuality has spread everywhere, it is urgent that we resolve this problem" (Uchida 1911:3–4).

The influence of the dualism of sexuality is seen in media statements in which sexuality was divided into a binary—namely, abnormal homosexuality or normal heterosexuality. Based on this discourse, the continuity of women's sex/gender/sexuality was an absolute demand of heterosexist society that excluded not only lesbians, but also the anti-*ryôsai kenbo shugi* group, such as Seitô members. It is evident that there were close connections between the discourse of binary sexuality and the ideology of compulsory heterosexuality discussed by Rich (1980). In short, the discourse of Western sexology was a convenient tool with which to discipline Japanese female students' sexuality under both the doctrine of "good wives, wise mothers" and patriarchy's compulsory heterosexuality. Lesbianism inevitably became known as a "revolting sexual inversion" within this context.

Same-Sex Love in the Seitô Society

Since its inception the Seitô Society had been seen as a hotbed of vices that stood in opposition to women's virtues. Because they failed to support the doctrine of "good wives, wise mothers," the group became a target of attack by the media and by society in general. Seitô Society members' activities were reported in scandalous terms. Both *Taiyô* (The Sun) in June 1912 and *Chuô Kôron* (Central Review) in July the same year published special issues titled "Women's Issues" to attack "new women" represented by the *Seitô* members. An article published in the Tokyo Daily Newspaper, November 29, 1911 called the Seitô members "hensei no onna" (perverted women) (Nichinichi 1912). The main reason for the media attacks was that its members transgressed what was considered men's territory by visiting prostitutes in the pleasure quarters and drinking with other women in bars.[12] Scandals about their sexual relationships and the issue of lesbianism among its members received especially keen attention from the press.[13] It was zealously reported that Hiratsuka Raichô was a bisexual as well as a sex addict and that Otake Kôkichi was a natural lesbian (see next section).[14] Seitô members' "outrageous" behavior constituted a form of rebellion against the compulsory heterosexuality forced on women by educators and mostly men intellectuals of the patriarchal gender/sexuality system.

Why was the sexuality of the Seitô members, particularly their lesbianism, attacked by the mass media? For one thing, the social context within which it was attacked—namely, the complex of the doctrine of "good wives, wise mothers" and the binary theory of sexuality—influenced those working for the press, which produced a distorted image of lesbians as "abnormal," "sexual inverts," and "ill." Within this context, the amorphous sexuality of the Seitô members was regarded as definitely "freakish." But how did the Seitô members view their own same-sex relationships? In what follows, the real nature of the lesbian relationships among Seitô members is pursued by analyzing some members' love affairs.

To shed light on the situation of Japanese lesbianism in the 1910s—and on the gap between the real situation and the discourse of Japan's lesbianism in the same period—I focus here on two well-known lesbian couples of the Seitô Society: (1) Hiratsuka Raichô, the founder of the Seitô Society and of *Seitô*, its magazine, and Otake Kôkichi; and (2) Tamura Toshiko, who was married to Tamura Shôgyo, and Naganuma Chieko, the wife of the poet Takamura Kôtarô and thus also known as Takamura Chieko. As I argue, Toshiko and Chieko represent the heterosexual paradigm in that they constructed the hierarchical binary gender roles of male and female, whereas Raichô and Toshiko tried to build their same-sex love relationship but failed because both fought for the male role in their relationship.

Both Tamura Toshiko and Naganuma Chieko had attended Japan Women's College and been members of the Seitô Society since its inception. Tamura Toshiko published her novel *Akirame* (Resignation) serially in *Osaka Asahi Shinbun* (Osaka Asahi Newspaper) from January 1, 1911, to March 31, 1911 (figure 5.1).[15] Thereafter, the lesbian issue was one of the main themes of her writing. This can be seen especially in her later works, *Wakai kokoro* (The fresh heart), *Samuke* (Chills), and *Nikki* (Diary). "The fresh heart," published in *Shin Shôsetsu* (The New Novel) in May 1916, is about an admirer of a female writer (supposedly Toshiko herself) who is eager to monopolize the writer's love. Chills and Diary focus on same-sex love between Toshiko and Seitô members Chieko and Raichô.

To the initial issue of *Seitô* magazine, Toshiko contributed her novel *Ikichi* (Liveblood), a powerful work protesting the female "virtue" imposed on women by Japan's phallocentric society. Chieko, an artist, drew a design for the cover of the first issue (figure 5.2). Their relationship began at that time, though Toshiko was already married. Chieko then left

Figure 5.1 Tamura Toshiko (1911).

Figure 5.2 Takamura (Naganuma) Chieko (1912).

Toshiko and took Takamura Kôtarô as her partner, later marrying him. Toshiko wrote the novel Chills in an epistolary style, with Chieko as the intended reader; it was published in *Bunshô Sekai* (The World of essays) in October 1913. In this novel Toshiko expresses her hatred of the female role and her passion for living with Chieko:

> I would like to let this man [Toshiko's husband, Tamura Shôgyo] have a modest wife, a lovely and obedient woman to live with him. However, every time this thought strikes me, I cannot help crying out, because I can do nothing. (Tamura 1988, 1:275)

Toshiko knew that she could not be a "modest wife" and "lovely and obedient woman" and so expressed her hatred of the role forced on her by the heterosexual codes. Moreover, her desire to live with Chieko was intense:

> I want to get out of here and start a new life only for you and me. If we are together, I think I will be released from the current situation and have a free life. I have forgotten the fact that I am a woman and the requirements for being a woman since I met you. I try to draw a picture of our happy life, which we might enjoy if we were to live together. Every time I recall that we can live the women-only life without "man," I feel so happy, as though my body were sailing out over the wide open sea. (Tamura 1988, 1:272)

Toshiko's description of her hoped-for life with Chieko is remarkably romantic. Romantic idealization of female same-sex attachment was not rare in literary works by both men and women in the Meiji era. In the case of Toshiko, I take her idealization of love between Chieko and herself as a case of defiance against the gender ideology that forced women to be obedient wives.

Toshiko wants to build a women-only land with Chieko and dispel all kinds of oppression, including the female role dictated by compulsory heterosexuality. Yet does this mean that Toshiko was totally free of the typical patriarchal values of Japanese society that sanctioned a dominant role for men in heterosexual relationships? It seems to me that she was still bound by patriarchal codes even while struggling against them. We can see this contradiction in her admiration of Chieko's "virginal" beauty:

> Even if you have had a lot of boyfriends until now, I know you have never fallen in love with any one of them. You are just like a little bird; so soft, lovely, and dear to me. When I hold your hands, your pure heart beats. It reminds me of the touch of a bud. (Tamura 1988, 1:270)

Perhaps Chieko awoke Toshiko's awareness of virginal beauty despite the fact that it was based on a standard put forth by heterosexual codes of beauty and thus was, arguably, an ideological construct of the heterosexist patriarchy. If so, what does it mean that Toshiko, who hated the gender role assigned to her by society, still admired Chieko's "feminine" beauty?

In another instance Toshiko writes of "the colorful parasols we bought: a red one matches you and a blue one me" (Tamura 1988, 1:270–271). Toshiko's color choice shows her consciousness of a dichotomy of gender roles. Blue symbolized the male and red symbolized the female (Suzuki 2000). In other words, she clings to the dichotomy of masculine/feminine, as symbolized by blue and red, even while trying to transcend the gender role assigned to her by the patriarchal society of Japan. This passage suggests that Toshiko tried to take on the "masculine" role in relation to Chieko.

It is also illuminating that Toshiko is repeatedly depicted as a "charming and feminine" woman by her contemporaries. By knowingly assuming a "charming and feminine" appearance, Toshiko tried to subvert the binary logic inherent in heterosexism-in which men remain superior to women—even though this subversion only exposed her "poor imitation." Thus the relation between Chieko and Toshiko cannot be defined as a classic case of butch-femme lesbians, in which the "mannish" woman takes the manly role and the "feminine" woman takes the passive, womanly role. Yet it must be admitted that Toshiko partially depended on the masculine-feminine dichotomy by imagining her lesbian relation with Chieko in terms of blue and red. Thus Toshiko played the man's role in her relationship with Chieko, which was also the role she would never claim in her heterosexual relationships.

To expand an understanding of the contradiction inherent in Toshiko's gender/sexuality, I look at the association between Toshiko and Raichô. Raichô and Toshiko tried to build a lesbian relationship but failed because their gender identities conflicted with each other. Toshiko contributed a short essay to *Chuô Kôron*, "*Hiratsuka San*" (Miss Hiratsuka), about her impressions of Raichô. This essay focuses primarily on Raichô's physical characteristics and stresses her "masculinity." In it, Toshiko notes that someone else had commented that Raichô's "Adam's apple is too big for a woman and a beard can be seen on her jaw. If we examine it carefully, we will find that her beard is long and thick, differing from the downy hairs of women" (Tamura 1988, 3:339). Toshiko implies that Raichô was a lesbian, as rumor had it, and that Raichô took the male role.

Toshiko's Diary published in the magazine *Chuô Kôron* in July 1913 is a record of same-sex love in the Seitô Society. The Diary begins with an interesting description of a one-day get-together with Raichô, whom Toshiko bumps into when seeking a new place to move into with her husband. Raichô then invites Toshiko to go out and they leave Toshiko's husband behind. The description shows how Toshiko herself prefers the "relationship" between women to her relation with her husband. The fact that she leaves her husband behind to join Raichô can be seen as a shift from the heterosexual world to the world of same-sex love.

What follows in Diary is an enlargement of the essay "Hiratsuka San." Toshiko describes not only Raichô's physical features but her attitudes, behavior, and gestures in ways that stress her masculinity. She emphasizes Raichô's "masculinity" by pointing out her custom of wearing *hakama* (a divided skirt) and wooden clogs.[16] In Toshiko's observation of Raichô's bodily features she uses the term "danseiteki" (masculine) repeatedly. By describing Raichô as a woman with masculine features, Toshiko emphasizes a contradiction between Raichô's sex and her gender:

> H[iratsuka Raichô] crosses her hands *like a man* while she is on the train. It is her habit; today she does the same as usual, and keeps silent with a solemn look. (Tamura 1988, 3:341, emphasis added)
>
> Widening her *hakama* and leaning on the wall and with her thick eyebrows, she undoubtedly looks just *like a man.* (Tamura 1988, 3:347, emphasis added)

Writing about Raichô's mental characteristics, Toshiko also repeatedly focuses on Raichô's masculinity:

> On her face without make-up there is nothing indicating that she is in love. As usual, the destructive, shaking passion shows up from the circles of her eyes to her cheeks (Tamura 1988, 3:344).

By emphasizing Raichô's masculinity and her emotions, Toshiko seems to predict the possibility of having a lesbian relationship with Raichô. When she gets drunk, she confesses to Raichô: "I feel so released that I can give kisses to anyone's heart" (Tamura 1988, 3:347). She continues: "While I told H [of my passion], H urged me eagerly to be her 'swallow.'"[17] However, the relationship between them does not develop. Toshiko says:

> I am drunk and my senses are working in my puppy love. I feel so free, but there are no special feelings between H and me. I did not have the slightest idea of holding her hand when I walked with her. (Tamura 1988, 3:347).

No matter how much Toshiko feels released and that she "can give kisses to anyone's heart," Raichô is never her choice as a lover. This seems to be related to Raichô's masculinity, as incessantly emphasized by Toshiko. Toshiko's comparison of Raichô and Chieko makes it even clearer how Toshiko and Raichô's gender identities conflict with each other. For example, Toshiko describes how Raichô made her feel as frozen as *sekkô* (plaster) and then writes:

> N[aganuma Chieko] can make her companion happier. I believe that N and I can achieve an artistic oneness through various illusions. This is also the reason I feel more familiar and closer to N. Even though I see Raichô's soft hands just beside me, I do not have any idea of holding her hand. Even if I take her hands, her body will not easily get used to my hands. (Tamura 1988, 3:344–345)

The gender role that Toshiko chose in her relation with Raichô was ultimately a "masculine" one despite the fact that Toshiko was often described as a "charming and feminine" woman. From this we might expect that the relation between Raichô and Toshiko would follow the classic paradigm of butch-femme with Raichô playing the "male" part and Toshiko playing the "female." But this type of relationship with Raichô was impossible for Toshiko precisely because she refused to take the feminine part despite Raichô's "masculine" characteristics.

At the end of Diary, Toshiko sentimentally recalls Chieko—"I cannot help thinking of the sadness N showed on her face while in the train on my way home" (Tamura 1988, 3:347)—whereas nothing happens between Toshiko and Raichô in the end. For Toshiko, the male role in gender play was the only choice in her lesbian relationships. She was convinced that because both she and Raichô sought that role, they had to break up. Soon after separating from Raichô, Toshiko recalled the feminine Chieko as the opposite of the masculine Raichô. Yet it may be more accurate to say that Toshiko missed her own male part in her relationship with Chieko, rather than Chieko's femininity per se.

Toshiko's attitudes toward her female partners in Chills and Diary reveal that her choice of the male gender role, her "feminine" appearance, and her resistance to Raichô's masculinity are full of paradox. In Chills, Toshiko's masculine feelings toward the "virginal" Chieko are apparent, whereas she and Raichô struggle to occupy the male position in Diary. For example, even though Toshiko masqueraded in her physical appearance as typically "feminine," she refused to take a female part even in her lesbian relationship with Raichô. She preferred Chieko's femininity undoubtedly because she could perform the male gender role in their same-sex love relationship. Through examining Toshiko's relations with Chieko in Chills and with Raichô in Diary, the contradiction in her gender/sexuality identity becomes clear.

Absolute versus Flexible Gender-Play

If we treat same-sex love from Toshiko's point of view, the binary construction in the gender play that she emphasized in her relationship with Raichô should not be overlooked. For Toshiko, both the male and the female parts in gender play existed due to her strong consciousness of the structure of heterosexuality. For this reason Toshiko tended to force her partner to take the female part in their sexual relationship. In contrast, Raichô did not hold to the heterosexual paradigm as a model for her relationships with women. The most evident example is her same-sex relation with Otake Kôkichi, which was often compared to *danshoku* (male-color), the "male-gay" relationship.

Figure 5.3 Hiratsuka Raichô (1911). She founded the Seitô Society that year.

Hiratsuka Raichô's (1913) essay "Ichinen kan" (One year) describes her one-year relationship with Otake Kôkichi.[18] Her relationship with Kôkichi was more like a male-color relationship than a lesbian one in that both took on the masculine identity (figure 5.3). Only by examining their gender play can light be cast on their gay-couple-like relationship. Butler's gender theory is enormously useful in conceptualizing the relationship between Raichô and Kôkichi, who tried to subvert gender dichotomy by "imitating" the roles of homosexual men.

Both women were cross-dressers, who smoked and drank like men. Kôkichi describes her own history as a cross-dresser:

> I (*Boku*) wore the male student's hat, straightened my mantle's collar, put on the dark blue *tabi* and a man's wooden clogs, and smoked while I walked with my sister. People teased and made fun of me. I think I did really look like a man. (Itô 2000:140)[19]

The image that Raichô had of Kôkichi can be seen from Raichô's writing: "My boy, Raichô's boy, I will never forget how you hurt yourself and left a scar on your body for me" (Hiratsuka 1912:85).

In this situation, their lesbian relationship was naturally seen as an imitation of "male-color" (*danshoku*). Toshiko composed the poem "*Atta ato*" (After seeing you two) to mock their "gay male" relationship:

> Kôkichi, your body is so huge,
> while you and R[aichô] are together,
> who is the one to embrace the other?
> While R embraces you, your bulk will get bulkier
> (Tamura 1912:135)

This poem depicts not only Kôkichi's masculine body but also Raichô's active male role in their relationship as well (figure 5.4). For this reason, Raichô and Kôkichi were a "gay male couple" rather than a lesbian couple in Toshiko's eyes.[20] Lesbian identity was influenced by the male-color concept of homosexuality at this time. Under this influence, Raichô and Kôkichi were seen as a gay male couple rather than as lesbians.

Their "male-color-like" relationship and Raichô's active and dominant role are also manifested in Raichô's essay, "Marumado yori" (From the round window):

> How passionate my kisses and hugs were to make Kôkichi become part of my world, I don't know, I don't really know. How Kôkichi's whole heart burned out like a flame in a snap. (Hiratsuka 1912:85)
>
> I put all of Kôkichi's letters and postcards into boxes in order. I cannot even put myself together. There are twenty-nine letters and thirty-eight postcards that I have received since November 30 last year [now it is May 1912]. The night of the thirteenth is unforgettable [the night they spent together for the first time]. I selected the letters including the express ones delivered after that night and read them again. I stared at the letters and kept sitting there till dawn. I could not help thinking of the issue of same-sex love. (Hiratsuka 1912:89)
>
> The night, all night long, Kôkichi cried in my arms. What kind of dream did he (*kare*) have? He seemed to be frightened by something and his body shivered several times. (Hiratsuka 1912:105)

Figure 5.4 Otake Kôkichi (Tomimoto Kazue) seated in the first row on the far left (1926).

In these excerpts, Raichô's active role in their same-sex love relationship is clear. Kôkichi's passion for Raichô is symbolized by the number of letters she sent Raichô in half a year. From the excerpts, a vivid image of a "gay" rather than a "lesbian" couple appears. Raichô's and Kôkichi's imitation of male-color not only challenged and mocked the traditional view of homosexuality as men's privilege in Japanese patriarchal society, but also asserted women's right to sexuality through demonstrating this parody of male color.

Raichô then left Kôkichi to live with Okumura Hiroshi, a man who was often described as a "sissy," though they did not marry.[21] She later had two children with him. This relationship was one of the reasons for the split in the Seitô Society. Yuasa Yoshiko comments in her diary: "Why did she fall on account of her relation with a man? Once she starts to live with a man and has children by him, even though she does not follow the system of marriage, nothing will change in her life. The freedom which women can get should not be sought in men and children" (Sawabe 1990:121).

Did Raichô compromise herself by adhering to the compulsory "woman's role" enforced by the dominant masculine ideology of Japan? She refers to Okumura in a letter entitled "*Dokuritsu suru ni tsuite ryôshin ni*" (To my parents: About my independence):

> I think both of you have already known a man who incessantly visited me since early last summer. I would like to inform you that I am going to start a simple new life with this young painter, five years younger than me, whom I call "little swallow," "younger brother." For me, he is composed of five-tenths of a child, three-tenths of a woman and two-tenths of a man. (Hiratsuka 1914:110–11)

In this letter Raichô imagines that Okumura is extremely feminine. Both Raichô herself and other members of the Seitô Society mention Okumura's "feminine" image. Commenting on how Kôkichi was upset by Raichô's relationship with Okumura, Itô Noe writes, "Kôkichi cannot forget Raichô nor she cannot forgive Okumura. Okumura's gentle, modest, and somewhat *feminine* attitudes irritate her" (Itô 2000:156, emphasis added).

For Raichô, Okumura's part as a man is just "two-tenths." Based on Raichô's description, Raichô is still playing the male gender role even in her heterosexuality. Thus even though Raichô's sexual option switched from homosexuality to heterosexuality, she did not play the female gender role as defined by the heterosexual codes of contemporary Japanese society.

Conclusion

I have examined the significance of the Seitô members' same-sex love in the historical context of the 1910s. There are contradictions and limitations in the Seitô members' "lesbianism": Toshiko, for example, seems to reintroduce the male/female, active/passive dichotomy in her same-sex relations with Raichô and Chieko. Yet I would argue that despite these contradictions, their relations show traces of Seitô member's resistance to absolute gender roles as disciplined by patriarchal, reproduction-centered heterosexism and the view of lesbianism as pathology. Their ambiguous sexuality not only challenged the dominant discourse on lesbianism in Japan but also overturned the doctrine of "good wives, wise mothers" supported by compulsory heterosexuality. By insisting that their gender was performatively constructed rather than biologically determined, they also dissolved the myth of the continuity of the sex/gender/sexuality system on which compulsory heterosexuality depended. Their defiance of the gender order can be seen as a powerful counter to the social hierarchy.

Through their rebellion, members of the Seitô Society arguably created the first lesbian continuum in modern Japan. Their gender performance succeeded in exposing the instability of the compulsory heterosexuality that had supported the Japanese patriarchal system. Even when there was a power struggle within this continuum—such as the conflict between Raichô and Toshiko on the issue of gender roles, which caused the split in their lesbian relationship—this female bonding still qualifies as a lesbian continuum. Through the various forms of sexuality played out in gender performance, *Seitô* members not only demonstrated their own sexual identity politics in reaction to the Japanese patriarchy, but also overturned the discourse of lesbian pathology invented by Japanese sexology.

Notes

This chapter is a revised version of an article published in the *U.S.-Japan Women's Journal* English Supplement No. 22 (2002). A preliminary draft of that article was read at the Fifth Annual Asian Studies Conference Japan held in Tokyo on June 23–24, 2001. I am grateful for comments made by Masazumi Araki, Elizabeth Balestrieri, Evelyn Blackwood, Sally A. Hastings, Noriko Hiraishi, Yoichiro Miyamoto, Yukari Yoshihara and Saskia E. Wieringa (in alphabetical order).

1. The February 1913 issue was prohibited from sale because of the article "*Fujin mondai no kaiketsu*" (The resolution for women's issues) written by Fukuda Hideko. Seitô journal published Ellen Key's "*Ai to dôtoku*" (Love and morality) in May 1913 and Emma Goldman's "*Fujin kaihô no higeki*" (The tragedy of women's liberation) in September of the same year.
2. Mass media developed the discourse on the degenerate female students in the following cases. In July 1901, *Yorozu Chôhô* (Yorozu National Newspaper), *Keika Nippo* (Keika Daily), *Hinode Kokku Shinbu* (The Rising Sun National Newspaper) and *Jinmin* (People) reported on "*Nippon joshi daigakko fuzoku jogakusei ensho jiken*" (The incident of the love letter to the female student in Japanese Women's College). Afterward, *Heimin Shinbun* (Commoners'

Newspaper) serialized a story called the "The Pleasure Quarter in Mejiro" (January 20 to February 13, 1907). Mejiro is the location of the Japanese Women's College. Each of these reports stigmatized female students in the Japanese Women's College by labeling them as sexual degenerates.

3. The gender theory here adopted comes from Butler's definition of feminist analysis that "gender is the cultural or social construction of the sex" (1992:140). For sexuality theory, I adopt Lacan's assertion that "for Freudian psychoanalysis, sexuality, situated between phallic desire and feminine jouissance, knows no other law than the logic of the unconscious" (Brousse 1992:409).
4. This news was reported under such headlines as "Ni shôjo jôshi o hakaru" (Two girls attempted love-suicide) in *Asahi Shinbun* (July 30, 1911); "Nishôjo idaite nyushui, shimai no gotoku shitashiki gejodôshi" (Two maids as close as sisters embracing each other committed double suicide) in *Yomiuri Shinbun* (July 30, 1911); and "Onna no dakiai shinju, shimai yorimo shitashiki naka" (Women who embraced each other committed love-suicide) in *Yorozu Chôhô* (July 31, 1911).
5. Coverage of the couple who were women's school graduates began as follows: "Suishi seru nibijin, kyokutan naru dôsei no ai" (Two beauties drowned themselves, extreme same-sex love) in *Tokyo Asahi Shinbun* (July 11, 1911); "Osoru beki dôsei no ai, Sone Okamura ni reijo no tôshin, joshi kyoiku kai no ichidai mondai" (Revolting same-sex love, Sone and Okamura, two ladies' double-suicide a serious problem of women's education) in *Yomiuri Shinbun* (July 31, 1911), and "Reijo dôshi no jôshi" (Two young ladies' love-suicide) in *Yorozu Chôhô* (July 31, 1911). Both *Yomiuri Shinbun* and *Yorozu Chôhô* printed a picture of the couple.
6. In Japanese, *senritsu* and *osoru* literally mean "revolting." The fact that these words were used shows how the contemporary patriarchy was threatened by the appearance of this counter power.
7. More research has been done on the history of male same-sex love in Japan than on female same-sex love (see Vincent and Kazama 1997). In the Seitô movement studies, although a number of scholars have referred to same-sex relationships between the Seitô women, the topic of lesbianism among them has not received the attention it deserves. For recent lesbian studies related to Seitô members, see Kurosawa 1985, Yoshikawa 1998, and Asano 2001. From my point of view, Asano's argument about lesbianism in the 1910s is too pessimistic.
8. In Japanese, "male color" can be inscribed as either "danshoku" or "nanshoku." See Sanseidô 1992.
9. The *Fujo Shinbun* articles of August 11, 1911, and September 8, 1911, both cited educators of women's schools. However, the commentators are generally anonymous.
10. This article partly overlapped with Havelock Ellis's "Sexual inversion in women" (1897). It is highly possible that Kuwaya adopted Ellis's work.
11. See *Fujo Shinbun*, August 11, 1911. Also see Robertson 1998:73.
12. Kôkichi's uncle, Otake Chikuha, a well-known painter of classic Japanese painting, was a supporter of the Seitô Society. He suggested to Kôkichi: "If the

purpose of *Seitô* Journal is for women's study, then it is necessary for you members to know the situation of 'women in the underworld.' " On his advice, Kôkichi and Raichô visited the pleasure quarter Yoshiwara to better their understanding of "real society" (Watanabe 2001:49–50). Women visiting prostitutes in the pleasure quarters in the Edo period was not uncommon. However, women of the Meiji period were disciplined to have "correct" sexuality and gender. For this reason, Kôkichi and Raichô's visit to the pleasure quarters was seen as outrageous behavior and a challenge to contemporary Japanese patriarchal society.

13. Before the Seitô Society was established, its founder Hiratsuka Raichô had been the focus of mass media for her attempted love-suicide with her male lover Morida Sôhei (Sasaki 1994).
14. These stories were reported in several newspapers under titles such as "Literary women's plays in Yoshiwara" (*Yororzu Chôho*, July 10, 1912) and "The ambiguous love: Raichô, Kôkichi and Sôhei" (*Nichinichi* 1912).
15. Tamura Toshiko was born in 1884 and attended Nihon Joshi Daigaku (Japan Women's College) in 1901. She became the pupil of Kota Rohan and was given the pen name Satô Roei in 1902. The turning point of her writing career came when her novel *Akirame* (*Resignation*) won the second prize in *Osaka Asahi Shinbun* in 1910. She gave up her writing career and followed Suzuki Etsu, her second husband, to Vancouver, Canada, in 1918. After living there for 18 years, she went back to Japan in 1936, leaving for China in 1938 and founding the women's journal *Nü-Seng* in Shanghai in 1942. She devoted herself to this Chinese women's journal until her death in April 1945. Her selected works are available in English (Yukiko 1987).
16. For the development of female students' fashion in the Meiji period, see Honda 1990. In Hiratsuka Raichô's case, she wore a male student's style *hakama* instead of *ebicha hakama*, which was the female students' uniform in the late Meiji period and which symbolized female students.
17. "Swallow" (*tsubame*) signifies a younger lover, usually male. Okumura Hiroshi, who became Hiratsuka Raichô's husband later, was said to be Raichô's *tsubame*.
18. Raichô writes in the preface, "I hope someday this record will become a research resource for women's studies done by women themselves" Hiratsuka (1914).
19. In the Japanese language, *boku* is a term for "I" that is used exclusively by men.
20. Tamura Toshiko's sensational work *Resignation* (*Akirame*) was another example of the male-color concept in contemporary Japan. After the female protagonist Tomie spent one night with her junior, Someko, Tomie recalls a scene in Ueda Akinari's narrative *Aozukin* about male same-sex love between a monk and his dead young servant, as follows: "After the death of the boy he adored, the monk was in a frenzy to lick the boy's bones and flesh, even though the boy's corpse had become rotten" (Tamura 1988, 1:102).
21. See Watanabe 2001:61–73.

References Cited

Asano, Masamichi. 2001. Yagate owaru beki dôseiai to Tamura Toshiko: Akirame o chushin ni (The almost terminated same-sex love and Tamura Toshiko—in *Resignation*). *Nihon Kkindai Bungaku* (Modern Japanese Literature) No. 65:163–178.

Brousse, Marie Hèlèn. 1992. Sexuality. In *Feminism and psychoanalysis: A critical dictionary*. Elizabeth Wright, ed. Pp. 140–145. Cambridge, MA: Blackwell.

Butler, Judith. 1992. Gender. In *Feminism and psychoanalysis: A critical dictionary*. Elizabeth Wright, ed. Pp. 140–145. Cambridge, MA: Blackwell.

———. 1993. Imitation and gender insubordination. In *The lesbian and gay studies reader*. Henry Abelove, Michèle Aina Barale, and David M. Halperin, eds. Pp. 307–320. New York: Routledge.

Ellis, Havelock. 1897. Sexual inversion in women. In *Studies in the psychology of sex*, vol. 1: *Sexual inversion*. Havelock Ellis and John Addington Symonds, eds. Pp. 77–103. London: Wilson and Macmillan.

Fukaya Masashi. 1988. Ryosai kenbo shugi no kyôiku (The education of good wives, wise mothers). Tokyo: Reimei shobô.

Furukawa Makoto. 1995. Dôsei ai ko (Studies of same-sex love). *Imago* (May):201–207.

Hiratsuka Raichô. 1911. Sokan noji (The satement of the initial issue). *Seitô* 1(1):1.

———. 1912. Marumado yori (From the round window). *Seitô* 2(4):76–108.

———. 1913. Ichinenkan (One year). *Seitô* 3(2):87–100.

———. 1914. Dokuritsu suru ni tsuite ryôshin ni (To my parents: About my independence). *Seitô* 4(2):102–116.

———. 1973. Genshi josei wa taiyô deatta (In the beginning, woman was the sun), 2 vols. Tokyo: Ôtsuki shoten.

Honda Kazuko. 1990. *Kaze no itazura* (The mischief of wind). Jogakusei no keifu: Saishoku sareru Meiji (The genealogy of the female students: The colored Meiji period). Tokyo: Seido sha.

Itô Noe. 2000. Zatsuon: Seitô no shui no hitobito—"atarashî onna" no naibu seikatsu (Noise: The people surrounding Seitô—The internal life of the "new women.") *Itô Noe zenshu* (Itô Noe collection), vol. 1. Tokyo: Gakugei shorin.

Koyama Shizuko. 1993 [1991]. *Ryosai kenbo to iu kihan* (The discipline of good wives, wise mothers). Tokyo: Keisô shobô.

Kurosawa Ariko. 1985. *Onna no kubi: Gyakkô no Chieko shô* (The woman's head: A reflection on Chieko's memoirs). Tokyo: Domesu shuppan.

Kuwaya, Sadaitsu. 1911. Senritsu subeki joseikan no tentôseiyoku (The revolting female sexual inversion). *Shin Kôron* (New Opinion), (September) 26(9): 35–42.

Nichinichi Shinbun Sha. 1912. Myôno koi: Raichô to Kôkichi to Sôhei (The ambiguous love: Raichô, Kôkichi, and Sôhei). *Nichinichi Shinbun Sha* (Tokyo Daily Newspaper), November 29–December 9.

Rich, Adrienne. 1980. Compulsory heterosexuality and lesbian existence. *Signs: Journal of Women in Culture and Society* 5(4):631–660.

Robertson, Jennifer. 1998. *Takarazuka: Sexual politics and popular culture in modern Japan*. Berkeley: University of California Press.

Roden, Donald. 1990. Taishô culture and the problem of gender ambivalence. In *Culture and identity: Japanese intellectuals during the interwar years.* J. Thomas Rimer, ed. Pp. 37–55. Princeton, NJ: Princeton University Press.

Sanseidô. 1992. *Daijirin* (Great dictionary). Tokyo: Sanseidô.

Sasaki Hideaki. 1994. *"Atarashî onna" no tôrai: Hiratsuka Raichô to Sôseki* (The arrival of the "new women": Hiratsuka Raichô and Sôseki). Nagoya: Nagoya daigaku shubba sha.

Sawabe Hitomi. 1990. *Yuriko, Dasuvidanya: Yuasa Yoshiko no seishžn* (Yuriko, Dasuvidanya: The youth of Yuasa Yoshiko). Tokyo: Bungei shunjû.

Shin feminizumu hihyo kai. 1998. *Seitô o yomu* (Reading *Seitô*). Tokyo: Gakugei shorin.

Suzuki Masahiro. 2000. Jendâ furî kyôiku no kiso chishiki (The basic knowledge of being gender free). Electronic document, http://www.ne.jp/asahi/seikyokyo/2000/sp–21.htm.

Tamura Toshiko. 1912. Atta ato (After seeing you two). *Seitô* 2(10):135.

———. 1916. Wakai kokoro (The fresh heart). *Shin Shôsetsu* (The New Novel), May:44–87.

———. 1988. *Tamura Toshiko sakuhin shu* (Selected works of Tamura Toshiko), 3 vols. Hasegawa Kei, ed. Tokyo: Orijin sentâ.

Uchida Roan. 1911. Seiyoku kenkyž no hitsuyô o ronzu (The discourse of sexology studies). *Shin Kôron* (New Opinion), (September) 26(9):56–61.

Vincent, Keith and Kazama Takayuki, eds. 1997. Gei sudadizu (Gay studies). Tokyo: Seido sha.

Watanabe Sumiko. 2001. *Seitô no onna: Otake Kôkichi den* (The woman of the Seitô: The biography of Otake Kôkichi). Tokyo: Fuji shuppan.

Yorozu chôhô shinbun sha. 1912. Jobunshi No Yoshiwara Yû (The literary women's plays in Yoshiwara). *Yorozu Chôhô* (Yorozu National Newspaper), July 10.

Yoshikawa Toyoko. 1998. Kindai nihon no rezubianizumu—1910 nendai no shosetsu ni egakareta rezubian tachi (Lesbianism in modern Japan: Lesbians in novels of the 1910s). In Seigensô o kataru (Talking about the sexual imagination). Konô Kazuko, ed. Pp. 75–110. Tokyo: Sanichi shobô.

Yukiko Tanaka, ed. 1987. *To live and to write: Selections by Japanese women writers, 1913–1938*. Seattle: Seal Press.

Chapter Six

"But no one has explained to me who I am now . . .": "Trans" Self-Perceptions in Sri Lanka

Shermal Wijewardene

> For me the prefix "trans" is a signal to be ready for anything, to allow others to define themselves regardless of my own preferences in defining another's appearance or characteristics.
>
> —Jamison Green 2000:8

This chapter sets out the self-perceptions of gender identity expressed by Shanthi and Manel, two "trans" persons from lower-middle-class village environments in the Western Province of Sri Lanka, who are biologically female and "trans" in their gender presentations.[1] Its focus is on the importance of acts of perception for Shanthi and Manel—others' perceptions of their gender expression as well as their self-perception of their gender behavior. The main objective of the chapter is to explore how Manel and Shanthi are continuously thrown back on their own imaginative resources to frame their gender difference. Self-perceptions have served as the only resource in their lives to represent themselves with dignity in a society violently intolerant of gender diversity. Our conversations in four in-depth unstructured interviews conducted separately approximately six months apart focus on the reactionary, radical, and creative aspects of these self-perceptions.

I use the pronoun "he" to refer to Manel and "she" to refer to Shanthi to suit their self-perceptions. At the time of the study, these two individuals displayed their "trans" identities quite differently. Manel consciously controls any evidence of femininity in his appearance and continues to dress, behave, identify himself, and work as a man in Colombo. Shanthi's appearance and behavior present a conflict of the conventional feminine and masculine gender presentations in the country. She believes that stereotypical "femininity" predominates in her appearance and is reconciled to it as evidence of her decision to love women as a woman. At the same time she displays ambivalence over the gradual submergence of her "masculine" gender expression.

Focus/Objectives/Context

Focus: The Quarrel with Terms

The term "passing women" is frequently employed for individuals like Manel and Shanthi to mean "people who have female bodies but who live their lives as men" (Green 2000:4). I resist the use of this term for my study due to the conjunction of "passing" with "women": this study clearly indicates that both individuals reject how the coherence implied by the term "woman" may be applied to them. I also share Judith Halberstam's reservations about the term's potential to connote the idea of women "masquerading" as the so-called "opposite" gender. Halberstam has noted that "For many gender deviants, the notion of passing is singularly unhelpful. Passing as a narrative assumes that there is a self that masquerades as another kind of self and does so successfully; at various moments, the successful pass may cohere into something akin to identity. At such a moment, the passer has *become*" (Halberstam 1998:21).

I consider the idea of an essential self that impersonates another self ideologically problematic as an understanding of any "trans" identity. "Trans" should represent the revolution in our thinking of gender as an unstable category of identity that is regulated through the play of power; it should not reinforce universalist notions of essential selves. Jamison Green highlights the value of the prefix "trans" above as an unstable signal that places responsibility on the "readiness" of the perceiver to allow the play of meaning. The prefix "trans" in conjunction with "gender" to form "transgender" can, from this point of view, signal a shift from the literal definition of over/across/through gender to the more politically dynamic idea of receiving, or the act of reading, gender expression when confronted with the all-important act of self-definition performed by "trans" individuals. Leslie Feinberg has defined the term "transgender" as "an umbrella term to include everyone who challenges the boundaries of sex and gender" (1996:x). As such, it is a term that is in danger of being used as the convenient shorthand for this unintegrated range of nonconformist gender expressions and sexual practices: it can be received as finally inclusive of marginal gender expression and, thus, can become the politically safe definition that can mean everything and nothing. Green's statement, which alerts us to the unpredictability and instability of the prefix "trans" in conjunction with the noun "gender," reminds us that even if "gender" is reassuringly familiar, the prefix "trans" will only foreground the process of perceiving and interpreting it. What is glibly termed a "range of nonconformist gender expressions" is determined as much by what is permitted as "trans" expression within the bounds of possibility available to the perceiver within culture as it is by the "trans" performance of the individual. This perspective places the act of perception under scrutiny and forecloses the possibility of "prefixing" the meaning of "trans."

The proliferation of gender identities stemming from the strong dimension of self-identification in transgender studies can yield other, more politically sensitive descriptive terms for my study. Stephen Whittle's definition of "cross-gendered" individuals is one such:

> There were many historical characters who "cross-gender lived" for significant parts of their lives at a time when hormonal and surgical reassignment treatment was not yet developed. Certainly for a lot of these characters there is no evidence at all of their sexual preference or practices; there is evidence that they lived their lives as men or women in opposition to their anatomical sex, just as many people who do not undergo gender reassignment nowadays. (Whittle 2000:15)

Whittle's reading of "cross-gendered" identities presents an "opposition" between anatomical sex and culturally constructed gender expression which, apart from my ideological objection to it, is not useful for my study. Perceptions of gender transgressions such as this commonly take the stability of sex and the fluidity of gender for granted. My conversations with Manel and Shanthi indicate very clearly that the nonsurgical challenge to biological polarities of male/female is a crucial part of their self-perceptions of gender identity. Halberstam's writing on "masculinity without men" is compelling for its proposal to discuss "female masculinities" not as mimetic of "masculinity" but as suggestive, especially in their marginalization, of the construction of masculinity itself (1998:1–43). "Female masculinity" is ultimately too partial a term to define both Manel's and Shanthi's gender expressions. I deliberately use the term "trans" for Manel and Shanthi because it is the only term that is inclusive of their gender atypical behavior and at the same time expressive of how the gender presentation of each differs from the other.

Focus: Why Self-Perceptions?

The quick and easy explication and use of terms such as "trans" or "transgender" or "cross-gendered" in this chapter should not conceal the fact that Manel and Shanthi continue to manage the emotional and psychological violence of incomprehension that is forced on them by a society largely unaware and intolerant of gender difference. More damaging than incomprehension may be interventions meant to investigate and "diagnose" this difference in their gender presentations, as Manel and Shanthi have experienced with physicians and mental health experts in Sri Lanka. Using terms of definition should not also blind us to the violence associated with the activity of prescribing (or conferring meaning on) through describing gender atypical behavior.

Manel's and Shanthi's testimony of the dysfunction bred by this lack of comprehension may be affirmed at a general level by all women and men who choose nonconformist gender behavior and can admit to the constant grim pressures of gender policing in Sri Lankan society. This lack of comprehension can be linked to what Judith Butler has termed "cultural intelligibility." According to Butler,

> "Intelligible" genders are those which in some sense institute and maintain relations of coherence and continuity among sex, gender, sexual practice, and desire. In other words, the specters of discontinuity and incoherence, themselves thinkable only in relation to existing norms of continuity and coherence, are constantly prohibited and produced by the very laws that seek to establish causal or expressive lines of connection among biological sex, culturally constituted genders, and the "expression" or "effect" of both in the manifestation of sexual desire through sexual practice. (Butler 1990:17)

Very simply, the cultural intelligibility of gender behavior entails how a person's gender behavior can/cannot be "intelligible" in terms of a particular culture's normative understanding of the continuity of sex, gender, and sexual practice. The gender presentations of both Manel and Shanthi problematize "cultural intelligibility" because they do not validate the perceiver's reference to the "coherence" and "continuity" of a sex identity, a stable gender identity, and sexual practice. Instead, the confusion generated by the apparent discontinuity in these connections in their gender expression serves to make cultural norms apparent and, as Butler has stated, they can "expose the limits and regulatory aims of that domain of intelligibility" (Butler 1990:17).

Objectives

My interest in foregrounding self-perceptions of gender identity in my study of Manel and Shanthi stems from two strong convictions that I explore in this chapter. I believe that this focus is necessary to publicize that Manel's and Shanthi's stories suggest the ways "trans" persons in Sri Lanka inevitably resort to self-perceptions for a personal philosophy of their difference in the absence of any self-affirming cultural props. The lack of means to understand oneself can be disempowering. However, the self-perceptions that frame this difference and fill a vacuum can give rise to subversive possibilities, as Judith Butler claimed it does in relation to her idea of the matrix of intelligibility by which gender is made culturally intelligible. It can "open up within the very terms of that matrix of intelligibility rival and subversive matrices of gender disorder" (Butler 1990:17). The "corruption" of the normative framework by which gender is comprehended is a vastly subversive outcome. At the same time, I also believe that the existence of alternative forms of self-definition can force Sri Lankan culture to confront gender deviance and its own violent repression of these differences at a very fundamental level. An analysis of self-perceptions requires psychological insight; however, I have not explored this area except at the most general level. I have wished to maintain a non-intrusive, sensitive method of analysis to allow Manel's and Shanthi's voices to emerge.

Context: The Women's Support Group

I was first motivated to engage with these issues to address the lack of knowledge resources on "trans" identities in Sri Lanka. As a volunteer of the Women's Support Group (WSG), the only lesbian, bisexual, and transgender (LBT) group in Sri Lanka, I was involved in 2003 in the group's setting up of the Transgender Research Project (TRP) in collaboration with a psychologist with relevant experience who was interested in our work with "trans" people. In its five-year history, the WSG has received three "trans" individuals into the group—Shanthi, Manel, and Dinusha—and has worked with one other person. All were biologically female and expressed a gender identity that they broadly named "masculine." Each sought peer support from the WSG at difficult moments in their lives.

Context: No More Playing Safe

Despite our mandate that included "trans" issues, our preparedness as a group had not been actively challenged until then. Despite the predominance of "gender-inappropriate" behavior amongst lesbians in our membership of 30 or so, "transgenderism" had not been raised at a personal level. It was clear that the most daunting challenge for the group lay in realizing the unexamined attitudes, motives, prejudices, and behavior that, for us as comparatively privileged women and as lesbians, informed our tactics for self-preservation and fed into our activism. Concealing our sexual difference and conforming strategically to less-compromised gender role-playing may be abhorrent to us, but they were still possibilities available to us, and necessary, particularly for personal security and effectiveness in our activism. In fact, we had become so practiced in these strategies as to be almost unaware of them. We offered these same possibilities of "strategic conformity" to Manel and Dinusha for reasons of safety. When our efforts met with rejection and failure, the group realized the extent to which it must actively depart from an implicit acceptance of these everyday concessions to gender norms.

Dealing with Incomprehension 1: The Perceptions of Family and Society

Manel

Dealing with incomprehension has involved, for both Manel and Shanthi, a search for the language to frame their difference. My conversations with Manel revealed that his choices in dress and behavior as a man aroused suspicion and intrusive curiosity for their "inappropriateness" in his village. "My family is confounded by my behavior. My sisters could not bring me into our village society as a girl because of my manner of speech and behavior. The society I grew up in drew back in fear—is this a girl, is this a boy?" Conforming to conventional feminine dress and behavior has only resulted in more confusion. Manel is aware that his manner of wearing skirt and blouse makes him even more obtrusive in his society as the clothes do not confer femininity on him: his identity is perceived as even more piquant.

Perceptions of Manel's gender identity also engender desire. He receives much attention from young girls in his village even when dressed in skirt and blouse. Manel believes these links are thwarted because homosexual sexual activity is largely underground. However, it is clear that Manel's sexual conduct with women in his village is viewed with derision due to his being perceived as an "oddity," or a "man," rather than a lesbian. He is convinced of the rivalry of young men in the pursuit of women. Manel is unable to feel desire unless he is perceived by his female partner as male. Realizing that his presence is embarrassing, Manel shuns the society of his neighbors and confines himself to his home.

Home provides the only safe space for Manel in his village, although his masculine gender presentation is a constant source of inquiry and worry for his family members. Manel's account indicates that a significant part of his struggle for self-definition arises from his strategies for coping with the powerful reinforcement of gender stereotypes in his domestic space. Marriage and motherhood are urged on Manel as a "corrective" to his gender ambivalence and a means of gaining social acceptance—with the persuasive possibility of divorce as an escape clause. Although Manel is able to resist most such overt injunctions to demonstrate stereotypical femininity, gender stereotyping operates in domestic space in more insidious ways to obtain his consent. Manel's apparent gender difference does not allow him to escape from the everyday domestic duties traditionally performed by wives and daughters in his society. Manel is derided for his "emasculation" in his own house by his male friends from the bazaar who observe his family's expectations of him. To counteract this disparaging of him as "henpecked" and unable to assert his traditional prerogatives as a male within the family, Manel offers them stories of his difference or challenges them on their "masculinity."

Caught between these expectations to validate one gender stereotype or the other, Manel has learned the provisionality of the scripts for feminine or masculine behavior. He recognizes which script would be most effective for his survival under the particular circumstances, while pursuing his own desired gender presentation. However self-affirming, this is also a lonely knowledge that has not given him a sense of integration in his family. Manel draws strength from performing the duties conventionally assigned to male members of the household and realizes his worth as a "man about the house" in the eyes of his mother. However, he is fundamentally cut off from family life through the living arrangements of the house, which seem to him to be deliberately designed to deny him the possibilities of communication and emotional connections with his mother and sisters. "There are two beds in my room, and my mother and sister occupy one bed. Now they have begun to use the other bedroom when I am home. They do care for me. I realized that I have never seen my mother and sister naked. I thought about it. I realized that they had arrived at a mental crisis with me." Manel is unable to reconcile the conflict of love and revulsion he receives from his home. His family has attempted to address their own anxieties and meet his desires to present a masculine gender identity by consulting medical opinion in Colombo for sex reassignment surgery for him to acquire a male body. Although this objective was ultimately frustrated by the obtuseness of doctors, Manel perceives this chapter as an important turning point in his relations with his family. He realizes that their motivation arises from wishing him to be "one thing or another"—even if it is to be male—instead of in-between, but views this attitude as positive.

Manel realizes that home offers more security for his difference than the world outside and is convinced by his family's arguments that his poor economic means, lack of education, and low social status confirm his marginalization. At the same time, he is keenly aware of his outsider status within the family and the mental distress of all concerned. Manel has chosen escape as the best coping strategy, frequently leaving home without a fixed destination in mind and sleeping rough in Colombo when all options of accommodation have failed. He has worked at many jobs in Colombo, but has not yet succeeded in gaining a permanent footing in the city.

Shanthi

My conversations with Shanthi, revealed similar anxieties over her place in her family with her growing knowledge of her gender difference and sexual attraction to women. Shanthi recalls her early isolation within her home due to her inability to express her difference and desires. She recalls dressing and behaving as a boy from a very young age and pursuing her desires for girls in a self-enclosed fantasy world where in secret she was able to explore romance and sex. Although Shanthi saw herself in her fantasies as a schoolboy in a relationship with a girl, she avoided the company of boys her age, fearful that they would "find her out" to be what she thought she was—that is, homosexual. "I was not afraid of their physical violence. I was afraid that they would label me. Can I say whatever I want? Even dirty words? Do you know the term '*aappa*/hoppers' (a Sinhala word for breakfast food which in vulgar use means 'lesbian') I was afraid they would label me that." Shanthi's fears arise from the memory of the public humiliation of a schoolgirl in her area over an alleged lesbian affair. Shanthi took to sports at the girls-only school she attended and had a number of female fans and friends. However, her lack of interest in boys and her reluctance to mingle in mixed-sex society isolated her from her female friends at school. Her education was disrupted and she retreated into an increasingly marginal existence, wary of insults and abuse. Faced with failing mental health when still young, Shanthi began medical consultations.

In her first job at a bank in her village, Shanthi resolved to conform to a feminine appearance. "I let my hair grow out. I thought to myself: I appear manly. I create problems for my mother. I cannot take my place in my society, I face discrimination, boys call me '*aappa*.' " Shanthi worked well at the bank and was appreciated for her efficiency. However, her new feminine appearance generated more unwelcome interest among the bank's customers and caused her much confusion, anxiety, and anger. "I think many men were attracted to me because I wore shirts and I appeared—I don't know how to say it, do I mean 'dominant'? I appeared to be like a masculine woman, or like a boy who had long hair. Men who liked that look paid me attention. There were women too." Shanthi is convinced of the truth of these recollections despite suggestions from mental health professionals that they may be delusions.

Dogged by mental health problems from her late teenage years, Shanthi still has doubts whether her "trans" identity is a manifestation of her schizophrenia. Estranged emotionally from her sister and her brother, Shanthi's only confidante is her mother, who is ambivalent about her perception of herself as a "man." She has faced violent reactions from some family members over the crisis created for them all by her gender difference. Shanthi's mental health problems rendered her especially vulnerable to the perception of her gender difference as an abnormal condition within the family. "On my return from Ward 59 [the psychiatric clinic of the state-run General Hospital], I resumed my course of medication at home. My brother told my mother 'Admit this thing in Angoda [a state mental health institute].' I swallowed [painkillers] and was taken back to Ward 59." With the help of a psychologist in Colombo, Shanthi was able to win her mother's support for sex reassignment surgery to realize her wish for a male body. Due to high medical costs and a fragile mental state, Shanthi gave up actively pursuing this wish. Shanthi now chooses to live at home, balancing hostility from some family members with her mother's understanding and support.

Dealing with Incomprehension 2: Perceptions of Self More Masculine than Men

Manel's sense of self is deeply rooted in his perception of his body and sexual desire. He rejects the physical features he perceives as feminine and therefore psychologically disabling—his face, his breasts—and takes comfort in his body, which he feels to be masculine. He perceives himself to be "masculine" and claims to have no understanding or use for the concept of "transgender" identity. He understands the existence of gender-typical behavior in his society but perceives it to be naturally linked to biological identities. "I don't perform or make a show of masculinity. I behave naturally. I only behave according to the dictates of my body. I will face marginalization if I act like a girl because I would appear strange in society." Manel's perception of his gender expression is of a hypermasculinity demonstrated by physical strength, aggression, and uncontrollable libido. He defines this gender identity as the polar opposite of "femininity," which is demonstrated by frailty, reserve, and sexual passivity. Manel's self-perception of his gender identity is clearly linked to notions of power and privilege that his patriarchal society confers on men. Thus, the subversive parody and caricature of gender stereotypes in Manel's behavior does not concern him; he is unwilling to accept that his own gender presentation may issue a strong challenge to the stability and coherence of "male/masculine." However, his self-perception of his gender expression as a rival, "unique," and more authentically masculine identity that relegates the masculinity of biological men to a weaker position has the potential of Butler's "subversive [matrix] of gender disorder." Manel claims,

> Men cannot equal me, though they may have a penis. I am 100 per cent certain that I have more gust [guts] than men. I can fight any man. Also I am

> superior to a man in matters of sex. When I was a man amongst other men in the bazaar, I used to ask them about their sexual appetites. I am stronger than a man. They are men only in name, I used to tell them. I used to think that they only looked like men.

Although Manel may appear to demonstrate the unthinking "heroic masculinity" discussed by Halberstam, which depends on the subordination of other masculinities, he has used his position as an "insider" in male-dominated circles to secure for himself the powerful role of the perceiver and access the anxiety and instability over norms that link biological male bodies to masculine gender-typical presentations. He has sensed that the "masculinity" of any "man," biological or nonbiological, can be validated only if it is *perceived* to be so, and that it must, therefore, be continuously actively demonstrated for affirmation and self-affirmation.

Telling Stories

Manel's personal philosophy of masculinity is empowering for him because it allows him to resist any challenge that his own gender presentation is "false" based on his female body. However, Manel is only willing to voice this perception of self when aware of the security of his circumstances. When faced with incomprehension or challenges to his identity, Manel has become practiced in narrating "stories" of his difference, which he denies are lies. For Manel, telling the "truth" about his sex identity is complex and does not involve a strict moral division between truth and lies. His truth is "provisional," depending on circumstances and his judgment of the sympathies of others. He realizes the main concern of most interlocutors is to discover his "true" biological identity and expose the "lie" of his gender expression; he feels the pressure to be either male or female. It is within the terms of his story that Manel deals with his listener's incomprehension by claiming the prerogative to be male or female depending on the situation. Manel's conflicting stories have forced those who are approached by him for mental and material support to engage with the history of these narratives and make links with previous listeners to do so. The apparent lack of credibility of these stories has led to a difficult and uncertain process of "cross-checking" and linking, resulting in more ambiguity and a constant deferral of the answer to the "mystery" of his biological identity. It is this situation that provides Manel most psychological security.

We may question the fairness of gauging the "truth value" of any one story of Manel's gender identity without, at the same time, inquiring about the "truth" of the stories told to him, especially by authorities in the medical profession. It is difficult to believe that any originally accurate account of gender identity could have remained intact through Manel's history of medical consultation in both the physiological and mental health sectors. Medical "diagnoses" of Manel's gender difference as related by him provide bizarre, absurd, and exploitative stories that more than surpass those related by him about himself. One such medical opinion had claimed his gender-deviant behavior to be the result of physical exercise, which could be cured by a full body massage to be administered by the doctor himself! Manel is disillusioned by the prejudiced attitudes of medical practitioners to his difference. He claims they were uniformly dismissive of his own perceptions, disrespectful, amused, or intent on physical examinations to check for biological identity.

In rejecting a medical solution to his conflicted sense of self, Manel has also rejected the medical diagnosis as a source of self-knowledge and sought alternatives. He has found some validity for his difference in his association with the WSG. "I still continue to tell you [the WSG] that I am a man," Manel said.

> Even though it may not be so, you may understand it whichever way you like. I don't mind that you think of me as a girl. But I only make an exception for you. I jumped a big hurdle, mentally, when I came to the WSG. I only realized that homosexuality exists in Sri Lanka when I came here. Because of this, the mentality I had about hospitals and wanting operations has gone away. I don't feel alone anymore.

Though he claims to be disgusted by male homosexual practices, Manel's perceptions of lesbianism intrigue him and afford him the means to make a fair comparison with his own body, gender presentation, and sexual behavior.

> I am fascinated by the fact that you are women [who love women]. Masculinity is very important for being in touch with my body. You may tell me "We are homosexual, and we have sex with women as women. You should also live as a woman, say that you are a woman." But I can't do that because I am not homosexual. I don't know how to live as a homosexual, I don't understand it. I can't do women-with-women. I have my own unique method of sexual practice which suits the pleasures of my body.

Manel's conviction should remind us of Whittle's observation on the submergence in gay and lesbian histories of the lives of "trans" people who do not undergo sex reassignment surgery (Whittle 2000:15). However, Manel's self-perceptions of his inimitable difference remain firm even in his identification with LBT allies, stemming as it does from his personal narrative of his body, and his sexual desire that makes him unique.

Manel's strength of conviction in his difference is affirmed by his own strategies to sustain his gender presentation. Manel's care of his own body has replaced his search for medical solutions. He camouflages his breasts with expensive surgical bandages that give him a sense of power and strength. However, Manel is sometimes vulnerable in situations which require him to reveal his body, such as sharing bathrooms with men. In such situations, Manel claims to be "on both sides, having breasts and a penis," and secures privacy for bathing. Dealing with incomprehension requires more than just stories, however, as gender is conventionally viewed as an identity that does not require explanation because it is non-negotiable and "already known." On occasions when Manel's identity card has provided indisputable official evidence of the falsity of his claims to be a man, he has narrated the following story:

> I underwent a physical transformation when I was young. I didn't have a vagina when I was little, but I used to urinate, although it was not clear from where. Therefore, I was identified as a woman. By age 11, my penis began to grow. My father consulted doctors at length on this. My physical transformation was successful to the extent that it was not possible to tell of the previous state. I began to develop the physical characteristics of a man. However, I still have a slight swelling of the breast, and therefore I am a little feminine in my behavior. Therefore, I can't undress or bathe with other men.

Manel claims that god inspires him with these stories, which are not lies but personal myths that will never change. His stories are ultimately meant to protect him from discrimination and violence; they reveal much of the price he pays for sacrificing these inalienable rights guaranteed by Sri Lanka's constitution.

The Search for Equilibrium

Shanthi's perception of bodily identity has changed throughout her life. For most of her life, Shanthi has seen herself as a man and was frustrated by her female body. She has a fragmented perception of bodily identity which marks buttocks, thighs, and breasts as "feminine," and hands, face, hair, and feet as "masculine." Shanthi is troubled by her rejection of her body and is also very sensitive to what she perceives to be inappropriate contact with certain areas of her body. She is aware of how homophobic harassment and her fear of it have affected her mental health and shaped her life. Shanthi's search for answers to her gender difference in the scanty resources available in Colombo has been motivated by her wish to regain some equilibrium in her life.

Unaware of the existence of a few structured support systems in the state health sector, Shanthi had begun her search intuitively through independent research in newspapers. These early initiatives rendered her vulnerable to the risk of sexual exploitation. Shanthi recalls the advice of an "effeminate" male counselor at a state-run youth center in Colombo that she "desire men at all costs; fantasize about men while masturbating, and find effeminate men desirable" as an answer to her confusion. Still other avenues explored confounded her in different ways, as in her encounter with a hypnotist in Colombo who had assured her heterosexuality through hypnosis. "He made me join hands with a boy who had arrived for a consultation. Then he chanted 'may your two souls be joined together' and uttered a pack of lies. Neither the boy nor I was hypnotized." Shanthi was finally able to receive some serious consideration of her questions at the General Hospital, Colombo.

In her interactions with medical officers at the General Hospital, Shanthi had only possessed the term "homosexual" to define herself. It was a term invested with her deepest fears of her difference. In discussions with medical officers, Shanthi acquired other terms to define herself, such as "gender identity disorder," "mind out of body," and "transsexual," which were more acceptable to her. Shanthi's perception of these terms as less stigmatized than "homosexual" encouraged her to adopt them as protection in public. A violent incident at a training institute where Shanthi was enrolled provides a scenario of the consequences of this perception. Fearing that a chance remark made by another trainee of an "*aappa*/hoppers smell" in the room had been meant as an insult directed at her, Shanthi had dashed a chair on the ground in rage and confronted the nurse, saying "How can that be? Although I appear masculine, I am not someone like *that*. I have gender identity disorder, I am not homosexual." Shanthi's actions were interpreted as "abnormal behavior" and she was referred back to Ward 59 for treatment. It is uncertain whether her statements were viewed with sympathy.

Changing Identities from "Trans" to "Lesbian"

Shanthi has explored the option of female-to-male sex reassignment surgery with psychologists and plastic surgeons in Sri Lanka. Her mental health was a serious consideration in her assessment for surgery. Finding little reassurance in conflicting medical opinions that link her "trans" identity and schizophrenia, Shanthi perceives that the psychological pressures of hiding her transsexual identity in Sri Lanka caused her mental deterioration. After carefully weighing her options, Shanthi has decided against surgery in Sri Lanka as it would not achieve a significant physical transformation for her. "I was told that the process involved constructing a penis from flesh taken from my body. I was told that it would be like a piece of meat. They do not construct testicles. I think this would be more mentally troublesome than my present state. I wouldn't be able to enjoy sex either. I have now reconciled myself to my choices as Buddhism has taught us to do." Shanthi's philosophical outlook has emerged from a personal process of Buddhist spiritual self-reflection that she perceives to be a self-made alternative that guarantees her mental stability. Perhaps the most empowering aspect of her choice is the liberty it provides her to pursue non-surgical alternatives to shape her body according to her desires.

Shanthi took up exercise and lifted weights at a local gym to gain a muscular V-shaped sportsman's frame and to reduce the body fat that gave her a feminine appearance.

Shanthi's growing relationship with a woman who perceives her as a woman has led her to re-evaluate the choices she has made for her body and her mind in the following manner: "No one has explained to me who I am now," she says. "I am a transsexual, I may also have schizophrenia. I am now reconciled to my choice to live my life out in this female body. I will live as a lesbian and choose another lesbian as my partner." This statement is a powerful reminder of the primacy of Shanthi's self-perception in comprehending her gender difference. Despite the finality of the statement, its strong element of personal choice only emphasizes future possibilities.

Celebrating What is Unfinished and Repeated

This chapter is the outcome of one of the primary aims of the Transgender Research Project, which is to reexamine the requirements that "truth" about gender identity places on transgender persons in Sri Lanka. Although postmodern knowledge accepts that gender identities—or any identity—can only be known through unauthentic and provisional stories, this awareness offers only elusive support, even for those who have it, with the daily demand for verification. Manel's and Shanthi's narratives are a reminder that gender-atypical behavior must be defended with ready responses to questions, stated or not, on why an individual looks "boyish," or "mannish," or "unfeminine," or "eccentric," or like a "butch lesbian," depending on the vocabulary available to frame this difference. These stories must be reiterated almost as testimonies of the right to the freedom of choice to express a gender identity and be respected for this difference.

While it is true that this awareness is oppressive for "trans" people, a too-narrow focus on their vulnerability to incomprehension and regulation will miss what is important in their response. In continuously reaffirming their commitment to the choice of gender transgressive behavior, "trans" people produce perceptions of self which introduce the knowledge of their difference. Responding to incomprehension can be viewed, therefore, as a creative act by which a "gender difference" that had hitherto been unthinkable in terms of hegemonic knowledge is allowed—in fact, demanded—to be produced. The status of these perceptions as "lies" and "fragments" is very important; they signal the importance of irreconcilability in a gender narrative. Rather than checking for authenticity, it is necessary to validate their inauthenticity as the sign that any gender expression, from the normative to the transgressive, is never finished or pre-fixed. Carol Queen and Lawrence Schimel have noted that "[t]he problem with any ascribed and adopted identity is not what it includes, but what it leaves out. Indeed, there are so very many ways to live in the world, countless sources of affinity, that our sexualities and gender/identities only go so far in describing, constructing, and supporting us" (1997:21). Queen and Schimel's thesis is borne out by the inadequacy and incompleteness of the narratives of the "trans" speakers in this study. Though these narratives may be excised or suppressed, they may also expose the contradictions and ambiguity of the hegemonic and the terms of the interrogation.

This process is already underway in Colombo through "trans" persons who have openly presented their perceptions of themselves through the media and the arts. Colombo-based dramatist Indu Dharmasena's interviews on his transition from female-to-male were broadcast over local television and radio in both English and Sinhala in 2003. Indu has since received many inquiries from within the country for information on the process of transition, ranging from the actual surgery to emotional support. A range of sociopolitical reasons may allow some "trans" persons to attain the public image that others cannot. However, there is evidence that the narratives of more marginal "trans" figures do not entirely disappear.

The story of Dinusha, a "trans" individual who entered into "marriage" as a man and was arrested on charges of deceiving society when found to be biologically female, had its cinematic parallel in Sri Lankan filmmaker Asoka Handagama's "Flying with One Wing."[2] Handagama's film (also reminiscent of "Boys Don't Cry") was premised on a fear psychosis over the exposure of the "trans" protagonist's biologically female identity; it was rejected by most lesbians in Colombo. It also had a powerfully disorienting effect on Manel. However, the film generated much debate in the city, and even became the subject of a book-length study by a local political study group (Gunarathna, Manuratne, and Priyadharshana 2003). An analysis of the correspondence between the film and Dinusha's life supports the main assumption of this chapter and its participants—that is, that "true" histories owe little to "narration" and much to creative assembling.

Notes

I would like to acknowledge the contributions of my fellow volunteers at the Women's Support Group (WSG): Rosanna Flamer-Caldera for her participation in the documentation process; Upeksha Thabrew for facilitating my investigations and hands-on assistance to Manel and Dinusha; Kaushalya Perera for invaluable intellectual input; Revathi Chawla for her efforts in the legal interventions of WSG;

Sunila Abeysekera for providing me with resources in a much-neglected area in Sri Lankan scholarship, and for inspiration. My thanks to Parvani Pinnewala, Clinical Psychologist, for referral of subjects, providing critical input into the case studies and psychological aspects of transgender work. My thanks to Anushaya Collure for unflagging encouragement. I thank Dr. Nivedita Menon of the University of Delhi for leading me to see areas of potential in this study and Nehama Jayewardene for her enduring support and care. Special thanks are due to Himali de Silva for emotional support and resources. It is also important to acknowledge the contribution of Companions on a Journey, a Sri Lankan lesbian, gay, bisexual, and transgender group that facilitated the WSG in its work with transgender persons.

1. All names have been changed for reasons of confidentiality.
2. The individual's name has been changed for reasons of confidentiality.

References Cited

Butler, Judith. 1990. *Gender trouble: Feminism and the subversion of identity*. New York: Routledge.

Feinberg, Leslie. 1996. *Transgender warriors: Making history from Joan of Arc to Dennis Rodman*. Boston: Beacon Press.

Green, Jamison. 2000. Introduction to transgender issues. In *Transgender Equality: A handbook for activists and policymakers*. Paisley Currah and Shannon Minter, ed. Pp. 1–12. New York: The Policy Institute of the National Gay and Lesbian Task Force.

Gunarathna, D., P. Manuratne, and M. Priyadharshana. 2003. *Kruthiya Metharam Nisa Nove, Ape Hadarima Metharam Nisa* (Not depending on the extent of the work, but depending on the extent of our knowledge of it). Mount Lavinia: X Group Publications.

Halberstam, Judith. 1998. *Female masculinity*. London: Duke University Press.

Queen, Carol and Lawrence Schimel, eds. 1997. *Pomosexuals: Challenging assumptions about gender and sexuality*. Pittsburgh: Cleis Press.

Whittle, Stephen. 2000. *The transgender debate: The crisis surrounding gender identities*. Reading: South Street Press.

Part III

Female Masculinities

Chapter Seven

Gender Subjectivity: Dees and Toms in Thailand

Megan Sinnott

Introduction

In a Thai linguistic practice that emerged in the 1970s, female-bodied individuals who hold a masculine identity, or are marked as masculine by others, are called "tom," a term that is derived from the English word "tomboy." Toms are paired, both linguistically and romantically, with feminine-identified women who are called "dees," a shortening of the English word "lady" (lā-dee).[1] Popular use of the terms "tom" and "dee" has largely overridden regional linguistic variations and has formed a national Thai language discourse on sexual/gender subjectivity.[2] Tom and dee are "subject positions" in that they serve as meaningful ways of categorizing one's experiences and sense of self in culturally recognized terms. Thai women use these terms (in particular the term "tom" for reasons discussed below) to refer to themselves and to define central aspects of their life narratives, that is, in the formation of their "subjectivities."[3]

The concepts of tom and dee dominate discourses concerning female same-sex sexual/romantic relations in Thailand and thus any female-female relationship that is recognized as sexual or romantic is by definition a form of tom-dee pairing. Tom-dee categories are also ideological in that women interested in finding female lovers are pressured to position themselves within this paradigm. The pairing of female same-sex sexuality into masculine and feminine identities is so prevalent in the Thai social landscape that it is typically described as a "natural" and obvious dimension of female same-sex romantic relationships. For example, during an interview with a group of Thai toms, one tom asked me what "farang" (Westerners) were like—if they were the same as Thai toms and dees. I said that as far as I knew gender divisions within female couples were not particularly strong anymore among American women—not the same as tom and dee in Thailand. The group seemed at a loss for words at first and then laughed at the absurdity of no toms and dees. "How do you know what to do then?" one tom wondered.[4]

Analysis of the gendered politics of subject formation has been the topic of perhaps the most enduring and profound contributions of feminist thought in the twentieth century. Feminists and queer theorists, in their project to understand the cultural production of categories of sexuality and gender, have developed and interpreted the theories of subjectification by figures such as Hegel, Freud, and Lacan. While not attempting so bold and hubristic a project as a thorough integration of these theories into the study of tom and dee dynamics and subject formation in Thailand, this chapter is informed by the feminist insights concerning the politics of "intersubjective theories of subjectivity."[5]

Women produce and claim tom and dee subject categories in the formation of their subjectivities (their sense of self) within larger cultural frameworks. This process, while constrained and limited within the cultural meaning system, is a strategic one that challenges and destabilizes these subject positions as it reproduces and reasserts them in ways that make tom and dee seem to be natural and self-evident categories. The resulting apparent stability of these resultant subjectivities is what Judith Butler calls a "performative accomplishment" (2003:415). This chapter is an exploration of the culturally framed ways in which the dominant forms of female homoerotics are performed in Thailand, with particular attention placed on the strategic manipulation of gendered discourses by Thai women engaged in tom and dee relationships.

Performativity

Queer and feminist theories of subjectivity currently rely heavily on the linguistics-based notion of performativity, most notably articulated by Judith Butler (1990, 1993, and 2003). Butler appropriates phenomenological approaches to subjectivity in which the subject is understood as constituting the social world through the production of symbolic acts (language, discourse, and bodily movement). Butler, influenced by Michel Foucault, goes further and proposes that gender, as an element of subjectivity or "identity," is a product of these acts and not a preexisting entity from which meaning systems emerge: "In this sense, gender is in no way a stable identity or locus of agency from which various acts proceed; rather, it is an identity tenuously constituted in time—an identity instituted through a stylized repetition of acts" (2003:415). Butler applies speech-act theory (as formulated by John Searle and J. L. Austin) with its focus on the productivity of reiteration—the linguistic act cannot be understood in terms of its relation to an objective truth that exists outside the statement. Rather, the speech act, or utterance, is a constituting agent that does not describe reality but brings it into discourse (see Hall 2000). Through repetition the speech act produces the reality it appears to describe. The outcome of the performance of the utterance is not completely predictable and slippage occurs. Butler appropriates this analysis of language as a means to understand gender performativity more generally through the range of discursive possibilities, including dress, bodily movement, and speech. The presumed naturalness of gender identity is revealed as the imperfect and continual reiteration of the identities of man and woman, challenging the presumption that they are natural categories that preexist the symbolic order. Butler's explications of performativity reveal subjectivity as continually emergent and inherently unstable.

Jacques Lacan's theories of subjectivity, based on an interpretation of Sigmund Freud's work of the tripartite subject (id, ego, and superego), also have had a profound influence on queer and feminist theory that resonate with Butler's notion of gender performativity. Lacan postulates that the individual acquires a self-perception and identity (ego) as an extension of the infantile "mirror stage" in which the child is able to recognize itself in the mirror. The self is thus only solidified through its reflection from an outside "other." The reflected image is illusory and its coherence and stability can never be fully achieved, thus leading to a continual dialectic of desiring the self in the mirror/other and rejecting the alienated Other/self. Lacan's notions of the resulting "decentered self" (the reality behind the illusion of a whole and bounded self) and "fragmented body" (the image of the castrated or incomplete body that haunts the subject) have proven useful in the articulation of the social and political construction of self—identity and subjectivity are always dependent on external forces that define and reflect the self back to the individual. The fragmented self continually seeks the wholeness that is promised in the ideal image presented in the mirror/other. Subjectivity is not a thing achieved, but is rather a continual process of reassertion dependent on the mirroring of those people who surround the subject.

Butler's concept of the emergent and performed self combined with Lacan's notion of the fragmented and interactive basis of subjectivity has been greatly influential in contemporary feminist and queer work on the issues of subject formation (see Weir 1996). This chapter focuses on the interactive and continually emergent nature of tom and dee identities. The subject positions tom and dee are in continual dialogue, embedded within a system of gender politics that validate or challenge particular narratives. While scholarship has rendered visible transgender/third-gender categories (see Herdt 1994), there is a risk that focus on these isolated categories of subjectivity will erroneously position them as stable Cartesian subjects that belie the contested and emergent qualities of all subjectivity. I argue that the transgender category of "tom" can only be understood in the context of interactions with other subjectivities and subject categories, in particular their romantic partners—dees. This chapter focuses on the dynamic, interpersonal, and interactive foundation of tom and dee subjectivities by examining the mutual construction of tom and dee. First, I review sexual and gender categories in the Thai context, followed by sections on the importance of gender binarism for toms and dees, the politics of tom masculinity and dee femininity and the sexual politics of "untouchability."

Sex, Sexuality, and Gender

Tom and dee subjectivities are particularly interesting forms of sexual subjectivity because they exist in a social and cultural context in which the concept of "homosexuality" is largely absent, or at least poorly defined. The categorization of people based on sexual orientation (homosexual, heterosexual, and bisexual) is a relatively recent concept that has been introduced to Thai society through the translation of medical, psychological, and academic discourses from English. "Homosexuality" has been translated into Thai as "rak-ruam-pheet," but this term is somewhat academic and formal and is not commonly used by ordinary Thais.

While the possibility of sexual relations between women has long been recognized in Thai discourse, women engaged in these acts were not marked as particular kinds of beings in Thai discourse before the division into tom-dee categories.[6] Sexual relationships between normatively feminine women are still largely nondiscursive. In other words, such relationships are usually not discussed at all and do not lead to societal labels or categories of subjectivity (such as "lesbian"). These women often do not identify themselves as lesbian or homosexual, or even describe these experiences as sexual.[7]

For many Thais, the concept of homosexuality is new and is largely incorporated into traditional Thai discourse in which people are classified in terms of gender rather than sexuality (see Jackson 1997a). Recognition of "third-gendered" (*pheet-thii-saam*) individuals or intermediary-gendered people is an integral part of Thailand's sex/gender order. In Thai, such individuals have been called "kathoey." *Kathoey* can be used to refer to physically hermaphroditic individuals, but is more commonly used to refer to people who seem to transgress or blend gender categorization in any behavioral context. Over the past 20 or 30 years the usage of the term has changed and now "kathoey" is used almost exclusively to refer to transgendered males; transgendered females are categorized by the recently invented term "tom."[8] Although the term "tom" is new, transgendered females have existed in the past, according to oral histories I gathered from people between 60 and 80 years of age (see Sinnott 2004).[9]

These transgendered people are understood to pair sexually with gender normative partners. In other words, a transgendered male will be partnered with a gender normative man and a transgendered female will be partnered with a gender normative woman. The gender normative partner is not typically understood as homosexual—in fact, until recently there was no signification for these people—there was no word to describe them as being different from men and women engaged in "heterosexual" relationships (heterosexuality is also a new term in Thai: *rak-tang-pheet*). Thus transgendered toms are understood as naturally partnered with gender normative women—dees. The gender normative partner of the "misgendered" (*phit-pheet*) person (referred to here as "transgendered") tends to be ignored in Thai analyses of homosexuality in Thailand because they do not fit the presumption of misgendering. Homosexual relations between two gender-normative men or women are also largely invisible; Thai discourse cannot account for same-sex sexual relationships in which neither partner is transgendered. Thus one's sexuality, sexual identity or subject position are understood as an extension of one's gender. The English terms "sex" and "gender" are commonly conflated in Thai; both are referred to as "pheet." Gender (*pheet-saphaap*), as a form of knowledge independent of sex or sexuality, is a new academic-inspired concept that is only peripherally and loosely integrated into Thai discourse. People's sexual behavior is largely assumed to be a natural extension of one's gender (not one's sexed body). A female-bodied person who has a masculine identity will be understood to have a masculine gender and therefore to be attracted to feminine women.

A specific linguistic signifier for female masculinity ("tom") is new—perhaps only 30 years old. However, the truly novel concept in the Thai cultural landscape is the labeling of a specific identity for feminine women engaged in homosexual relationships—"dee." Dees are not discursively distinguished from "women" by nature of their homosexuality; these women are dees by virtue of sex with toms, not sex with "women." The result is an ambivalent position of the dee in the sex/gender order; they are gender normative yet sexually ambiguous in that they do not neatly fit the trans-gender-normative gender pair model. The term "dee" distinguishes them, however indistinctly, from the category "women," yet incorporates them as kinds of women. Dees are understood to be potentially involved in relationships with either males or toms, both of whom are masculine beings. Thus, the use of the term "identity" may be misleading. The dee subject category resides in the combination of gender normativity with a sexuality that can include female partners, as long as those partners are masculine. They are not notably distinct from any woman in Thai society; all "women" (that is, non-toms) are potential dees. Yet, relationships with toms do not necessarily invoke an identity shift to "dee-ness." The nature of dee-ness is its ambivalence, as the degree to which women *own* dee identity and use it as a self-conscious self-referent varies widely.[10]

Tom masculine subjectivity depends on a distinction from the femininity of "ordinary women" embodied in the dee subject category. Toms thus often reassert the common understanding in Thai society that dees are no different from women in general. This discursive sameness between "dees" and "women" is also commonly asserted by dees. Dees can avoid being categorized as sexual or gender "deviants" by supporting this discourse that dees are "ordinary women" even as they engage in romantic/sexual relations with toms.

Toms and dees engage in a kind of rhetorical dance deploying discourses of femininity and masculinity that serve to define the other, and by so doing, to define the self. The genders of toms and dees are so intertwined that tom masculinity may be most fully articulated in the expectations of a dee; it is she who most convincingly patrols the borders of what it is to be an appropriate partner of a dee. Toms are compelled to distinguish their masculine subjectivity from normative femininity. In other words, they must demonstrate that they are not "ordinary women." Toms actively position their masculinity against other gendered alternatives (ordinary women, men, and lesbians).

Gender Dualism

Contemporary theories of identity (whether these identities are sexual, national, ethnic, or gendered) are heavily influenced by the structuralism of linguistic and social theory that posits meaning and language as constituted through sequences of binary oppositions (man/woman, self/other). The structural anthropology of Claude Lévi-Strauss was informed by the structuralism of Ferdinand de Saussure and in turn influenced a host of leading theorists of gender and sexual subjectivity, including Simone de Beauvoir. In her path-breaking feminist work *The Second Sex*, Beauvoir critically applied the dialectics of subjectivity explicated in Georg Hegel's *Phenomenology of the Mind* and Lévi-Strauss's concepts of the binary distinction of nature/culture. Beauvoir describes gender as a hierarchical binary in which "Woman" serves as the oppositional Other to the male subject (Weir 1996).

Allison Weir (1996) reintroduces Hegel's dialectic back into this primary binary that informs de Beauvoir's work. In place of de Beauvoir's rigid Self/Other, Man/Woman hierarchical binary, Weir reasserts Hegel's Self and Other categories as existing in dialectical flux; everyone's object (other) is a subject that is further objectifying others in a process Hegel has termed the "master/slave" dialectic. Weir recuperates this Hegelian dialectic as an important dimension of feminist theory of subjectivity:

> The master-slave story demonstrates the inadequacy of the Enlightenment conception of ourselves as individual, finite subjects, isolated consciousnesses, who exist in opposition to the world, to other subjects, to our own bodies.

> The struggle between the two subjects who become master and slave is one step toward the recognition that self and other, subject and object, are in fact not opposed but united, integrally related. (Weir 1996:21)

The relational, binaristic, and dialectical basis of tom and dee identities are evident in the normative rendering of masculine-feminine pairings, the positioning of dees as separate and distinct from toms, and the performances on which these distinctions are continually played out. The oppositional nature of gender identity does not mean that there can only be two genders, a point that has been convincingly argued by the sizable literature on third genders. Rather this dialectic points to the relational and oppositional quality of subjectivity that is defined against a negative or oppositional quality.

Gender duality is hegemonic in Thai same-sex relations; tom-tom, or dee-dee couples are rejected from the dominant discourse. Most toms and dees found the idea ludicrous and unsettling when I suggested it. Same-gendered (dee-dee, tom-tom) sex is considered by toms and dees to be as "deviant" as same-sex sexuality is commonly considered in Anglo/American discourse. Both toms and dees usually said they felt it was "unnatural" to change from a tom to a dee or for two toms or two dees to be in a relationship, although some had heard of such cases. Chang, a 26-year-old dee who had recently moved to Bangkok from southern Thailand, described the clear-cut distinctions that she and others make between toms and dees ("women"):

> I have never had any lover who is a woman [*phu-ying*]. I usually meet toms. I don't know why I usually have a very tom lover. I think it may be because our society thinks that toms have to be with dees. I've never seen any dee being with a dee. I don't think there are any. I think 99 per cent are very tom and very dee. My 20 or 30 friends are all dees and toms. I saw two toms together but one tom changed herself to be a dee. Once I saw an older friend at . . . [a] party. She had her hair cut short and didn't put on any make-up but she had no bra [that is, she did not bind her breasts as some toms do] and dressed the same as a woman. I was confused at first but finally I saw her with a tom so I knew that she actually was a dee. I remember that at first she was a tom but when she loved a tom she had to change herself to be with her tom lover. She looks happy. If one is very tom and then she totally changes herself to be a dee, I think that would be too much! I don't think I could handle that.

For Chang, it is a truism that "women" cannot be with "women" (in contrast to the idea that females cannot be with females). Chang reasserted hegemonic notions of gender duality within the context of tom-dee relationships by claiming that gender binary coupling is a social norm (toms *should* pair with dees) and natural (toms *do* pair with dees). Identity becomes nonsensical without a binaristic, mutually defining pair of subjectivities and subject positions. Chang made sense of the anomalous situation where two apparent toms are in a relationship by explaining that one tom was fluid in her gender identity and could adjust her identity/gender to be in accordance with normative expectations.

Tom Identity: Serving Women

Feminist theorists, drawing on the Hegelian dialectic and object relations theory, assert that subjectivity is essentially a social relationship; no subjectivity can exist if one is not recognized as a subject (Weir 1996). The need for mutual recognition leads to an interdependent and interactive basis for subject formation. Tom and dee subject categories, as central organizing categories for social and sexual relationships, are appropriated by women as meaningful ways to understand the self and connect with others. These subject categories are merged with individual subjectivities ("I am a tom") in an interactive context in which toms distinguish themselves from other subjects, such as "woman" and "man."

The primary way of defining one's "tom-ness" is to distinguish oneself from "ordinary women" or dees. Secondarily, tom masculinity is often consciously positioned against male masculinity, resulting in a hybrid gender formulation between normative masculinity and femininity. The commonly heard truism that "toms are similar to men" must be reexamined with an awareness of the actual complexity and variability of tom masculinity. Female masculinity cross-culturally is an under-researched topic but the work that exists demonstrates that forms of female masculinity are produced in complex, nonisomorphic relation to male gender categories.[11] For example, Gayle Rubin has argued that "butch" masculinity for American women does not mean necessarily that butches want to be men, are similar to men, or identify with men:

> The term [butch] encompasses individuals with a broad range of investments in "masculinity." It includes, for example, women who are not at all interested in male gender identities, but who use traits associated with masculinity to signal their lesbianism or to communicate their desire to engage in the kinds of active or initiatory sexual behavior that in this society are allowed or expected from men. It includes women who adopt "male" fashions and mannerisms as a way to claim privileges or deference usually reserved for men. It may include women who find men's clothing better made, and those who consider women's usual wear too confining or uncomfortable or who feel it leaves them vulnerable or exposed. (1992:467)

Being a tom relied on distinctions between toms' masculinity and men's masculinity. The most important distinction was in toms' ability to "serve" women in ways that men were thought to be unlikely to do. Toms said that "serving" women was a way to compensate their feminine partners for the tom's lack of manhood. The masculinity that emerges is a blend of stereotypical Thai feminine characteristics and a rejection of femininity:

> Khem (tom): Toms must dress coarsely. I think that toms are womanizers, they drink and take drugs. Dees are ordinary women [*phu-ying thammada*]. As for me, I am a tom because I don't like to wear skirts and I have short hair. Frankly, I want to be just a bit of a tom, like a fake tom, because sometimes I want to be a woman. You know that there are toms and dees, these toms are completely like men, but I am not. Sometimes I want to be strong, but I have a weakness at the same time. To summarize, I am a blend, in the middle, but I am more tom-like because I like to serve. (Matthana 1996:129)

Khem defined her masculinity somewhat ambivalently, but as most firmly residing in her need "to serve" others, which is the most stereotypical requirement of normative Thai femininity. Thai women are taught from an early age to be of service to others and to be attentive and sensitive to others needs.[12] Toms have appropriated this stereotypically feminine quality as the cornerstone of their masculinity. Toms often described this kind of caretaking in terms of masculine norms, such as the norm that men should protect women or be family leaders. However, tom caretaking almost always involves putting a dee's emotional and sexual needs before their own, which is not a masculine norm.

Chang, a dee, positioned toms as having a blend of masculine and feminine characteristics; she said they were strong but also able to care for her in ways that men would not, such as performing housework:

> I understand that a tom is a woman so they don't have to do everything like a man. I don't like toms who act like a big bully or drink or smoke. That's why I prefer older toms who are more mature. I've heard of so many friends of mine who are toms but they can do housework and don't have to act like a man. Actually my tom now is doing my laundry at home and she can do everything like a housewife. But she takes care of me and acts tough outside of the house.

Dees develop a discourse in which toms *are* equivalent to men, *are not* equivalent to men, *should be* equivalent men, or *should not* be equivalent to men, depending on the rhetorical imperatives of their discussion.

Many of the dees I interviewed said the qualities most often sought in toms were attentiveness and service. Um, a professional woman in her mid-30s who had relationships with both toms and men, defined "successful" dees as being in need of toms' attentive service:

> Dees that are successful in being dees have to be helpless. They need to need help. For example, they should not like to drive so that toms have to pick

> them up everyday, so they are together every day. They [successful dees] don't like to go anywhere by themselves, they need someone to take them out every day. So the dee cannot be without the tom, and that is what a successful dee will think.

The "successful" dee will fit well with the tom because she will allow the tom to express and perform her masculinity by taking care of the dee. For Um, the definition of dee also resided in this caretaking dynamic. When asked if she could ever see herself attracted to a dee, she answered "no," and said that she would not enjoy taking care of a woman:

> Women seem like they cannot take care of themselves. If I had a dee girlfriend, I wouldn't want to bother taking care of her. I wouldn't like it. It's annoying; they are so fussy. If I have a tom, she will take care of me and be worried about me. She will find nice presents for me and pay a lot of attention to me . . . I can be friends with dees, but I don't want to be lovers with them, it wouldn't be fun. Toms are fun. Toms will take me out, take care of me, that's fun. They will help me carry things. When I went abroad with that tom it was such great fun both times we went. She drove me around. I didn't have to do anything. If I had a dee lover, I would have such a burden. But I wonder why toms like to take care so much?

Most dees interviewed agreed that an older, capable tom on whom they could rely for advice and guidance was their ideal. Cot, a dee in her mid-20s, exemplified what dees expected of toms in terms of their ability to care for dees: "I like them because I feel that they are strong, and I can depend on them. I feel that I am weak and so I want somebody who is strong."

Both toms and dees construct a discourse in which tom masculinity is understood to reside in an ability to serve women. Dee subjectivity is premised on supposed weakness and neediness that necessitate particular kinds of masculine performances from toms. Tom and dee subjectivities require mutual recognition in that dees have to provide a means for toms to perform their masculine subjectivity through which a woman can form a relationship with a tom, and thus become a dee. While tom and dee subjectivities are interdependent, they also entail conflict and strategic manipulation in the interpretation and application of these subject categories.

Sexuality and "Stone Butch" Toms

While the discourse of toms as caretakers was an important part of constructing tom masculinity, the most contentious aspect of toms' "service" was the sexual practice of "untouchability" of many toms.

"Untouchability" means that it is considered masculine and proper for toms to perform for dees sexually, while not allowing their feminine partners to touch toms physically. Untouchability is based on the distinction made between the "active" partner (*fay ruk*) and the "passive" partner (*fay rap*). According to Thai norms, men are understood to be active in sexual activity, while women are passive, receiving the man's actions. Thus, toms are expected to be active and perform for the dees sexually (such as oral sex or manual stimulation). The irony is that in the tom-dee model, the dee is the partner who is expected to achieve orgasm, not necessarily the tom.

While actual sexual behavior between couples varies, the dominant discourse requires that toms at least present themselves as exclusively sexually "active" by never allowing themselves to be touched sexually. Dees play an important role in maintaining this discourse. For example, a dee wrote in a letter to a lesbian/tom-dee newsletter, *Anjareesaan*:

> I can't accept it at all. I can't accept a tom that lets a dee do it for her. If it is like that, why are you a tom? Go and be a dee instead. Normally when I have sex with my girlfriend, she will do it [sex] for me always, which she has said that she enjoys. Just to see me enjoy myself and she is happy already, something like that. So I have never done anything for her [sexually]. Another thing, like I have said, I cannot accept a tom that lets a dee do it for her. (Quoted in Matthana 1996:141–142)

Cuk, a tom, also adhered to the untouchability rule and explained that if she allowed her dee girlfriend to touch her body, Cuk would be uncomfortably reminded of her femaleness:

> My girlfriend has never touched my breasts. Mostly I will be the one who does it [to/for her]. At least I wear a bra and a shirt and I wear pants. I have never taken it all off. I asked her if she wanted me to take it all off. If she wanted me to, I would have taken it all off because it was taking advantage of her too much, because she took all her clothes off and I didn't. But she said if I took all my clothes off it wouldn't be the same, it [my body] will become a woman. I understand that she will feel like that. We have been together for a long time, I will get that feeling from her. If I take all my clothes off, I'll look like a woman, and I won't be confident in myself. I'll feel embarrassed, something like that. I've had orgasms without taking off my clothes. Everyone is different. I always ask my partner if it feels good there. If she says yes, I immediately will have the same feeling. Just this and I feel good, I don't need her to touch my body . . . We hug, but once we hug, [my partner] will feel it, but at least there is a shirt covering me. I've asked her, and she thinks that I am a man, it's just that I can't have children with her. (Matthana 1996:142–143)

Baimai, another tom, stressed her belief that the untouchability practice is right and proper for toms and dees:

> With my girlfriend (*faen*) who is a dee, she is the one who goes along with my wishes always, so I have never asked her to do it [perform sex] for me. She is the one who takes off all her clothes. As for me, it depends on whether I feel like it or not. She never complains. She just lies there. I think that's good. I don't think anything of it. I don't want anything more than that. I just go ahead and do it for her; there is no time to notice if she does it for me or not. I just try to do my duty the best I can. I just do it until I think she is satisfied. I estimate the time that I think is right. (Matthana 1996:142)

However, other toms described the practice as oppressive. Piin, a middle-class tom in her 30s operated a web site in which hundreds of toms and dees discussed their lives on an ongoing web board. In an interview, she described untouchability as a way that dees manipulate toms into one-way sexual practice:

> Some women say they can't tolerate it if toms ask her to be "doers" or if toms take off their clothes. I say that is selfish. You want to have happiness but the "doers" are tired too. Why can't you let them [toms] feel happy too? I would say that that woman is selfish. I blame so many dees in the web site. Some dees say, no, I can't accept that. In my experience, I have had so many girlfriends when I was young. I met so many kinds of women. Some don't want me to do them but they want to do me instead. [laughs] They are so dee, very womanly, but still active. I met some dees who do nothing, just lie down. Some love me so much but if I ask them to do me it will affect our relationship in a bad way. I met them all so I have learned from that. And I also have gained some experience from talking to Lesla members on the web. I have to accept the reality that I am physically a woman. I don't think the same as many Thai toms, maybe I am a dee! [laughs]

The discourse of untouchability is the site of contestation and of strategic claims between dees and toms for feminine or masculine subjectivity. Some toms and dees admit that they do not conform to this practice themselves, but it is very difficult for a tom to admit this in the presence of other toms or dees. Rather than being "passive," in actuality dees play an active role in the deployment of this discourse. For many dees their role as the receiver of sexual attention was an important part of their attraction to toms. The dee category is thus based on a contradiction; by construing oneself as gender normative and properly feminine, dees can ironically engage in a more active pursuit of sexual satisfaction than would be considered proper in sexual interactions with males.

Dees as "Ordinary Women"

The "stability" of the dee identity, in terms of it being identifiable *as* an identity, lies in the relative ease in which a Thai woman can *become* a dee. One has only to find a tom lover or partner and one is a de facto dee. Toms do not seek out dees necessarily—they find "women" who become dees by engaging in a relationship with a tom. *All* "women" (that is, nonmasculine women) are potential dees; never having had a tom lover before is no reason to discount a particular woman as a partner for a tom. Similarly, having a male lover does not necessarily disrupt the dee subjectivity. Dees are expected to be what Anglo/Americans think of as bisexual. As "ordinary women," having male lovers reaffirms dees' femininity and therefore their distinction from toms.[13] Toms position dee identity as situational and embedded in the typical life trajectory of "ordinary women."

One way in which toms positioned dees as "ordinary women" was by asserting that for a dee to get married was correct and largely inevitable. Toms said they recognized that dees, as ordinary women, would want to get married and live with a man. Nuu, a tom in her 40s, was representative in this often heard refrain: "I am not selfish. If a woman says she can go on living an ordinary life with a man, I'll say please go—to go is better, because I probably can't give her very much." Cuk, a tom, agreed that for a woman to marry was natural and should be encouraged:

> We broke up because she went and got married. We separated because I think its better to get married. I didn't feel that bad because it is the best for her. I think it is naturally the best for her. Her parents wanted it, and she can find real happiness. If she really is in love [with him], let her go. I think about myself too, but what can I do? It is better than her having another woman—that I couldn't accept. (Matthana 1996:108)

Dees also often positioned themselves as "ordinary women." Bua, a dee (who had been involved with both men and women) described her previous relationship with a tom. I asked her if she felt that toms were in some way disadvantaged by not having the same opportunities that men had. She answered, "I am sorry about it, but that's their problem." I asked her if she felt she was different from her tom lover:

> I feel I am normal, but she is abnormal and I feel sorry for her. I'm with her to be friends, to help her. I want her to feel she can have a partner like anybody else. I'm normal, part of society. She is the one I must take special care of, because she is delicate, has lots of problems, which makes her abnormal. Sometimes I think she is like a man, because sometimes she treats me like a man would, takes care of me, is very gentlemanly. I just want her to be a real man, so I could be with her all our lives.

While many dees positioned themselves as "ordinary women" and thereby essentially different from toms, not all dees felt comfortable with the presumed sameness between themselves and "ordinary women." Toms often insisted that dees were no different from heterosexual women even if a woman would try to establish her dee identity as a stable and core aspect of herself. For example, Nuu, a tom, introduced me to two dees for conversation and potential interviews. Jaeng, in her 20s, told us about her recent breakup with a tom lover. Jaeng was devastated by the breakup. She told Nuu and me that she had always loved toms and had never been interested in men romantically. Jaeng even used the expression that toms often used to describe themselves, saying she was "born this way [as a dee]." To reinforce the point that she felt incapable of forming a romantic relationship with a man, Jaeng told me she had remained married for a short time to please her parents. She explained that she just could not bear her husband because she had never had any sexual or romantic feelings for men, and so divorced him shortly after the marriage.

After Jaeng finished her story, Nuu tried to comfort her over her recent breakup by saying, "You should look for somebody good, you don't have to think whether they are a man or a woman." I was struck by the comment for two reasons. First, the comment seemed to purposefully ignore Jaeng's claims to be solely interested in toms. Second, I had never heard the advice that one should look for someone "good" regardless of the gender/sex given to a tom. Nuu's comment illustrates the dynamic and relational aspect of constructing tom identity. Toms position themselves in contrast to "real" men, while they also position themselves as essentially different in nature from dees, who they often claim are not "born to be."

Building a stable sense of oneself as dee, or a stable dee identity, therefore, depends on contradicting the dominant discourse of dee as "ordinary women" that toms appropriate so readily. Some dees describe themselves as exclusively dee; it is precisely these women who are integrating a notion of sexuality with gender as the basis for personal identity (as is found in "lesbian" identity in the United States). These women find it difficult to convince toms that they are more similar to toms than they are to "ordinary women." They are constructing a discourse that there are "true dees," women who are exclusively interested in toms as lovers and can form life-long relationships with toms.

The notion of "true dees" has met with considerable scepticism among the toms I interviewed. Um, a dee who has had both male and female lovers, distinguished dees from other women in an interview:

Um: A dee is someone who also likes women. Dees have the characteristics of being gentle. But if you are talking about a tom, they are strong like men. But an "ordinary woman" must like men.

MS: So dees aren't "ordinary women?" Are they another category?
Um: Yes. They can go back and forth [between male and female lovers].
MS: But toms say dees are "ordinary women."
Um: But dees like women. Is that ordinary? That's not so ordinary. Why don't they like men if they are ordinary?

Chang, another dee, also claimed that dees were not the same as "ordinary women." She said that dees were actually more misgendered (*phit-pheet*) than were toms since they chose to be with a woman when it would be relatively easy to be with a man:

> Sex [*pheet*] means to have a female sex or a male sex. So people are confused if you are a woman but don't marry a man. So being mis-sexed/gendered [*phit-pheet*] means to go against your masculinity or femininity. Dees are very mis-sexed/gendered since they don't act like men but they *still* want to be with a woman. Actually they can be with a man since they are very feminine. But for toms, to be with men is harder since they are not cute and girly.

Chang is making a rather radical declaration. For her, dees constitute the more disruptive category in the Thai sex/gender order and are truly more "mis-gendered/sexed."

Chang agreed with the discourse that to be a tom was difficult and even tragic because dees could easily abandon them for men. However, she made a distinction between "fake" and "real" dees:

> There is a good chance that the dees who are not real dees will dump the good toms to have a boyfriend. But I think they are women so if they want to have boyfriends just let them go and be happy, since it's their nature and it's the right way for them and society will accept that. The old and good toms will be hurt by this more seriously than the young toms since the young toms just like to play around anyway. I think there are so many dees now who will change and have boyfriends so I say you shouldn't make a promise to a tom [to be together] if you are not sure you are a real dee. But I know myself that I don't want men, so I can guarantee myself.

The discourse of "real" versus "fake" dees indicates a point of rupture with the dominant tom-dee discourse. This dominant understanding of female same-sex relationships polarizes "misgendered" toms and "ordinary women," placing these two subject categories as oppositional, relational, and exclusional. To be a "real dee," "ordinary woman," or "fake dee" are ways in which women are engaging the dominant gender framework, manipulating its codes of masculinity and femininity to make claims for tom and dee subjectivity.

Conclusion

For Lacan and Butler, the process of subject formation begins with the entry in the cultural symbolic order that is, at its core, an entry into gender categories. For these theorists, gender is not a peripheral or secondary characteristic of subject formation—it is subjectivity itself. While the categories of "tom" and "dee" are not the only meaningful ways that Thai women in same-sex relationships understand their own life narratives, gender subject categories—tom, dee, man, woman—are of central importance to the understandings of self.

Gender, rather than sexuality or sexual orientation, is the dominant discourse through which tom and dee subjectivities are formed. These gendered categories are not static or wholly agreed upon by toms and dees themselves. Tom and dee subjectivities are embedded in the performative politics that construct gender as a system. The binary of masculinity and femininity in the context of tom and dee relationships has the appearance of being natural and self-evident, but an exploration of the ways this gender duality is deployed reveals that it is contested, performed, and often ambiguous.

A significant shift in the Thai sex/gender order can be found in the creation of a linguistic category "dee" to refer to feminine women engaged in relationships with masculine women. Within tom and dee communities, women are identifying themselves in traditional gendered terms but with new sexual accents. The previously nondiscursively recognized partners of "misgendered" females (toms) are now called "dees." This shift is partial and contested; dee is not a fully formed identity and is not appropriated by all women engaged in relationships with toms. The dee identity is born in the interstices between gender normativity and the largely permissible zone of female same-sex erotic activity. Dee subjectivity is marked by strategic disavowal of sexual sameness with toms. The degree to which dees are an identifiable identity, as distinct from "ordinary women," marks the degree to which one can say there is transformation in the dominant discourse that has asserted that homosexuality is indistinguishable from "misgendering." In the search for discursive shifts occurring in non-Western discourses of gender and sexuality, the changing status and identity of the "normative" gender/sexual partner in same-sex relationships assumes much significance.

Notes

This chapter heavily relies on data collected during my dissertation research in Thailand from 1992–2001. My research consisted mainly of interviews with and observation of communities of toms and dees (approximately 100 interviews). Much of my interview material is published elsewhere so in order to provide fresh information to supplement my own interviews, I have also relied on several important Thai texts that are not otherwise available in English. Matthana Chetamee's Master's thesis (1996), on the subject of family life and women who love women in Thailand, contains fascinating and richly detailed interview material that needs to be incorporated into the English literature on female same-sex erotics cross-culturally. I also have relied on Anjaree's newsletter/magazine (entitled *Anjareesaan* or *An*). Anjaree is a Thai lesbian organization that campaigns on a national level for lesbian and gay rights and also provides social functions for its members. All names used in interviews are pseudonyms and are in the form of a Thai "nickname." Nicknames published in the Thai source material are repeated here for ease in tracing references, should the reader wish to do so.

1. A thorough analysis of the use of English to label these gender categories is beyond the space of this chapter, but a few words of explanation are in order. Jillana Enteen 2001 argues that the use of English terms is a common Thai practice to create a new word in Thai when there is no Thai equivalent available. For example, the Thai term "faen" was created to refer to the recently formed categories "boyfriend" or "girlfriend." These temporary romantic relationships did not involve the commitments, financial and otherwise, of marriage. Thais adapted the English word "friend" or "fan" into a new Thai word—"faen" to label these casual relationships. Enteen points out that the new English-derived Thai word does not hold exactly the same meaning as its English referent (Enteen 2001:103–104). The Western world (Anglo-European nations), and its representative language of English, is commonly held to be synonymous with social change. Any perceived new social category will be tied symbolically to the West through the use of English terminology.
2. Use of the national languge, Central Thai, extends beyond the national borders to Laos, many of whose residents are exposed to Thai media and can speak or understand the Thai language, which is closely related to Lao. On a trip to Laos in the summer of 2005 I found the words "tom" and "dee" were the terms Lao speakers used to refer to female same-sex couples.
3. I am indebted to Tom Boellstorff for this language of "subject categories" and "subjectivities" in place of the term "identity." See Boellstorff 2005: 10–11.
4. The word "tom" is a self-description in this context and is used in the same sense that "woman" might be. When I refer to a person in the text as a "tom," as in "the tom answered," it has the same connotation as, "the woman answered." In contrast, using the phrase, "the lesbian said," sounds overly totalizing and inappropriate. The choice of the word "tom" to refer to a third person is based on the inadequacy of the term "woman," which is problematic in this context because toms identify themselves in contrast to the gendered category "woman," for reasons discussed below.
5. See Allison Weir 1996 for a comprehensive and insightful comparison of the theories of subjectivity by Simone de Beauvoir, Georg Hegel, Jacques Lacan, Jacques Derrida, Judith Butler and others.
6. Female same-sex sexual behavior is termed "len pheuan," which is a set expression that can be translated directly as "play [with] friends." This term has been

found in Thai literature dating back several centuries. See Sinnott 2004; also Loos 2005.

7. The nondiscursive quality of erotic acts experienced between women who do not identify as tom-dee raises an important question about the possibility of objective or transcultural usage of the term "sexuality" or "sex." If these acts are not described as "sexual" by either the participants or by social conventions, which is often the case in the Thai context, can they be reasonably labeled as nondiscurive forms of female-female *sex*? At what point can physical contact be understood as "sexual" in disregard to local meaning systems? See Elliston 1995 for a critique of the usage of "sexuality" as a cross-cultural category of analysis.
8. See Morris 1994, and Jackson 1997a, 1997b, for a history and description of kathoey and transgenderism in Thai society.
9. The history of transgenderism in Thai culture is not well known; the degree to which it was a lived identity versus a textual symbol in the past is not clear. See Morris 1994 for a discussion of the history of textual representation of kathoey.
10. See Ara Wilson 2004 for a discussion of recent transformations of tom and dee relationships in the context of globalizing economic forces and their impact on commercial spaces. Wilson analyzes the types of homosocial spaces that toms and dees use.
11. For discussions of female masculinity, see Nestle 1992; Kennedy and Davis 1993; Gremaux 1994; Halberstam 1998; Blackwood and Wieringa 1999.
12. Young girls working and helping their mothers while their brothers play is a common sight in Thailand. Also, women do constant caretaking activities for those around them, such as serving food and drink. For detailed description and analysis of Thai women's social training, see Muecke 1984; Mills 1995, 1999; Taywaditep, Coleman, and Dumronggittigule 1997; Thaweesit 2000.
13. Dees differ from American femmes who are understood to be "lesbian" or distinct from heterosexual women. My thanks to Evelyn Blackwood for this insight concerning the differences between Western femmes and Thai dees.

References Cited

Blackwood, Evelyn and Saskia E. Wieringa, eds. 1999. *Female desires: Same-sex relations and transgender practices across cultures*. New York: Columbia University.

Butler, Judith. 1990. *Gender trouble: Feminism and the subversion of identity*. New York: Routledge.

———. 1993. *Bodies that matter: On the discursive limits of "sex."* New York: Routledge.

———. 2003. Performative acts and gender constitution: An essay in phenomenology and feminist theory. In *Feminist theory reader: Local and global perspectives*. Carole R. McCann and Seung-Kyng Kim, eds. Pp. 415–427. New York: Routledge.

Elliston, Deborah. 1995. Erotic anthropology: "Ritualized homosexuality" in Melanesia and beyond." *American Ethnologist* 22(4): 848–867.

Enteen, Jillana. 2001. Tom, dii and Anjaree: "Women who follow nonconformist ways." In *Postcolonial, queer*. John C. Hawley, ed. Pp. 99–122. Albany: State University of New York Press.

Gremaux, Rene. 1994. Woman becomes man in the Balkans. In *Third sex, third gender: Beyond sexual dimorphism in culture and history*. Gilbert Herdt, ed. Pp. 241–281. New York: Zone Books.

Halberstam, Judith. 1998. *Female masculinity*. Durham: Duke University Press.

Hall, Kira. 2000. Performativity. *Journal of Linguistic Anthropology* 9(1–2): 184–187.

Herdt, Gilbert, ed. 1994. *Third sex, third gender: Beyond sexual dimorphism in culture and history*. New York: Zone Books.

Jackson, Peter. 1997a. Kathoey><gay><man: The historical emergence of gay male identity in Thailand. In *Sites of desire, economies of pleasure: Sexualities in Asia and the Pacific*. Lenore Manderson and Margaret Jolly, eds. Pp.166–190. Chicago: University of Chicago Press.

———. 1997b. Thai research on male homosexuality and transgenderism and the cultural limits of Foucauldian analysis. *Journal of the History of Sexuality* 8(1): 52–85.

Kennedy, Elizabeth Lapovsky and Madeline D. Davis. 1993. *Boots of leather, slippers of gold: The history of a lesbian community*. New York: Penguin.

Loos, Tamara. 2005. Sex in the inner city: The fidelity between sex and politics in Siam. *Journal of Asian Studies* 64(4): 881–909.

Matthana Chetamee. 1996. Withi chiwit lae chiwit khrorp-khrua khorng ying-rak-ying. (Lifestyles and family life of women who love women). M.A. thesis, Thammasat University, Bangkok.

Mills, Mary Beth. 1995. Attack of the widow ghosts: Gender, death, and modernity in northeast Thailand. In *Bewitching women, pious men: Gender and body politics in Southeast Asia*. Aihwa Ong and Michael Peletz, eds. Pp. 244–273. Berkeley: University of California Press.

———. 1999. *Thai women in the global labor force: Consuming desires, contested selves*. New Brunswick: Rutgers University Press.

Morris, Rosalind C. 1994. Three sexes and four sexualities: Redressing the discourses on gender and sexuality in Thailand. *Positions* 2(1):15–43.

Muecke, Marjorie A. 1984. Make money not babies: Changing status markers of northern Thai women. *Asian Survey* 24(4): 459–470.

Nestle, Joan, ed. 1992. *The persistent desire: A femme-butch reader*. Boston: Alyson Publications Inc.

Rubin, Gayle. 1992. Of catamites and kings: Reflections on butch, gender, and boundaries. In *The persistent desire: A femme-butch reader*. Joan Nestle, ed. Pp. 466–482. Boston: Alyson Publications.

Sinnott, Megan. 2004. *Toms and dees: Transgender identity and female same-sex relationships in Thailand*. Honolulu: University of Hawaii Press.

Taywaditep, Kittiwut Jod, Eli Coleman, and Pacharin Dumronggittigule. 1997. Thailand (Muang Thai). In *The international encyclopedia of sexuality*, vol. 3. Robert T. Francoeur, ed. Pp. 1192–1265. New York: Continuum.

Thaweesit, Suchada. 2000. *From village to factory "girl:" Shifting narratives on gender and sexuality in Thailand*. Ph.D. dissertation, University of Washington.
Weir, Allison. 1996. *Sacrificial logics: Feminist theory and the critique of identity*. New York: Routledge.
Wilson, Ara. 2004. *The intimate economies of Bangkok: Tomboys, tycoons, and Avon ladies in the global city*. Berkeley: University of California Press.

Chapter Eight

Hunting Down Love: Female Masculinities in Bugis South Sulawesi

Sharyn Graham Davies

I'm going hunting
I'm the hunter
I'll bring back the goods
But I don't know when
—Bjork, *Homogenic*

Introduction

Before sitting down to begin work on this chapter, I randomly selected some music to provide inspiration. The CD I chose was Bjork's *Homogenic*, the first song of which is entitled "Hunter." I had listened to this album many times before, but it was only this time that I actually listened to the lyrics and realized how familiar they sounded. Just the previous year I had been sitting in a house in Makassar, the capital of the province of South Sulawesi in Indonesia, talking to an informant-cum-friend about issues of identity and sexuality. Dilah was telling me how s/he does not like the term *lesbi* because it does not fit hir idea of who s/he is. S/he does not want hir identity to be limited to sexual desire, which she sees the term lesbi as implying. Moreover, Dilah wants to present hirself as someone who actively pursues relationships and is in control of hir movements. In applying a label to hirself, Dilah stated that s/he likes the term *hunter* because s/he hunts down love and pounces on it.[1]

Dilah is from a Bugis farming background and finished school when s/he was 16. Two years later s/he moved to Jakarta and began working in a hair salon. It was there that Dilah met many politically active people and became increasingly interested in issues of sexuality and identity. While in Jakarta, Dilah had the opportunity to engage with popular national and international discourses of sexuality and gender that s/he accessed through mass media and association with other hunter and with *gay* and *waria* (transgender male) friends. Now back in Makassar, Dilah continues to engage in broader discourses of gender and sexuality through hir work as a DJ in a city nightclub and through hir support of various events organized by waria, such as fashion parades. Dilah has thus had the opportunity to think through, and discuss with others, notions of erotic desire and subjectivity. For Dilah, being assertive and hunting down what you want, is part of being hunter.

In this chapter I explore the subject positions of female-born individuals who do not identify with the category woman (*wanita, perempuan*, Indo.; *makkunrai*, Bug.), and do not aspire to be men (*laki-laki*, Indo.; *oroané*, Bug.). Rather, such individuals refer to themselves, and are referred to, as *calalai* (Bug.), or a variant term such as hunter. To explore calalai subjectivities, this chapter is divided into three sections. In the first section, I examine notions of ideal Bugis masculinity and femininity and analyze the impacts of local and national ideologies and Islamic discourses on Bugis gender ideals. This section provides a context in which Dilah and other calalai negotiate gender identities. In the second section, I use ethnographic data to specifically explore calalai subjectivities. Because of the pervasiveness of dominant gender ideologies, calalai often feel that their only option is to follow forms of masculinity. In this section I assess ways in which calalai emulate such ideals and thus reinforce normative gender systems. Calalai generally do not consider themselves men, though, nor are they considered as such, and so in the final section I analyze ways in which calalai engage and rework dominant gender discourses.

While some calalai have specific engagement with wider notions of genders and sexualities, such as those circulating though email, Internet, activist organizations, travel, and personal connections, for many calalai such access is limited. As Blackwood notes for lesbi in West Sumatra, "Because their location limits access to certain circuits of knowledge, their lesbi subjectivities reflect the particularities of place" (2005:237). Part of the aim of this chapter is to explore calalai subjectivities as they are located within South Sulawesi.

A dilemma inherent in emphasizing locatedness, though, is that larger global processes have a tendency to be downplayed. Moreover, as Boellstorff (2002) argues, ethnolocality (a term he coined to name a spatial scale where ethnicity and locality become a single concept) can obscure notions of similitude and community that exist at a national, or even global, level. As Boellstorff (2005) notes, for many gay and lesbi Indonesians their subjectivities are developed at a national level and they feel themselves part of a gay world (*dunia gay)* that supercedes ethnolocality. As such, a critique of ethnolocality opens up a space from which we can imagine new geographies of identification and equip ourselves to better respond to an already globalized world (Boellstorff 2002:38). Acknowledging the centrality for many individuals of national and global queer discourses, Blackwood (2005:222) asks how then "do researchers make sense of the complex relationship between cultural locatedness and global connectedness without recreating hierarchical dichotomies of traditional-modern and indigenous-global practices?" This is a particularly relevant issue in South Sulawesi where most calalai are unable to engage directly in national or global queer discourses and dominant referents for gender ideals are disseminated through hegemonic heteronormative frameworks.

While this article looks at how calalai engage with and rework dominant national, local, and Islamic norms of gender (under whose rubric falls sexuality), there is scope for research on ways in which calalai more specifically engage with, and also impact, Indonesian and global queer discourses. For instance, while dominant gender norms suggest that calalai should be the most sexually assertive partner, it is *linas*, femme partners of calalai, who are often considered as such, a position that reworks notions of calalai masculinity. How do linas expectations of being sexually dominant correlate with tombois' relationships in West Sumatra, for instance, where tombois see themselves as men and expect to take a dominant role in sexual play (Blackwood 2005)?

Before starting, a note on language is necessary. While the issue of language is a tricky one, Boellstorff (2001) remarks that debates concerning terms provide a context in which new ways of thinking about gender and sexuality emerge. While Dilah prefers the term hunter, others favor the term *tomboi* or calalai. No one I met in South Sulawesi, however, used the term lesbi to refer to themselves, although other people did use this term. As Murray found, individuals in Indonesia do not like to use the label lesbi to describe themselves as it is connected with "unpleasant stereotypes and the pathological view of deviance derived from Freudian psychology (1999:142)." On the contrary, however, Blackwood found that individuals in West Sumatra privately use the term lesbi and for them it does not call up "Eurocentric notions of a sexual orientation or identity that is a core aspect of one's self," although for other members of society the term does carry a strong connotation of deviance (Blackwood 2005:223). This contrast in interpretations reveals just one way in which a single term is imbued with different meanings, showing the diverse appropriations of queer discourses.

While I could have used either "hunter" or "tomboi" in this chapter, I have chosen to use the Bugis term "calalai" for two reasons. First, calalai in more rural settings are not familiar with these other terms because they have limited contact with (and influence from) people outside their immediate village. Second, while it may not be possible to talk of calalai identity being wholly indigenous or local, because for most calalai their identity is formed at the intersection of various influences, there are certain factors, such as the particular understanding of gender, which I explore elsewhere (Graham 2004), that makes it possible to see differences between calalai and, say, tomboi in West Sumatra (Blackwood 1998). Use of "calalai" does not negate that some individuals see themselves as national subjectivities rather than in ethnolocal terms (Boellstorff 2005). The use of "calalai" acknowledges that notions of self are also culturally contextualized (see further, Blackwood 2005). Etymologically, the term "calalai" means "false man" (Pelras 1996:165). It may be more appropriate, though, to interpret this as indicating that calalai are masculine females, rather than that calalai are inauthentic men.

Gender in a Cultural Setting

In order to provide a context for calalai identity negotiation, it is useful to have an understanding of ideal gender types and how they are presented. In doing this, I analyze four factors. First, issues of social location are discussed to provide an image of ideal Bugis masculinity. Second, I introduce the concept of *siri'* (Bug., shame/honor) to tease out notions of ideal Bugis femininity. In the third and fourth sections, I examine national and Islamic gender ideals represented in dominant discourses to show their respective representations of masculinity and femininity. One of the points drawn out in this section is the lack of alternative ways of presenting a legitimate gendered self in Bugis South Sulawesi.

In reality, it is often difficult to disentangle religion, cultural custom, and national discourse, and indeed international influences, as they converge and mutually reinforce each other. Moreover, people negotiate discourses differently in their subject creation and may combine these respective influences into an unproblematic Bugis self. While I separate local, national, and religious discourses for heuristic purposes in the first section of this chapter, in everyday gender negotiations the boundaries are often blurred. Therefore, in the second and third sections of this chapter, I refer to Bugis masculinity and femininity, suggesting that these be taken to refer to the incorporation of not just localized gender ideals but of the multitude of influences that combine in the constitution of Bugis gender norms.

Social Location: Ideals of Bugis Masculinity

During my field work I attended many weddings. One of the most frequently discussed topics at such events was which eligible woman would make a suitable partner for which eligible man. While many matters such as their character, occupation, age, and looks were discussed in determining the potential compatibility of the two individuals, one of the key determinants of compatibility was the individuals' relative social status. Even when discussants had quickly concluded that two individuals were an appropriate match, if someone then mentioned that the woman's social status was higher than the man's, the match was dismissed as unsuitable and the conversation quickly turned to assessing the potential compatibility of a different couple. While these conversations were generally light-hearted affairs, they suggest the importance many Bugis place on social status.

Because status is an issue of concern for many Bugis, in this first section I want to explore the relationship between status and gender with a view to extrapolating notions of ideal Bugis masculinity. To do this, I draw on the work of Susan Millar, who conducted fieldwork over two decades ago. Although her theoretical analysis occurred before advances in gender theory and queer theory, Millar's work is still one of the very few published sources on status in Bugis society; ironically, because Millar downplayed the significance of gender, it reveals a great deal about the importance and clarity of Bugis gender ideals.

Millar argues that a cultural preoccupation with hierarchical social location eclipses concerns of gender in Bugis society. Millar goes on to note that social location "is an attribute of each individual and has far less to do with gender than with individual characteristics distributed without reference to gender" (1983:477). While the importance of social location in Bugis society should not be underestimated, I want to show how, rather than being less important than social location, gender delineates acceptable means by which people can obtain or lose social status. As Geertz recently emphasized, gender "can be embodied in and reflective of finely graded and subtly expressed status differences" (2006:327–328). Indeed Millar herself notes that the gender system "is constructed, and patterns of male-female behavior function, in accord with the overarching concern of the Bugis to learn and maintain their social locations" (1983:482). By epitomizing masculine ideals a man can improve his relative social location. Bugis ideals of masculinity are thus evident in contests for social status; while class dynamics are involved in these contests, certain masculine qualities are generally desirable.

In understanding social location in Bugis society, *lahireng* (Bug.) and *bateng* (Bug.) are central concepts. Millar (1983, 1989) gives a detailed analysis of these terms, which I briefly summarize. Lahireng refers to outward displays of behavior and accomplishments. Society's interpretations of how well a person acts and their level of social achievements in part determine where a person will be placed on the social ladder. Lahireng is linked to a person's ability to be rational and reasonable; a person, who acts accordingly, especially in the most trying of times, will be conferred a relatively high social status by their community. Moreover, rational and reasonable individuals raise their level of social accomplishments and succeed in accumulating wealth and education. They are able to enhance both their mental and physical self-defenses, such as inner and outer strength. In addition to lahireng, *bateng* helps determine an individual's social standing; it signifies a person's constantly changing state of inner experience. Bateng does not refer to the essential character of a person; bateng is created in relation to a person's lived experiences. Individuals should strive to reach a balance between their bateng and lahireng. If a person can balance these two factors, then they may become known as a "person densely filled up," which in Bugis is referred to as a *tau malisé* (Millar 1983:479).

Tau malisé are highly respected in Bugis society. They are individuals who are self-disciplined, rational, and reasonable, who show great physical strength in hazardous circumstances, and who command admiration and reverence from their companions. Millar does not use the concept of tau malisé to elucidate ideal notions of masculinity, but she does note in a footnote that Bugis do not consider it to be in a woman's nature to become tau malisé; instead women should win the affection and protection of a tau malisé (1983:491n6).

Bugis men, then, can become tau malisé by exemplifying desirable aspects of masculinity, developing their lahireng and bateng complex, embodying traits such as authority, discipline, physical strength, and assertiveness. In this way, men secure and improve their relative social location. If a man does not obtain and display these desirable qualities, society may consider him a person not "densely filled up"; in Bugis such a person is called a *tau massissi lalo* (Millar 1983:479).

For many Bugis the image of ideal masculinity is embodied in tau malisé. Many individuals feel they need to adhere to this model in order to improve their relative social location (Davies 2006). Calalai fashion parts of their behavior on this model of masculinity embodied by tau malisé.

Siri': Ideals of Bugis Femininity

Official prescriptions for being a woman in Bugis society are in many senses quite strict; failure to conform to ideals of femininity risks causing *siri'* (Bug.). Siri' is a complex word that has a range of meanings, including shame, ashamed, disgrace, diffident, shy, and a sense of honor (Matthes 1885:583; Pelras 1996; Collins and Bahar 2000; Idrus 2003). Even this list of words does not fully capture the meaning of siri'. If someone causes a person to feel siri', or if they themselves are made to feel siri', immediate action is necessary to ensure the matter is resolved. If there is no quick resolution, an entire family may be made to feel siri' and this could have negative consequences for their social status. It is little wonder then that strict regulations are in place to try to ensure that siri' transgressions never occur. In Bugis society a woman signifies a family's siri'; an entire family's social status may be measured by the position and behavior of women family members. Thus, women, particularly, are made aware of what is expected of them in terms of ideal femininity.

Bugis women are expected to be modest in dress, which generally entails covering their knees and shoulders in public. Indeed, the term *makkunrai* (Bug., woman) literally means to "become covered" (Idrus 2003). Becoming covered not only protects a woman's body from public view, but also helps ensure the maintenance of her honor. Bugis women are also expected to marry because it is through marriage that they have the legitimate opportunity to bear children. Having children increases a woman's status to that of an adult and it grants her the title *Indo'* (Bug., Mother). Children are desired to ensure the continuation of a family's bloodline and to act as a form of security for aging parents. It is not usually enough, however, for a Bugis woman merely to marry. A Bugis woman should marry a man of suitable rank, that is, a man of higher status than hers. Of course there are rare cases when women do not marry. The highest ranking woman in Bugis society, Puang Datu Peta Bala Sari, who sadly passed away recently, never married because there was no man of higher rank for her to marry. Generally, however, an unmarried self in Indonesia is considered an incomplete self (Boellstorff 1999).

By remaining unmarried and childless a woman threatens her family's siri'. A man named Puang Sulai told me there are very few calalai because Bugis women are carefully protected (*dipelihara*). In other words, women are restricted in their movements and behaviors. The consequences of openly contesting established norms of Bugis femininity are such that very few individuals are willing, or able, to radically contest gender ideals by identifying as calalai.

National Gender Ideals

Separating Indonesian gender ideals from Bugis ones is a challenging undertaking as the national government has disseminated certain key gender ideals that are variously interpreted and embodied by individuals in Bugis society and often reconstituted into a Bugis identity. However, national ideals of masculinity and femininity are evident in the government's discourse of the family. In Bugis, a wife is called and referred to as *bainene* A (wife of A), while the husband is called and referred to as *lakkaina* B (husband of B). These terms indicate that each partner equally "belongs" to the other (Idrus 2004). In the national language, however, a husband is referred to as *kepala rumah tangga* (head of the household) and a wife as *ibu rumah tangga* (mother of the household). As Millar states, "It is noteworthy that the term associating a married male with household headship is Indonesian, whereas the terms for husbands and wives which indicate an equal complementarity between the two partners are Bugis" (1983:485).

In relation to Indonesian masculinity, such usage suggests that a man must act as the head of the household and make decisions in the best interests of his family's welfare. A man is expected to be the main money earner, giving his wife and children financial support. Protecting the purity and morality of the family is also seen ideally as the function of the husband (Sullivan 1994). In official discourse, men's nature is thought to make them suitable for formal public engagements, interacting in the public sphere and representing their families. In order to do this, men are assumed and expected to embody and display self-discipline and rationality. These expectations intersect with Bugis ideals of masculinity.

In relation to Indonesian femininity, the government actively promotes the idea that a woman's natural role and her supreme accomplishment are to become a wife and mother. In undertaking these roles a girl becomes a woman and thus a rightful and valuable member of the Indonesian nation-state. In the period under President Suharto (1966–98), referred to as the New Order, women were considered to be the emotional heart of the family. Some scholars (for example, Sullivan 1994; Suryakusuma 1996) use the term *Ibuism* to refer to the national policy of endorsing nuclear families and motherhood. This policy hierarchically ordered the five major duties of women: wife; mother; procreator; financial manager; and member of society (Sullivan 1994:129–130). Only when a woman married and had children was she considered a member of society. As Blackwood (1995) notes, a woman may not even be considered an adult until she marries heterosexually. It is not surprising, then, that calalai feel pressure to marry men and have children.

The government plays a strong role in defining sexuality, especially in the case of its civil servants, over whom the government has a certain amount of control. The rationale behind this is that civil servants represent Indonesia and as such should uphold the principles of the nation and set an example for the rest of society. Suryakusuma noted that the sexual conduct of civil servants is seen as a gauge of both the morality of the nation's citizens and the legitimacy of the government (1996:92). While not illegal, female same-sex sexuality is considered contrary to the nation's aims and is officially frowned upon (Murray 1999; Blackwood 2005), an attitude which in part influences Dilah and others to use phrases such as *menjadi sakit* (Indo., became ill) to describe the point at which they initiated same-sex sexual activity.

The government promotes its vision of the ideal family, defined as a nuclear unit consisting of a male husband, female wife and children, in many different ways. Parker (1992, 2002) writes of the means by which this ideal is promoted through school curricula and health care clinics. The mass media and development agencies also promote familial ideals focusing on women as feminine wives and mothers and men as masculine husbands and heads of households. Such limited models mean that boundaries are defined and contraventions sharply highlighted. No legitimate models of alternative ways of being are promoted, making it hard for Dilah and others to break away from the expectations placed on them to be feminine wives and mothers.

Islamic Gender Ideals

Almost every morning during my fieldwork I was given a complimentary hour-long lesson in Bugis. Because I lived relatively close to the largest mosque in the area that broadcast prayers for many kilometers, the *imam*'s (prayer leader) sermons were hard to sleep through. The sermon would start around 4 a.m., broadcast through an incredibly crackly speaker system, which did not aid my understanding and learning. Indeed, for almost four months I thought the imam was continually talking about calalai until I finally realized how poorly my Bugis language acquisition was going; the imam was not talking about calalai, but rather *calalé* (myself). These daily sermons are just one way in which Islam is fused with daily Bugis life. Adherence to Islam is strong in Bugis South Sulawesi (Pelras 1996); various religious offices and both formal and informal Islamic groups promote ideals of Muslim femininity and masculinity. Marriage is advanced as a moral requirement of all Muslims; after marriage a couple is expected to have children. Indeed it is through children that a couple's duty as Muslims is largely fulfilled.

In respect to femininity, a Muslim woman's role is ideally centered on the home and her family's well-being. In ensuring this, Islam may be used to curtail a woman's movements and control her social conduct. During my fieldwork, it was usually expected that I, along with my host-sisters, come home before *magrib* prayers, which occur just after sunset at around 6 p.m. Prayer times are thus one way in which Islam is used to organize people's lives. In constructing images of Muslim women, Western-derived images may be used for contrast. For instance, depictions of scantily clad women, or women as individualistic and self-centered consumers, are juxtaposed with images of demure, and increasingly veiled, Muslim women (Hatley forthcoming)—indeed, within the last decade there has been reclamation of the veil as a symbol of empowerment (Brenner 1996; Lindquist 2004). In line with the thinking that heterosexual marriage and children are moral requirements of Muslims, Islam is drawn upon by certain individuals to assert that homosexual relations are sinful. For instance, some people in Bugis South Sulawesi told me that calalai are committing a sin because Islam explicitly prohibits same-sex sexual relations.

In respect to masculinity, Muslim men are officially considered to be the heads of households and their family's public representatives. Islam exhorts Muslim men to be the caretakers of women and to be their managers, leaders, and educators. Entrusted with providing for their wives and children, men are economically responsible for their families. Islam requires men to ensure the protection, provision, and development of their family, while fostering a home environment that is cooperative and equitable, rather than combative and competitive. Muslim men are required to pray at the mosque on Fridays; this large gathering of men often serves as a public forum for asserting and affirming notions of masculinity. In numerous ways, then, Islam shapes official ideals of both Bugis masculinity and femininity.[2]

Negotiating Masculine Norms

The above four sections outline official gender ideals as they are presented to individuals living in Bugis South Sulawesi. It is in this environment that calalai negotiate their identities. Individuals, such as Dilah, who are female-born but who do not conform to ideal prescriptions of womanhood, are left without a respected alternative model of being. Many calalai thus seek out the only other sanctioned model, that of masculinity.

For Dilah, being calalai is partly about performing the roles prescribed in notions of ideal masculinity. Dilah affirms that calalai work in many different areas, but primarily in those considered masculine, such as driving taxis, working in small businesses, and working as DJs in nightclubs. When I commented to Dilah that s/he works in a hair salon, a job where many women work, Dilah replied that cutting hair is often men's work, and moreover, it is important how a person approaches their work. Dilah said that s/he wears trousers and a shirt to work, keeps hir hair short, and wears a chunky watch, all signs for hir of masculinity. Dilah also consciously chooses not to learn other aspects of salon work, such as make-up application, that are considered feminine.

Rani's choice in clothing, way of walking, speaking and posturing, all affirm hir masculinity. Furthermore, Rani, who lives in a rural environment, smokes, gambles, and stays out late at night. Such behavior in women is severely frowned upon; as I mentioned earlier, my host-sisters and I were generally expected to be home before *magrib* prayers.

One area in which calalai often replicate masculine norms is in romantic relationships. In popular discourses, promoted through mediums such as magazines, television, and advertising, the only model of a sanctioned relationship is of a feminine-masculine couple. As Murray notes, "If the butch-femme stereotype as presented in the Indonesian popular media is the only image of lesbians available outside the metropolis, then this may affect how women express their feelings" (1999:143). This masculine-feminine archetype works to encourage calalai to present a masculine image to be complemented and reinforced by a feminine partner.

Rani is unofficially married (known in Indonesian as a marriage below the hand—*kawin di bawah tangan*) to a woman called Sia, and the couple has an adopted child. Within this relationship Rani performs the roles of a husband and father, including providing the main familial income, while Sia takes charge of the household and the raising of their child. Rani and Sia have made a pragmatic choice by recognizing both their own desires and the expectations of the society in which they live; delegating tasks along normative lines works well for them. In part because Rani and Sia have structured their partnership to conform to the dominant husband/father-wife/mother model, they find social acceptance that may not have otherwise been forthcoming. While their relationship does not create feelings of siri' for their families, people do comment on their relationship. On numerous occasions I heard visitors being made aware of a fact they may have missed: that Rani is female-bodied. While Rani's femaleness is certainly an issue worthy of comment, within their community I never witnessed or heard of Rani and Sia being harassed or disparaged. Some people sanction Rani's identity, and hir relationship with Sia, by saying that Rani has been given a certain fate, a fate that cannot be changed, and as long as Rani is a good person, s/he should be accepted as a worthy member of the community. In other cases, though, where a calalai and hir partner are not known to the community, where their family is not understanding, or where they challenge boundaries too radically, they can and do bring shame upon their family.

Negotiation of gender norms often results in creative responses. A calalai named Ance' wanted to have a child but s/he was not attracted to men, nor did s/he want to marry a man in a conventional sense. To this end Ance' married Wawal, a transgendered male (*calabai*), recognizing that this was one way in which s/he would be able to legitimately have children and continue hir life as a calalai. At the start of their relationship everything worked well. Wawal's assumption of the role of wife left Ance' free to pursue more masculine tasks. Not long into their marriage, though, Wawal started to get lazy and expected Ance' to be both husband and wife. Ance' was then forced to work all day in the fields as a farmer and then come home and be a mother to their daughter, do all the housework, and meet Wawal's rising living costs. Finally, when Ance' had had enough, s/he left the relationship, but s/he is grateful that s/he has hir daughter.

The marriages of Rani and Sia, and Ance' and Wawal, are instructive in a number of senses. In one respect they demonstrate how performative citations are never just the result of voluntary choices; subject positions are formed within particular discursive frameworks that simultaneously encourage and restrict identity formations (Butler 1993; Kondo 1997:7). Rani and Ance' defied norms expected of their female bodies, but conformed to heteronormative structures in their romantic relationships. This outward relationship structure can also flow over into sexual encounters, as Saskia Wieringa found while living in Jakarta. Wieringa noted that if she wanted to go out with femme women, she had to learn to be butch—and indeed the butches instructed her on how to be butch—while the femmes clearly expressed what they expected from her in terms of chivalry and lovemaking (1999:208).

In a sense, Ance' and Wawal, and Rani and Sia, performed the respective roles of ideal husband and wife. There is, then, value in using the idea of performativity to discuss calalai subjectivity. Performativity allows examination of dominant ideologies and the ways individuals emulate, modify, and resist these in daily life. Interwoven into such discourses are dramaturgical ideas of embodying a particular role. Redeploying the work of Austin (1955), Butler (1990, 1993) writes of the process of subject formation in terms of performativity, in which the enacting of identities in fact brings those identities into being, rather than expressing some predetermined essence. An initial reading of performativity theory in relation to calalai emulating normative Bugis masculinity might suggest that calalai gender is voluntaristic, optional, and imitative. However, Butler's insistence on the performative status of all gender allows a reconceptualization of calalai masculinity to see ways in which gender is more than mere recitation. Rani, for instance, is married to a woman and is in many ways like a man, yet s/he is not conceptualized as a man because s/he enacts a version of calalai masculinity, as we will see in the next section.

The relationships of Rani and Sia, and Ance' and Wawal, also show actions of agency, although not necessarily of resistance. While both relationships appear quite mimetic of heteronormativity, making it easy to dismiss any active negotiation, Parker's (2005) analysis of agency enables an appreciation of the ways in which calalai employ active subject negotiation. Parker (2005:65) suggests that agency is a useful term to refer to a capacity for pragmatism, for meaning- and identity-making, that is not necessarily radical or revolutionary in intent. Thus, agency can be seen as something that is deployed toward ends that may be self-serving and pragmatic, while resistance should be reserved for more direct challenges to power structures. Using this interpretation of agency allows an appreciation of the complexity of the context in which calalai subjectivity is given identity and meaning and the ways calalai negotiate particular structures. Calalai are not necessarily directly challenging social structures but moving within them, as for instance when Ance' married Wawal in a move that allowed hir to legitimately have children but continue to engage in masculine activities.

Calalai Masculinities

On one occasion I became involved in a conversation with Mina, the ex-girlfriend of a calalai named Maman. For most of our discussion, Mina and I sat on the balcony of Maman's house flanked by a number of children who sat playing games or ran up and down the stairs. After general small talk I ventured to ask Mina what it was like having a calalai partner. Although we had already discussed Mina and Maman's past romantic relationship, I was a bit wary of asking this question because there were a lot of people around, including Maman's father, and I was not sure how Mina would respond to such a personal, and potentially unapproved, topic. However, Mina immediately responded that having a calalai partner was great (*hebat*, Indo.). Mina then related one example of how Maman was able to go out at night on hir own to buy medicine, when Mina's father or brothers were not at home. While a boyfriend could have legitimately performed this task, Maman, unlike a boyfriend, was able to bring the acquired product into the house even if Mina's father was not at home. If a boyfriend had entered Mina's house when her father was not home, a siri' situation may have arisen. Indeed, the theme of calalai being relatively unrestrained in their relationships was also revealed by Dilah who told me that calalai are much freer (*lebih bebas*, Indo.) in their relationships with women than are men. If Dilah has a girlfriend, s/he said the two of them can go anywhere together and it is acceptable. Dilah smugly noted though that if s/he were a man, s/he would have to marry the woman before they were granted the freedom of movement s/he currently enjoys with women.

Mina and Maman were together for quite a few years but Mina's parents continually applied pressure on Mina to marry a man and have children. Finally, against Mina's protestation, her parents orchestrated her marriage. Upon hearing the news that Mina was engaged (*dijodohkan*, Indo.), Maman raced to her house, positioned hirself in front, and yelled for Mina to cancel the wedding and come back to hir. Mina told me that a man would never have acted like this because it was not appropriate behavior. Bugis men, Mina said, are expected to be rational, disciplined, and in control of their emotions. Of course Bugis men do act in inappropriate and emotional ways, but according to Mina, Maman was able to get away with these actions and not cause hir family to feel siri' because s/he is calalai. Another interpretation of this event might be that Maman was female-bodied and was therefore not considered able to control hir emotions as well as a male could. Because of the position Maman occupies hir behavior does not necessarily bring shame upon hir family as it would were s/he a man or a woman.

As noted above, calalai are often able to move freely in public places. When I attended weddings with Rani, I was struck by the freedom with which Rani was able to move about in different settings. Sometimes Rani would be in the kitchen with the women helping cook food and then s/he would wander out to the front of the house and sit chatting, smoking, and drinking coffee with the men. While there is no strict segregation of the sexes in Bugis society, it is rare for a lone woman—especially a woman smoking—to sit in the company of a group of unrelated men, or for a man to help with baking cakes for a wedding feast. That Rani moves with comparative ease between these two settings suggests that the expectations of social movement are more flexible with respect to calalai.

It is not just a matter of calalai choosing what roles they want to perform or how they want to present themselves. There are a number of prescriptions calalai are expected to adhere to. Dilah revealed that calalai should be identifiable by their style (*gaya*, Indo.). For instance, calalai should have short hair, never wear pretty or girlish clothing, and should not wear any makeup. Ance' also talked about the importance of calalai dressing in particular ways. For Ance, men's clothes provide freedom of movement, unlike women's clothes. For example, the way that a man's sarong is tied (rolled down) makes it far less likely to come undone, nor does it need continual resecuring as do women's sarongs that are tucked in. However, calalai do not necessarily aim to appear exactly as men; in many cases there are subtleties in their dress and accoutrements that suggest calalai identity. Dilah, for instance, wears just one earring to assert hir calalai identity.

In appreciating calalai negotiations of normative gender ideals, the potential of performativity theory becomes apparent. There is danger in suggesting that calalai subjectivity is merely mimetic of heteronormativity and heterosexuality. In this context, the language of play and performance may become dangerous, attracting further rejection and derision of alternative identities. However, in her work on butch-femme subject positions in England, Alison Eves (2004) draws on the work of both Bourdieu (1990, 1992) and Butler (1990) to show ways in which butch and femme resist and destabilize heteronormativity, even when their actions may be read as imitative. Eves suggests a method of theorizing gender as performative without suggesting that it is preferential, discretionary, willful, or role-playing. While it is hard for butch individuals to create a unique gender style, or at least one that is read as independent of normative masculinity, a deeper understanding of butch subjectivity reveals distinctive repertoires. Thus, Eves calls for more attention to be paid to the structural and to everyday social practices in relation to gender engagements. Similarly, even though calalai romantic relationships and subjectivity may resemble heterosexuality and heteronormativity, the performative nature of gender means that their subjectivities are unique, subversive, and resistant.

Conclusion

This chapter examined the subject positions of female-born individuals in Bugis South Sulawesi who, for a variety of complex reasons, do not identify as women or men but rather as calalai, or another cognate term. A key determinant of gender is the cultural setting where negotiations take place. In South Sulawesi, notions of ideal masculinity are clearly evident in quests for social location. Struggles for status form a key organizational principle in Bugis society. In order to assert and affirm their social location, men should exemplify ideal forms of Bugis masculinity. Through an analysis of social location, what it ideally means to be a Bugis man becomes clear: men embody self-discipline, reason, authority, physical strength, aggression, and bravery.

Bugis femininity is articulated in the principles attached to the honor/shame complex called siri'. A Bugis woman is conceived of as being the primary symbol of her family's siri' (honor) and she is therefore under pressure to ensure she does not cause siri' (shame). In order to avoid this consequence, women should embrace models of ideal Bugis femininity: women should be modest in dress and behavior; they should not travel alone at night or entertain men unaccompanied; and they should marry heterosexually and bear children.

Government and Islamic discourses reinforce and combine with local ideals of masculinity and femininity. As a result, being Muslims and members of the Indonesian nation-state, calalai are presented with images of women as wives and mothers, roles they should embody to be considered full adult citizens. Similarly, strict models of masculinity are presented. Men are expected to be the primary breadwinners, providing financial support for their wives and children, and protecting the purity and morality of their families.

To an extent calalai emulate ideal forms of masculinity. As Blackwood (1998) similarly found in the case of tomboi in West Sumatra, the dominance and pervasiveness of these models convince some female-bodied individuals of their masculinity. However, while calalai present a model of masculinity, calalai tend not to be considered, or to consider themselves, men. One reason why calalai are not considered men is the particular Bugis understanding of how an individual comes to be gendered. For many Bugis because the body can never be forgotten in matters concerning gender, a female can never be conceived of as a man. A similarly important reason why calalai may not be considered men is that they rework dominant masculine discourses. For instance, the partners of calalai are often viewed as sexually assertive and demanding, reversing prevailing norms that suggest masculinity necessitates sexual dominance. In many ways, then, calalai assert particular gendered repertoires within a structured environment.

I have focused here on localized engagements because, as Blackwood notes, "Research on transnational sexualities cannot overlook the importance of particularities of localities" (Blackwood 2005:238). Locality remains an important site for examination and it can complement projects that examine larger issues of similitude at national levels (for example, Boellstorff 2005). Localized examinations show that calalai are not necessarily marginalized because they are often outside of direct transnational flows. Such explorations also reveal ways that localized notions of gender and sexuality may be taken to larger metropoles.

This chapter incorporates notions of performativity and agency to capture the complexity of issues involved in calalai negotiations of gendered subjectivities. There is no single calalai identity; each individual juggles, interprets, and reworks dominant discourses and personal desires in their daily embodied lives. Calalai take on aspects of ideal masculinity but rework these and play with them. Their gendered performances, however, are not simply a matter of picking and choosing which rules they want to observe because there are expectations placed on calalai. At some points, calalai are obliged to enact masculinity and discard feminine behaviors. At other times, though, calalai take on feminine performances or take advantage of their interstitial position, moving between masculine and feminine spaces. Calalai are tolerated and accepted in some situations, although at other times they face severe restrictions and discrimination. Throughout these various experiences of female masculinities, underlying calalai notions of self is, in Dilah's words, a desire to go out and actively hunt down what you want.

Notes

This chapter resulted from a panel on female same-sex relations organized by Saskia Wieringa and Evelyn Blackwood for the Third International Association for the Study of Sexuality, Culture and Society conference held in Melbourne, October 1–3, 2001. I would like to thank the following people who have helped me develop the ideas contained in this chapter: Evie Blackwood, to whom I am most indebted for providing many insightful and constructive comments and for her continuing support; Tom Boellstorff, Saskia Wieringa, Lyn Parker, Greg Acciaioli, Mandy Wilson, Romit Dasgupta, and Tom Graham Davies. The ethnographic material contained in this chapter is the result of 20 months of field work carried out in Indonesia between 1998 and 2005, and I thank my friends and informants there for welcoming me into their lives. I also want to acknowledge the financial support I received from the University of Western Australia, the Australian National University, Hasanuddin University, Leiden University, the KITLV, a Huygens Nuffic grant, a Wyn Hoadley Chancellor's grant, the Asia: NZ Foundation, and the Auckland University of Technology. Research in Indonesia was conducted under the auspice of the Indonesian Institute of Science (LIPI). Some ethnographic data has previously been published (Graham 2001, Davies 2007) or is forthcoming (Davies forthcoming), and I thank the editors for granting permission for me to build on this material here.

1. Following Blackwood (1998), I use "hir" and "s/he" to encourage readers to think of subject positions distinct from the binaries of his/her, he/she and to show the prospect of subjectivity outside of normative gender dichotomies. An additional motivation to use "hir" and "s/he" is that neither the Bugis nor Indonesian languages differentiate between masculine and feminine pronouns, rather they respectively employ the nongendered pronouns *i/na* and *dia*. All conversations recounted were conducted in Bahasa Indonesia, with some segments in Bugis. Indonesian words are initially identified with (Indo.) and Bugis words with (Bug.). All names used are pseudonyms.
2. For more information on Islam see also Abdullah and Siddique 1986; Istiadah 1995; Brenner 1996; Hooker 2003; Idrus 2003; Bennett 2004; Eliraz 2004.

References Cited

Abdullah, Taufik and Sharon Siddique, eds. 1986. *Islam and society in Southeast Asia*. Singapore: Singapore Institute for Southeast Asian Studies.

Austin, J.L. 1955. *How to do things with words*. Cambridge: Harvard University Press.

Bennett, Linda R. 2004. *Women, Islam and modernity: Single women, sexuality and reproductive health in contemporary Indonesia*. London: RoutledgeCurzon.

Blackwood, Evelyn. 1995. Senior women, model mothers, and dutiful wives: Managing gender contradictions in a Minangkabau village. In *Bewitching women, pious men: Gender and body politics in Southeast Asia*. Aihwa Ong and Michael Peletz, eds. Pp. 124–158. Berkeley: University of California Press.

———. 1998. Tombois in West Sumatra: Constructing masculinity and erotic desire. *Cultural Anthropology* 13(4): 491–521.

———. 2005. Transnational sexualities in one place: Indonesian readings. *Gender & Society* 19 (2): 221–242.

Boellstorff, Tom. 1999. The perfect path: Gay men, marriage, Indonesia. *GLQ: A Journal of Lesbian and Gay Studies* 5(4): 475–510.

———. 2001. HIV, sexuality, and gender in the Pacific and Asia: Observations from the Sixth International Congress on AIDS in Asia and the Pacific. Paper presented at the Sixth International Congress on AIDS in Asia and the Pacific, Melbourne, Australia.

———. 2002. Ethnolocality. *The Asia Pacific Journal of Anthropology* 3(1): 24–48.

———. 2005. *The gay archipelago: Sexuality and nation in Indonesia*. Princeton: Princeton University Press.

Bourdieu, Pierre. 1990. *The logic of practice*. Cambridge: Polity Press.

———. 1992. *An invitation to reflexive sociology*. Cambridge: Polity Press.

Brenner, Suzanne. 1996. Reconstructing self and society: Javanese Muslim women and the veil. *American Ethnologist* 23(4): 673–697.

Butler, Judith. 1990. *Gender trouble: Feminism and the subversion of identity.* New York: Routledge.

———. 1993. *Bodies that matter: On the discursive limits of "sex."* New York: Routledge.

Collins, Elizabeth and E. Bahar. 2000. To know shame: Malu and its uses in Malay societies. *Crossroads: An Interdisciplinary Journal of Southeast Asian Studies* 14(1): 35–69.

Davies, Sharyn Graham. 2006. Gender and status in Bugis society. In *Understanding Indonesia.* S. Epstein, ed. Pp. 93–106. Wellington: Victoria University of Wellington Press.

———. 2007. *Challenging gender norms: Five genders among Bugis in Indonesia.* Case studies in Cultural Anthropology Series. Boston: Wadsworth/Thompson.

———. Forthcoming. *Gender diversity in Indonesia: Beyond gender binaries.* London: RoutledgeCurzon.

Eliraz, Giora. 2004. *Islam in Indonesia: Modernism, radicalism, and the Middle East dimension.* Brighton: Sussex Academic Press.

Eves, Alison. 2004. Queer theory, butch/femme identities and lesbian space. *Sexualities* 7(4): 480–496.

Geertz, Clifford. 2006. Comments on Transgenderism and gender pluralism in Southeast Asia since early modern times. *Current Anthropology* 47(2): 327–328.

Graham, Sharyn. 2001. Negotiating gender: Calalai' in Bugis society. *Intersections: Gender, History, and Culture in the Asian Context* http://wwwsshe.murdoch.edu.au/intersections/issue6/graham.html (accessed August 6, 2006).

———. 2004. It's like one of those puzzles: Conceptualising gender among Bugis. *Journal of Gender Studies* 13 (2): 107–116.

Hatley, Barbara. Forthcoming. Women, gender and popular culture in Indonesia. In *Encyclopaedia of women in Islamic cultures.* S. Joseph, ed. Leiden: Brill Publishers.

Hooker, M.B. 2003. *Indonesian Islam: Social change through contemporary Fatawa.* St. Leonards: Allen & Unwin.

Idrus, Nurul Ilmi. 2003. *"To take each other": Bugis practices of gender, sexuality and marriage.* Ph.D. Dissertation, Department of Anthropology, Australian National University, Canberra.

———. 2004. Behind the notion of *siala*: Marriage, adat and Islam among the Bugis in South Sulawesi. *Intersections: Gender, History and Culture in the Asian Context* http://wwwsshe.murdoch.edu.au/intersections/issue10/idrus.html (accessed August 10, 2006).

Istiadah. 1995. *Muslim women in contemporary Indonesia: Investigating paths to resist the patriarchal system*, Working Paper No 91. Clayton: Monash University Centre of Southeast Asian Studies.

Kondo, Dorinne. 1997. *About face: Performing race in fashion and theater.* New York: Routledge.

Lindquist, Johan. 2004. Veils and ecstasy: Negotiating shame in the Indonesian borderlands. *Ethnos: Journal of Anthropology* 69 (4): 487–508.

Matthes, B.F. 1885. *Makassaarsch-Hollandsch woordenboek* [Makassarese-Dutch dictionary]. 1st ed. Gravenhage: Martinus Nijhoff.

Millar, Susan. 1983. On interpreting gender in Bugis society. *American Ethnologist* 10: 477–493.

———. 1989. *Bugis weddings: Rituals of social location in modern Indonesia.* Berkeley: University of California Press.

Murray, Alison J. 1999. Let them take ecstasy: Class and Jakarta lesbians. In *Female desires: Same-sex relations and transgender practices across cultures.* Evelyn Blackwood and Saskia E. Wieringa, eds. Pp. 139–156. New York: Columbia University Press.

Parker, Lyn. 1992. The creation of Indonesian citizens in Balinese primary schools. *Review of Indonesian and Malaysian Affairs* 26: 42–70.

———. 2002. The subjectification of citizenship: Student interpretations of school teachings in Bali. *Asian Studies Review* 26 (1): 3–38.

———. 2005. Resisting resistance and finding agency: Women and medicalized birth in Bali. In *The agency of women in Asia.* Lyn Parker, ed. Pp. 62–97. Singapore: Marshall Cavendish.

Pelras, Christian. 1996. *The Bugis.* Oxford: Blackwell Publishers.

Sullivan, Norma. 1994. *Masters and managers: A study of gender relations in urban Java.* St Leonards: Allen and Unwin.

Suryakusuma, Julia. 1996. The state and sexuality in New Order Indonesia. In *Fantasizing the feminine in Indonesia.* Laurie J. Sears, ed. Pp. 92–119. Durham: Duke University Press.

Wieringa, Saskia E. 1999. Desiring bodies or defiant cultures: Butch-femme lesbians in Jakarta and Lima. In *Female desires: Same-sex relations and transgender practices across cultures.* Evelyn Blackwood and Saskia E. Wieringa, eds. Pp. 206–231. New York: Columbia University Press.

Chapter Nine

Lesbian Masculinities: Identity and Body Construction among Tomboys in Hong Kong

Franco Lai

Introduction

TB/TBG role-play is common among lesbian couples in Hong Kong. Lesbians in Hong Kong adopted the term "TB," which is an abbreviation for "tomboy," to signify masculine lesbians. Conventionally, "TB" is the one who plays a masculine role and "TBG," which is an abbreviation for "tomboy's girl," plays a feminine role. A "tomboy's girl" means a tomboy's girlfriend.

TBs in Hong Kong face a paradoxical situation: they are both socially tolerated and socially undesirable. On the one hand, TBs can have a masculine appearance, such as having a short haircut and wearing men's clothes in everyday life; on the other hand, they are perceived as deviant because conventional gender norms do not expect females to be masculine. Many TBs report that they encounter unpleasant experiences, such as being shouted at in women's toilets and being teased by classmates or colleagues. Despite these experiences, TBs persist in displaying masculinities on their bodies. Due to the paradoxical situation that TBs are both socially tolerated and socially undesirable, I argue that TBs' masculinities are not simply their personal choices but products of negotiation between TBs, the lesbian community, and Hong Kong society.

In this chapter, I examine the negotiation process between these three groups. I select the workplace as one of the domains of investigation to illustrate TBs' masculinities because employees are expected to conform to conventional gender norms at the workplace. I argue that in their workplace negotiation, TBs do not conform to the mainstream gender norms that emphasize that women have to be feminine and only men can perform masculinities. Through the persistent display of masculinities, TBs attempt to normalize and naturalize their TB identity as well as their masculinities. In the negotiation process between TBs and Hong Kong society, the lesbian community plays an important part because it works as a form of empowerment for TBs. In their negotiation with the lesbian community I argue that TBs do not conform to all the values and norms of the lesbian community. TBs see the lesbian community as too restrictive because of the prevalence of norms and rules that limit TBs' performance. Instead of following the dress code and behaving exactly like a TB, TBs adjust their role and develop fluid role-playing with their girlfriends.

In this chapter, I first provide a review of relevant theories useful for this analysis. Then I explain the cultural context of Hong Kong as well as examine the lesbian community. Analyzing the relevant contexts provides a framework to understand why lesbians demonstrate certain kinds of behaviors, such as the persistent display of masculinities in the workplace, as well as why the negotiation processes take place.

Negotiating and Enacting Identities

Giddens's theory of structuration (1986) argues that both social structure and human agency constitute social life. Though the social structure exerts social forces on individuals, the behaviors of individuals are not dictated solely by the social structure. Human agents have the capacity to understand the contexts in which they move; they can deploy power to "act otherwise" and intervene in the social structure (Giddens 1986:14). Giddens's theory reveals that behaviors demonstrated by human agents are not solely individual choices but products of negotiation between social structure and human agency.

Hong Kong society expects men to be masculine and women to be feminine. Under this binary gender system, TBs, being human agents, "act otherwise" (Giddens 1986:14) and dress in a masculine way. Similarly, the lesbian community divides lesbians into either TB or TBG; TBs are expected to be masculine and TBGs feminine. Under this social structure, TBs, being human agents, act otherwise and practice fluid sexual relationships with their TBG lovers. Gidden's theory of structuration is applied to analyze the negotiation between TBs and the larger society and also the negotiation between TBs and the lesbian community.

Butler (1999) argues that gender identity is constituted through regulatory practices, while gender reality is created through sustained social performances. When a collective of biological females, who dress up like men and are attracted to women, begin to call each other "TB," the TB identity is constituted through these regulatory practices, which Butler (1999) argues, enable the coherent linkage between sex (that is, biological female), gender (that is, social male), sexual practice (that is, same-sex relationship), and desire (that is, passion for women) to be formed.

According to Butler (1999), individuals reinforce and naturalize gender reality by repeating the regulatory performances. Similarly, as I argue, TBs normalize and naturalize their identity, their sexual orientation, and their behaviors by repeating the regulatory performances. Although TBs are a minority group in Hong Kong, they negotiate with Hong Kong society by making an extra effort to normalize and naturalize their sexual orientation and behaviors. In Butler's view, TBs' persistent presentation of masculinities can be interpreted as a kind of strategy to achieve normalization and naturalization.

Goffman's (1959) discussion of impression management interprets the everyday interactions between individuals as performances carried out by individual performers. According to Goffman, the several selves owned by one individual may contradict one another. These contradictory qualities will give rise to role conflict and negatively affect an individual's presentation of himself or herself as a credible person to his or her audience. Goffman (1997) points out that individuals avoid role conflict by practicing role segregation that is facilitated by audience segregation.

I use Goffman to analyze TBs' interactions in the workplace, where they may be required to present a feminine image. Hong Kong society believes masculinity and femininity should be on opposite ends of the same axis. The required feminine appearance contradicts TBs' masculine identity. In order to solve the role conflict and to maintain masculine identity, TBs practice impression management, that is, role segregation and audience segregation, to maintain a persistent masculine image.

What is a "TB"?

According to the Oxford English Dictionary (Oxford University Press 1989), "TB" means tuberculosis. In Hong Kong, many people over 40 with good English understand that "TB" refers to tuberculosis; however, this understanding is uncommon among the younger generation. From the 1960s onward, girls from girls' schools extracted "TB" from the term "tomboy," which means "a girl who behaves like a spirited boy; a wild romping girl" (Oxford English Dictionary 1989), and used it to represent girls who were masculine and fell for girls. Nowadays, lesbians in Hong Kong use the term TB to represent masculine lesbians generally.

TB identity emerged as a process of collective self-naming in girls' schools. Female masculinity is tolerated more in girls' schools than in coeducational schools, where masculine duties (for example, carrying heavy things) and sports (for example, playing basketball) are usually performed by male students. In a girls' school, both masculine duties and sports are left to stronger and taller girls. In these schools, members of a basketball team were often popular students and had many fans crazy for them (Chou 2000:217–218; Kam 2002:19).

Apart from female masculinity, intimacy between girls is also tolerated in girls' schools. "[S]o far as there is no explicit sexual behavior, [it] can be seen as natural and normal" (Chou 2000:217). In a context where female masculinity and intimacy between girls were highly tolerated, girls with masculine appearance who had crushes on other girls became more and more popular. When more and more masculine girls became visible in girls' schools, the masculine girls became distinctive and began to name themselves "TB."[1] The term "TB" was gradually adopted by the lesbian community in Hong Kong to represent masculine lesbians.

Meanings of "Female Masculinities" in Hong Kong

According to Beynon (2002), masculinity is culturally defined and composed of social codes of behavior that men learn to reproduce in culturally appropriate ways. Though women are capable of presenting masculine behaviors, they are discouraged from doing so. Halberstam (1998) argues that this kind of discouragement is the manifestation of hegemonic male masculinity. To a certain extent, TBs' bodies are perceived as deviant under hegemonic masculinity; however, Hong Kong society positively evaluates females with masculine attributes. The conventional view of men's superiority interprets masculinity as superior to femininity; as a result, females with masculine attributes are perceived positively as strong, active, and easygoing. Girls are allowed to dress like boys and play "boys' " games, such as riding bikes and playing sports before adulthood. Many parents believe that their daughters' manifestations of early masculinity are signs of strong and healthy bodies. Some of my informants reported that they were allowed to dress like boys and play boys' games when they were small. Ah-man[2] (age 45) said that she began to wear cowboy clothes and play with toy guns when she was only six years old. Ah-fong (age 30) stated that she was like a boy and liked climbing trees and playing with model cars and planes since the age of nine.

After entering adulthood, however, girls must give up these masculine attributes because adult women are expected to be feminine, gentle, and ready to marry. A masculine body is an obstacle to finding a husband, who supposedly looks for a feminine woman to be his wife. If a daughter still dresses like a boy when she is close to adulthood, her parents begin to intervene. Kit-man was 16 at the time of the interview and she still dressed like a boy. Her mother and grandmother were always trying to persuade her to dress up in a more feminine way. Though female masculinity is accepted to a certain extent in Hong Kong because masculinity is associated with positive attributes, TBs' masculine bodies are undesirable under conventional gender norms, especially for adult TBs.

The lesbian Community in Hong Kong

Possessing an institutional base is the decisive feature of a lesbian community (Lockard 1986:94). A community provides continuity; even if one organization fails, there are others to replace it. Moreover, since the lesbian community is open to all, it is easy for new members to locate it (Lockard 1986:88–89). I argue that the lesbian community did not form in Hong Kong until the 1990s. Though lesbians had common places to meet in the 1970s and 1980s, those places lacked continuity and constituted "lesbian circles" only.

Lesbian Circles in the 1970s and 1980s

Ah-lik (age 45) said that private gatherings were held among middle-class lesbians in the late 1970s and continued through the 1980s. According to Ah-lik:

> One of my sister's friends looked like a TB. I asked this friend whether she was a TB, and we two disclosed our TB identity to each other immediately. This TB friend then took me to the private lesbian gatherings called *fit wuih*. *Fit wuih* was held at one of the members' homes, and there would be around 20 people. Six out of ten participants were TBs and the remaining were TBs' wives or girlfriends.

I asked, "What do you mean by *fit wuih*"? Ah-lik explained: "Literally, *fi* means matching or cruising; *wuih* means gathering. *Fit wuih* means the gathering for matching and cruising." However, the friends who met in these gathering were limited to a circle of friends because *fit wuih* was privately held.

Identity Change from Tomboy to TB

Before the 1990s, both the terms "tomboy" and "TB" were used to refer to masculine lesbians. Wai-ki (age 39) told me that the students from the girls' secondary school that she attended adopted the term tomboy in the 1970s. Ah-lik (age 50) and Ah-man (age 45) said that the term "TB" was already prevalent in their girls' schools in the late 1960s. However, from the 1990s onwards, only the term "TB" was used. Through investigating the process of identity change from "tomboy" to "TB," we can understand the changes in the cultural context of Hong Kong from the 1970s to the 1990s.

The concept of "homosexuality" was imported from the West to Hong Kong in the 1970s when the media reported illegal homosexual acts, that is, buggery, conducted by several male senior civil servants (Chou and Chiu 1995:146). Homosexuality, referring to buggery between men, was a crime before it was decriminalized in 1991. Ah-lik believed that homosexuality was perceived as a kind of abnormality then. She said, "When I was around ten I could read the newspaper myself. I learned from the newspaper that homosexuality meant buggery between men. Our society viewed homosexuality as a kind of abnormality, a social disorder."

The discrimination against homosexuals was severe in the 1970s. Ah-man, Ah-hing and Ah-lik said that many heterosexual people used the term "*nàahm yàhn pòh*" to describe masculine lesbians; they felt very bad about this term.[3] Literally, *nàahm yàhn* means a male adult, and *pòh* means an old woman. Culturally, *pòh* is often negatively used to describe a rough woman, for example, *baat pòh* means a bitch; *gàai síh pòh* means a rough female vendor in the market. Compared with "homosexual" and "*nàahm yàhn pòh*," 'tomboy' and "TB" are more acceptable names for masculine lesbians to call each other. Ah-man said, "Outsiders called us *nàahm yàhn pòh*, but we never used it to call ourselves. In my girls' school, we called each other 'TB.' " Ah-lik explained the advantage of using the term "TB." She said, " 'TB' is a short form so outsiders can't understand what it is when my friends and I talk about it publicly. Although 'tomboy' does not refer to lesbian directly, the 'boy' can make people guess it easily. 'TB' can avoid this kind of association."

The terms "tomboy" and "TB" helped to avoid the association with homosexuality, especially the term "TB," which was composed of two letters only. Moreover, "tomboy" is a Western term, so it sounds superior and fashionable. To a certain extent, tomboys thought that this Western term could enhance their status through resisting the negative naming of *nàahm yàhn pòh*.

As discussed before, different lesbian circles adjusted to the term tomboy differently. For example "tom-boy" was used in Wai-ki's school and "TB" was used in Ah-man's and Ah-lik's schools. The diverse naming of "tomboy" and "TB" reflects the lack of one single lesbian community in the 1970s and the 1980s. Lesbians from different circles did not have communication with one another. Due to the absence of a lesbian community in the 1970s and 1980s, lesbians had no place to gather and hence were limited to their own circles.

In the 1980s, discussion of the decriminalization of homosexuality started in Hong Kong. The death of John MacLennan in 1980 was the major incident that pushed the Hong Kong government to change the laws on homosexuality. MacLennan, a police inspector, was charged with engaging in illegal homosexual acts in 1978; he was alleged to have committed suicide before being arrested. His death caused a huge controversy, as some parties believed that MacLennan was murdered but the police insisted that he committed suicide in order to escape from being caught.[4] The court declared that MacLennan died from an "unknown reason" and recommended that the Hong Kong government change the laws on homosexuality (Chou and Chiu 1995:161). In 1980, the Attorney General and the Chief Justice asked the Law Reform Commission to consider changing the laws on homosexuality (Consultation Paper 1988:3). A consultation paper was released in June 1988; in July 1991, homosexuality was decriminalized and homosexual act committed in private by consenting men over the age of 21 was not a crime any more (Chou and Chiu 1995).

Although the issue of decriminalization focused only on homosexual acts between men, it implicitly influenced the identity change of tomboys. Soon after the decriminalization of homosexuality, nine major gay and lesbian groups were formed in the early 1990s (Chou and Chiu 1995:180–184). As more and more lesbians came out and joined those groups, they became more visible so that a lesbian community was gradually created. I argue that the reason why "TB" has become the only term that refers to masculine lesbians from the 1990s onwards was due to the formation of the lesbian community.

The Ten Per Cent Club, one of the major gay and lesbian groups in Hong Kong, recruited both gays and lesbians as their members; a subgroup that served lesbians solely was formed in 1991, but was dissolved in 1993. In 1994, there was an open and informal gathering for lesbians, called "XX Síu Jeuih" (*síu jeuih* means gathering) (Chou and Chiu 1995:193). King, the founder, shared her reason for organizing XX Síu Jeuih. She said, "I had participated in the sub-group for lesbians under the Ten Per Cent Club; however those gay men were never concerned about women. As a result, I quit in 1993. In 1994, some friends asked me to form a lesbian group together, and this was XX Síu Jeuih." The first lesbian pub was Smart S, which was opened around 1994 but closed down around 1998. Ah-man had been to Smart S once. She said, "Smart S mainly served lesbians, but it welcomed gay men as well."

The lesbian community took shape in the early 1990s with the establishment of lesbian groups under the Ten Per Cent Club, XX Síu Jeuih, and Smart S. The formation of the lesbian community helped to standardize the term "TB." Interestingly, because the lesbian community welcomed lesbians from all walks of life, and some lesbians were not good in English, the term "TB" was chosen to refer to masculine lesbians. Wai-ki said, "The term 'TB' was much more user-friendly to those lesbians who were not good in English. As you know, the lesbian community has lesbians coming from all walks of life. TB seems to be a more convenient term." This situation is very different from the *fit wuih* described by Ah-lik above, which only involved middle-class lesbians. TB is easier to pronounce, so more people in the lesbian community adopted this term. Moreover, as lesbians from different circles joined the lesbian community, this helped to spread the use of TB. As a result, TB became a common and standard term from the 1990s onwards.

Lesbian Community in the 1990s

In Hong Kong, lesbian pubs, lesbian service groups and lesbian websites provide a setting for lesbians to interact. TBs seldom restrict themselves to one lesbian community only. They sometimes go to pubs, sometimes join lesbian service groups, and sometimes browse lesbian websites. Each section of the lesbian community possesses its own features. As I discuss in the section that follows, lesbian pubs are a highly performative context where TBs usually drink beer and sing pop songs made famous by men singers. A typical masculine TB image is clearly displayed in the context of lesbian pubs. In contrast, in the warm and cozy context of lesbian service groups, TBs can share common experiences and difficulties. In lesbian websites, where people are invisible, a sexual identity (that is, TB or TBG) is like a pass—disclosing sexual identity is almost a must at the very beginning of a chat as well as in the friend-seeking columns.

Lesbian Pubs

There were four main lesbian pubs in Hong Kong, all of which were located in commercial buildings and coexisted with heterosexual nightclubs and gay pubs in the same building. These commercial buildings were small in size, so each pub could rent the whole floor for business. Upon stepping out of the lift, a person was already at the entrance of the pub. A board on which was written "members only" hung next to the entrance; its function was to screen out nonlesbian customers. In fact, official membership did not exist.

Lesbians usually went to lesbian pubs in groups, rarely alone. First, the setting of the pub discouraged single customers. There were no small tables. A single customer was usually asked to sit at the bar unless there were many empty tables. Second, customers were expected to participate in group activities, such as chatting and playing pub games. Single customers might feel strange to be alone while all others were in groups.

Ying-wai (age 32) shared her first experience of going to a lesbian pub in 1998:

> I knew a lesbian party was going to be held at a lesbian pub. I did not know any lesbian friends before, so I was desperate to join this party even though I had never been to a lesbian pub. In the pub, there were many people but most of them were in groups. It seemed that they had known each other for a long time. I didn't know anyone, so I just found a less crowded table and sat down. I was shy to chat with strangers, and I didn't know what I should do. I forget how long I sat at the table. Then a couple sitting at the same table began to talk with me. They said that I looked so bored sitting alone. They introduced themselves and asked me to introduce myself as well. After the party, we kept in contact, and we're still friends now.

The experience of Ying-wai revealed how easy it was to make friends at lesbian pubs. At a lesbian pub, people may approach you or you can approach other people. Customers felt it was easier to make new friends at the lesbian pubs. Why is that so? First, the setting pushes a single customer to make new friends because she is forced to sit with other customers. Second, a pull factor operates based on their shared lesbian identity. Once inside the pub, lesbians easily develop a trust in each other. Customers feel they are "members" and find it easy to talk and interact with strangers. They are rarely suspicious of the intentions of strangers at lesbian pubs. Friendship is quite easy to build up at the lesbian pubs based on this common "membership" and shared sexual identity.

Appearance and Manners

Customers in lesbian pubs were mainly young women. Singing karaoke was a popular pastime because every customer could see who was singing in the small pub. TBs, who outnumbered TBGs, usually sang men's pop songs. The collective preference that TBs should sing men's songs only gradually became a norm. Siu-kwan (age 32) said that singing karaoke in the lesbian pub helped her find dates: "Singing karaoke performs a function. When I see a girl I like, I will sing a male pop song to attract her."

At the pubs, people felt relaxed because of the alcohol and the dim environment. Moreover, the pubs were very crowded on Saturday night. Under the relaxed and crowded environment, people tended to have more bodily contact, such as putting a hand on a friend's shoulder, or shoulders touching shoulders while sitting down. This kind of bodily contact seemed to be unintentional; in fact, it was usually initiated by TBs. Kai-ming (age 25), a TBG, said that two TBs had touched her intentionally at a lesbian pub.

> I have gone to the lesbian pubs several times only. I still remember that two TBs touched my waist and my shoulders casually at the pub last Saturday. One of them was my friend and her girlfriend was present that night. She did not care about her girlfriend but hugged my waist. One of them was a new friend whom I had known for only two hours. My friends and I had formed a circle to play pub games. This TB approached us and stayed behind my back, and said that she also wanted to play with us. Then she took her right hand from my back to join the games and she put her left hand on my shoulder. Her face was just next to my face! I think her posture and my friend's hug were unnecessary. In this kind of situation, I do not push them away at once but move their hands away slowly. Of course I will speak out if they are being too offensive.

TBs are expected to play a masculine gender role, which is supposed to be active and aggressive. As a result, they display their active and aggressive attributes especially in front of the supposedly passive TBGs. As Kai-ming said, some bodily contact was unnecessary and could be avoided. However, TBs sometimes touched TBGs' shoulders or waist casually. Kai-ming said that she tolerated this kind of bodily contact to a certain extent because she could foresee that other people (most likely other TBs) might criticize her for being overprotective if she pushed away those two TBs and scolded them immediately. Surely, this kind of bodily contact happens only in the pubs. Tomboys rarely do so during dinner or barbeque; if they do the TBGs would shout immediately. Moreover, TBs do not touch TBGs who have a partner already.

Lesbian Service Groups

There were two main lesbian service groups that were nonprofit organizations. Although newcomers usually came alone the first time, it was easy to make new friends in lesbian service groups because committee members usually took the initiative to talk and break the ice. Moreover, the nature of the activities provided more opportunities for participants to talk with each other and the quieter environment enabled participants to chat freely. They could form their own circles after knowing each other for only a short time, that is, one to two hours. As I observed, participants usually paired up or grouped together by the end of the activity.

When several TBs grouped together, they usually shared their experiences, such as the problem with using the public toilet and their relationships with family. The following is a common dialogue:

A: Have you ever gotten into trouble using the public toilet?
B: Yes. About half a year ago, I quarreled with a woman fiercely because she mistook me for a man.

A: Last time, a woman shouted at me in the toilet. So embarrassing.
B: Next time ask a friend to accompany you and keep talking to this friend when entering the toilet. The women won't shout at you at once if you have a friend with you.

Dialogue regarding family relationships was also commonly heard:

A: Does your family know about your sexual orientation?
B: Yes. Several years ago, I brought my first girlfriend home for dinner many times intentionally because I wanted my parent to know my sexual orientation. They found out what the matter was finally.
A: You're so lucky. I dare not tell my parents.
B: My parents were unhappy with it at the beginning. We had communicated for a long time before they could accept my sexual orientation.

Through sharing common experiences and difficulties, TBs learned that they were not the only ones who faced the bathroom problem or hid their sexual preferences from their parents. Moreover, the practical suggestion of tackling the bathroom problem, for example, asking a friend to be a companion when entering the bathroom, encourages TBs to maintain a masculine image.

Lesbian Websites

By searching the Chinese phrase *néuih tùhng sing lyún* or *néuih tùhng ji* on the Internet, many web addresses of Chinese lesbian websites are generated.[5] As most of the Hong Kong lesbian websites are in Chinese, the search result of the word "lesbian" includes fewer Hong Kong lesbian websites.[6] The Hong Kong lesbian websites can be categorized into three types: (1) owned by lesbian service groups and aimed at promoting the group as well as its activities; (2) owned by individuals and aimed at providing lesbian information; (3) personal websites. Individual lesbians share their love stories and photos through writing in personal websites. In general, a lesbian website often includes a message board and a friend-seeking column.

A friend-seeking column usually has preset blanks such as name, gender, age, hobbies, and ICQ number for participants to fill in.[7] Participants can choose to leave their own details or contact the listed participants on ICQ. Lesbians rarely filled "female" in the gender blank but chose "TB" or "TBG" because every participant was assumed to be a female at the very beginning. Usually, "TB/ TBG" was listed next to the gender blank in order to prevent participants from filling "female" in it. Ah-chi (age 26) said that she stated her gender as "TB" when she filled in personal information in the lesbian friend-seeking columns. She explained: "I state my gender as TB in lesbian friend-seeking columns because people can guess what kind of person I am generally. For example, they can guess that I should look masculine instead of feminine and I should take a boyfriend role in a relationship." Wai-ping (age 15) also stated her gender as TB in lesbian friend-seeking columns:

> Lesbians usually categorize each other from appearance, for example, you look masculine you should be a TB, or you look feminine you should be a TBG. I think my appearance is quite masculine and like a TB. Moreover, I do identify myself as a TB. As a result, I state my gender as TB in lesbian friend-seeking columns.

In pubs or service groups, lesbians could categorize each other into either TB or TBG from appearance. As a result, it is uncommon and a bit rude to ask a lesbian whether they were TB/TBG directly. However, in virtual reality where people were invisible to each other, lesbians could not identify who were TBs and who were TBGs from appearance. As a result, they stated their sexual identity clearly in friend-seeking columns or simply asked whether people were a TB or a TBG directly on ICQ.

Diversity within the Lesbian Community

The Fluidity of TB/TBG Role-Play

In Hong Kong, the TB/TBG role-play seems to be prevalent because many lesbian couples consist of one masculine lesbian and one feminine lesbian. Conventionally, a TB has a masculine appearance and plays a masculine role in a relationship; a TBG, in contrast, looks feminine and plays a feminine role. A TB takes up "men's" responsibilities such as paying bills and carrying her girlfriend's handbag, as well as escorting her girlfriend home. Ah-kwan (age 24) claimed she was a TB and considered paying bills and escorting her girlfriend home as her responsibility. "When I went out with my girlfriend, I carried things and opened doors for her. I escorted her home every time after we went out, for dinner or movies. I felt satisfied after escorting her back to a safe place. Taking care of the girlfriend is my responsibility. I paid bills for my girlfriend and I never asked to go 'Dutch.' "

Yin-shing (age 35) shared similar views with Ah-kwan; she believed that a TB should play a man's role in a relationship and take care of her girlfriend.

> A TB must take care of her girlfriend; otherwise what's the point for her to keep a masculine appearance? It's so easy to cut one's hair short and dress like a man. But, a masculine appearance means nothing if this TB does not take care of her girlfriend and cannot afford her girlfriend's daily expenses.

According to Ah-kwan and Yin-shing, taking care of their girlfriend is a major responsibility of being a TB. Indeed their belief is similar to the conventional sexual division of labor in Hong Kong in which men provide money and strength.

The conventional division of labor, however, may be only a myth and may not work in lesbian relationships or in heterosexual relationships. Because a relationship is full of negotiation between the two parties, it seems impossible to clearly distinguish a masculine role and a feminine role within a relationship. Regarding the issue of division of labor, Ah-shun (age 30) said that she never refused to do housework although she defined herself as a TB. She said:

> I've identified myself as a TB for at least ten years. However, I don't limit myself to "masculine" behaviors only. I live with my girlfriend now, and I do cook and tidy the house every day. I like cooking so I don't mind doing the cooking every day. My girlfriend hates cleaning the floor so I just do it. I don't mind doing housework because I love her.

TB/TBG role playing is not always modeled after a heterosexual norm in today's Hong Kong. First, both parties have to work for an income. Second, a TBG may earn a higher salary than her TB lover. Though Ah-kwan and Yin-shing insisted on paying the bills for their girlfriends, the act of paying the bills can be seen as an item of expressive equipment for building a masculine impression rather than for fulfilling a girlfriend's actual financial needs. Moreover, it is uncommon to see a TBG quit her job and rely on her TB lover financially. When both parties have to work, the TB cannot leave all the housework to her lover.

Apart from paying bills and doing housework, it is also difficult to distinguish a masculine role and a feminine role among lesbian couples in their daily interactions. Yat-ching (age 37) and I had an interesting dialogue during an interview:

> *Franco:* Do you think you're masculine in your relationship?
>
> *Yat-ching:* My ex-girlfriend, Siu-fong, expected me to carry heavy things for her. She always took a bottle of water out from her bag and put it into my rucksack. I am not happy that I have to carry heavy things all the time, and I have lost my temper before. However, her temper is even worse than mine.
>
> *Franco:* How about your daily life?
>
> *Yat-ching:* When we had meals together, she usually picked up food and put it into my bowl. She also helped me to peel oranges.
>
> *Franco:* Don't you think helping someone to peel oranges is a feminine behavior?
>
> *Yat-ching:* No. I think picking up food and putting it into my bowl and peeling oranges are quite masculine. Although Siu-fong expected me to

> be a TB and required me to carry a bottle of water for her, she was a very independent and capable girl in fact. She seldom relied on me. In a social gathering, she would interact with people actively. As a result, it was difficult to say who was a TB or a TBG in our daily interaction.

A bottle of water, which was just 500 milliliters, should not be heavy for any adult to carry. Siu-fong employed a bottle of water as an item of expressive equipment to reinforce Yat-ching's masculine impression and her feminine impression. Superficially, Yat-ching was a TB and took a masculine role in the relationship. However, Yat-ching believed that Siu-fong also carried out some "male" responsibilities, such as picking up food, peeling oranges for her, and chatting with people actively in a social gathering.

The conventional division of labor still influences the TB/TBG role-play to a certain extent. As a result, some items of expressive equipment, such as paying the bills and carrying a bottle of water for her girlfriend, were used to highlight the role difference within the TB/TBG role-play. However, the "male" responsibilities and the "female" responsibilities are in fact contestable because they vary from relationship to relationship. As Yat-ching said, "It was difficult to say who was a TB or a TBG in our daily interaction."

Being a Pure

Apart from the predominant TB/TBG role-play, the identity called "pure" is adopted by some lesbians in Hong Kong. They refuse to put themselves under the either-or categorization. Chou translates the term into Chinese as *bu-fen* and into English as "unclassified" (2000:241). But the translations do not seem to be popular. Lesbians who refuse the TB/TBG categorization usually identify themselves as "pure."

Literally, "pure" means not mixed with other substances. The term was adopted because those lesbians do not want to be mixed up with TBs and TBGs. Pure is taken to mean "pure lesbian" without any role-playing. Regarding their appearance, because "pures" reject the TB/TBG role-play, they present neither a masculine (TB) nor a feminine (TBG) appearance. In other words, they try to present a gender-neutral appearance. For example, they seldom put on masculine icons, such as a tie, or feminine icons, such as wearing red lipstick.

Suet-ming (age 24) gave an interesting explanation of pure. She said, "The pronunciation of the word 'pure' sounds like a Chinese character *pìu*. *Pìu* means to float, and it just matches the underlying meaning of pure—rejection of any categorization." Suet-ming was not very serious when she gave me this explanation. She said it was just an idea that was spread among her friends. In fact, I have not heard this from other lesbians. Although Suet-ming's explanation is possibly a joke, her association of the term "pure" and the Chinese character *pìu* reflect their rejection of being categorized.

Siu-po is an interesting case: she embodies the diversity of the lesbian community. Siu-po identified herself as a TB in secondary school but abandoned this identity after Form Six.[8] About one year later, she learned about the pure identity and began to adopt it. When I asked her why she still maintained a masculine appearance, she gave me an unexpected answer. She said:

> I think it's funny to be a deviant person. A few years ago, the media liked portraying TBs as abnormal and deviant. I used to think, "I'm deviant, so what!" Now, I like challenging the definition of TB. I make myself look unisex intentionally. I don't wear a dress, but I like to do facial massage and I always tell my friends which brand of facial product is good. When people comment that I have an alternative style, I think it's very funny.

Siu-po shared with me the process in which she abandoned the TB identity and took up the pure identity. She recounted her experience:

> In secondary school, I thought that masculinity, such as being good at sports and having a masculine appearance, was superior. As a result, I cut my hair very short and claimed myself as a TB. However, the Hong Kong Certificate of Education Examination[9] woke me up! Many TBs in my school got bad results, and I began to recognize that TBs did not represent superiority anymore. As you know, academic performance is extremely important in valuing a person in school. After the HKCEE, my TB identity began to fade away. In Form Seven, I read books written by some local gays and lesbians, and I learned about the term "pure." Now I don't identify myself as a TB but a Pure. I found that I could be my true self after abandoning the TB identity. Although I still like to put my foot on the chair when I sit down, the purpose is different. In the past, I aimed at presenting masculinity; now, I aim at feeling comfortable.

Siu-po dressed up like a TB but at the same time she liked facial massage. She thought her "alternative style," a mixture of masculinity and femininity, could challenge the conventional norms and she enjoyed doing so. Her perspective is similar to Butler's view in *Gender Trouble*:

> This text [*Gender Trouble*] continues, then, as an effort to think through the possibility of subverting and displacing those naturalized and reified notions of gender that support masculine hegemony and heterosexist power, to make gender trouble, not through the strategies that figure a utopian beyond, but through the mobilization, subversive confusion, and proliferation of precisely those constitutive categories that seek to keep gender in its place by posturing as the foundational illusions of identity. (Butler 1999:44)

Butler argues that subverting regulatory practices can denaturalize the gender identity. Siu-po denaturalized the TB identity by displaying both masculinity and femininity on her body.

Persistent Display of Masculinities at the Workplace

If TBs want to maintain their "natural" appearance at work, they have to find a job that allows them to dress in a masculine way. Some employers do not care about their employees' appearance very much because the job does not require face-to-face contact with clients. In this situation, TBs can maintain their "natural" masculinities at work. How do they manage their impression at work?

Impression Management

Wai-yin was a high school graduate, and worked as an insurance salesperson. A salesperson usually gets only a short period of time, that is, one hour, to persuade a client to buy an insurance package; a client evaluates the credibility of a salesperson from the first impression. As a result, impression management is extremely important within the insurance industry. Most insurance companies in Hong Kong require their salespeople to dress formally. Wai-yin's company allowed female staff to wear men's business suits provided that they were formal; she chose to wear men's suits with a tie to meet clients.

Wai-yin did not wear a business suit unless she met clients. She usually wore a T-shirt, short trousers, and a cap in her leisure time. One day, Wai-yin had lunch with me before meeting a client. It was the first time I saw her wearing a business suit. Wai-yin was five feet seven inch tall; as a result, the man's suit fitted her very well. Her business suit, her leather shoes, and her briefcase were all in black. Wai-yin might employ the color black to establish a professional image; at the same time, the color black also intensified Wai-yin's masculinity.

At a dinner party of six lesbian friends, Wai-yin said that she insisted on wearing a tie when meeting clients. She explained that a tie was a nice accessory that highlighted her tidiness and sincerity. She further said that her supervisor at work was also a TB. According to Wai-yin, although her supervisor also wore men's business suits to work, she could not accept wearing a tie because she thought it would look too masculine. Surprisingly, her supervisor asked her why she wore a tie. Wai-yin explained the functions of wearing a tie to her, such as highlighting tidiness and sincerity.

Wai-yin said that she had developed her own strategy to prevent clients from mistaking her for a man:

> When I make cold calls, I introduce myself as "Miss Yeung" at the very beginning. When I meet the client, the client always doubt whether I'm "Miss Yeung." I will re-confirm and say, "I am Miss Yeung", purposely. If the client still feels strange about my appearance, I will ask, "How do you like my suit, is it nice?" or "Is my tie nice? I really like this color!" These kinds of questions can relieve a client's anxiety. It does work!

Wai-yin wore the most masculine man's suit, a black business suit, to work. She put much effort into presenting a capable impression. Moreover, she asked her client to comment on her appearance, which helped Wai-yin to establish an open and friendly impression.

Magic of the Changing Room

Margaret worked as a waitress in a Chinese restaurant that required her to wear a *kèih pòuh* uniform and red lipstick.[10] Even though the uniform was extremely feminine, Margaret could accept it. However, she could not accept wearing women's business suits to work. A few years ago, she was employed as a customer service officer and was required to dress formally. On the first working day, Margaret wore a man's formal shirt and trousers. However, her supervisor complained and asked her to wear women's formal clothes, that is, a woman's formal business suit. Margaret tried to persuade her supervisor to let her wear a man's business suit but failed. On the second day, Margaret did not go to work and eventually resigned.

Superficially, Margaret held a double standard toward the waitress' uniform and the formal dress code. Why did she accept the former but reject the latter? Margaret explained:

> I accept a *kèih pòuh* uniform because I only have to wear it at work. I can take it off once I leave the restaurant. After wearing the *kèih pòuh*, I can leave my TB identity aside and play the role of a waitress. However, I can't accept the woman's formal business suit because I have to wear it on my journey to the office and back home. I just can't wear those feminine clothes on the street.

I argue that the process of changing clothes in the changing room is the key to explain why Margaret can accept a *kèih pòuh* uniform but not a woman's business suit. Sassatelli (2000) studies why people who work out, such as CEOs and managers, can forget their senior position and follow the instructors to perform routine exercises. She reports that they go through a particular process of putting on T-shirts and shorts in the changing room in order to make themselves ready for the exercise class. Although this process is common sense, it does work and enables them to leave their busy daily duties aside and get ready for exercise class. The changing room is an important space for individuals to shift identities.

Although the context I studied is a workplace, Sassatelli's (2000) idea is useful to understand Margaret's situation. The space of the changing room and the process of changing clothes are like the "magic power" that is vital to shifting identity from a TB to a feminine waitress. As Margaret said, she could leave the TB identity aside after wearing the *kèih pòuh* uniform. The potential problem of role conflict did not arise because the "magic" of the changing room solved it, allowing Margaret to accept the *kèih pòuh* uniform. In contrast, the department of customer service would not allow Margaret to change clothes after arriving at the office. Margaret was in role conflict—the feminine women's business suit conflicts with her TB identity. Margaret chose to maintain her TB identity and so she quit the job.

Negotiation between TBs and Society: Naturalization of TBs' Masculinities

In the previous section, I illustrated how TBs negotiate conventional gender norms by insisting on a masculine appearance. In Hong Kong society where women are expected to be feminine, I argue that TBs try to normalize and naturalize their masculinities through persistent display of masculine appearance.

Ah-lik (age 50) said that she spent her whole life negotiating with society. She said:

> When I was still a teenager, I already identified myself as a TB. I liked cutting my hair short but my parents objected. I insisted and they could do nothing to stop me. I was so tough my parents used to call me *ngàuh wòhng muih*.[11] From my 20s onwards, I cut my hair even shorter and wore men's shirts and trousers. The stares from passers-by told me that I should not dress up like that. However, I have persisted up till the present. I've kept a masculine image for 30 years.

I asked Ah-lik why she insisted on keeping a masculine image despite the unfriendly stares from passers-by. She gave me a simple but straight answer. She said: "I want people to understand that it's okay for me to dress up in a masculine way."

TBs consider their masculine appearance as their original and natural appearance and they want people to agree with them. Ah-lik clearly explained that she has persisted in keeping short hair and wearing men's clothes for the past 30 years because she hoped that people might accept her one day. Ah-lik was rewarded after 30 years of persistence. She said: "In the 1970s and 1980s, most of the stares from passers-by were hostile. From the mid-1990s onwards, there were fewer stares on the street and the stares were less hostile. Nowadays, TBs are more visible than before so the stares are not as hostile as before."

Butler argues that the "truth" of gender is produced through regulatory practices that generate coherent identities (1999:23). Being a sexual minority, TBs want to normalize and naturalize their "unconventional" appearance and sexual orientation through regulatory and sustained practices. In line with Butler's argument, TBs persist in presenting a masculine image in order to achieve normalization. They believe that one day society will accept them and thus are proud to maintain their masculine appearance.

Conclusion

This chapter employs the empirical phenomenon of TBs' persistent display of masculinities as an entry point to study the negotiation between TBs and society, and the negotiation between TBs and the lesbian community. I argue that TBs persist in displaying masculinities because they want to achieve naturalization in society. According to Giddens, human agents have the capacity to understand the contexts in which they move and also know what they do while they do it; they can deploy power to "act otherwise" and intervene in the social structure (1984:14). Society expects its members to conform to gender norms, which means that men should be masculine and women feminine. TBs, being human agents, do not conform. TBs normalize and naturalize their identity, their sexual orientation, and their behavior by repeating regulatory performances, as Butler (1999) suggests. TBs' persistent presentation of masculinities can be interpreted as a strategy to achieve normalization and naturalization.

In addition to the negotiation process between TBs and Hong Kong society, TBs negotiate with the lesbian community over the form of their sex-role relationships. Masculinities are not static but contestable. Being human agents, TBs "act otherwise" (Giddens 1986:14) and do not conform to the expectations of the lesbian community. Though TBs display a masculine image, for example, by keeping short hair and wearing men's clothes, they negotiate with the lesbian community by creating a more fluid masculine role. At the same time the lesbian community controls and standardizes TBs' bodies. TBs have to follow the norms of the lesbian community and maintain their masculinities to a certain level, such as having a haircut above the ears and pairing off with only a TBG.

My informants who were in their 50s reported that Hong Kong society is friendlier than it was 30 years ago. This change in attitude shows that TBs are rewarded for their persistence. The larger society, the lesbian community, and the individual TBs all contribute to the production and reinforcement of TBs' masculine behavior and their persistent display of masculinities.

Notes

This chapter is taken from my M.Phil. dissertation, which was funded by the Chinese University of Hong Kong, HKSAR, China. The research for the chapter is based on ethnographic fieldwork conducted from June to August 2002. The major instruments of data collection were individual in-depth interviews and participant observation.

1. Note that some masculine girls in girls' schools displayed a masculine image in their teenage years but chose to marry and have children after leaving school.
2. Informants were given Chinese pseudonyms in Romanization.
3. All ethnographic terms are transliterated using Yale Romanization for Cantonese.
4. For more details see Chou and Chiu 1995.
5. Literally, *tùhng ji* means comrade. In the early 1990s, a few gay and lesbian activists in Hong Kong adopted the term *tùhng ji* to represent gays and lesbians. Chou (1995), a scholar specializing in *tùhng ji* study, explained the reasons for adopting the term. First, it avoided the negative meaning associated with homosexuality, such as buggery and abnormality; second, it transcended the boundaries between different sexual identities.
6. The Chinese lesbian websites mainly belonged to Hong Kong and Taiwanese people.
7. ICQ is short for "I Seek You." It is an internet-wide instant messaging service for people to chat online. Registered users have to login with assigned ICQ numbers.
8. Form One to Form Five are the first five years of secondary school.
9. The Hong Kong Certificate of Education Examination (HKCEE) is an open examination for Form Five students. Passing this examination is a pre-requisite for entry into Form Six and extremely important for students who want to go on to further study.
10. *Kèih pòuh* is the Chinese women's one-piece dress. The origin can be traced to the Qing dynasty. It was still prevalent even in 1950s Hong Kong. Nowadays, some restaurants and some schools have borrowed the concept of kèih pòuh to design uniforms for female staff or students.
11. Literally, *ngàuh wòhng* means the king of oxen and *muih* means a little girl. Culturally, the Chinese people consider the oxen to have a nasty temper and a stubborn character. The phrase *ngàuh wòhng muih* is used to describe a girl who is stubborn and loses her temper easily.

References Cited

Beynon, John. 2002. *Masculinities and culture*. Buckingham: Open University Press.

Butler, Judith. 1999. *Gender trouble: Feminism and the subversion of identity*. rev. ed. New York: Routledge.

Chou, Wah Shan. 1995. *Tùhng ji jaahm chēut lòih*. [Comrades coming out]. *Hong Kong Economic Journal*. January 29.

———. 2000. *Tongzhi politics of same-sex eroticism in Chinese societies*. New York: Haworth Press.

Chou, Wah Shan and Man Chung Chiu. *Yì gwaih sing sí*. [History of the gay and lesbian movement]. *Hèung góng tùhng ji yìhn gau séh*. [Research center for comrade study].

Giddens, Anthony. 1986. *The constitution of society: Outline of the theory of structuration*. Cambridge: Polity Press.

Goffman, Erving. 1959. *The presentation of self in everyday life*. London: Penguin.

———. 1997. The self and social role: Role distance. In *The Goffman reader*, Charles Lemert and Ann Branaman, eds., pp. 35–41. Malden, MA: Blackwell Publishers.

Halberstam, Judith. 1998. *Female masculinity*. Durham: Duke University Press.

Kam, Yip Lo. 2002. *TB je sing biht* [The TB identity]. Postgraduate student paper, School of Journalism and Communication, the Chinese University of Hong Kong.

Lockard, Denyse. 1986. The lesbian community: An anthropological approach. In *Anthropology and homosexual behavior*. Evelyn Blackwood, ed. Pp. 83–95. New York: The Haworth Press.

Sassatelli, Roberta. 2000. Interaction order and beyond: A field analysis of body culture within fitness gyms. In *Body modification*. Mike Featherstone, ed. Pp. 227–248. London: Sage Publications.

Chapter Ten

Transnational Sexualities in One Place: Indonesian Readings

Evelyn Blackwood

The term "transnational sexualities" has come into use to move beyond the limited and simplistic dichotomy of local-global. The term "local-global" in relation to sexualities suggests the difference between traditional or oppressed sexualities and a Western-defined liberated gay-ness (Manalansan 1997). "Transnational" in contrast points to the lines that crosscut the binary; it suggests that the "global" and "local" thoroughly infiltrate each other (Grewal and Kaplan 1994). "Transnational sexualities" insists on the recognition that particular genders and sexualities are shaped by a large number of processes implicated in globalization, including capitalism, diasporic movements, political economies of state, and the disjunctive flow of meanings produced across these sites.

In studies of transnational sexualities locality has remained a contentious but important site to disrupt the universalizing tendencies of queer academic and activist discourses. Following Ulf Hannerz, Grewal and Kaplan argued that transnational recognizes the "localized reception of globalization producing altered forms" (1994: 14). Manalansan (1997) calls for recognition of multiple localized articulations of sexualities. Bacchetta (2002) warns against transnational queer representations that erase a range of intranational queer subjectivities, including those marked by gender, ethnicity, class, or caste differences. Yet, even the use of "transnational" as a frame for exploring sexualities and genders makes it extremely difficult not to import and privilege Western understandings of lesbian or queer lives. Manalansan notes, "By privileging Western definitions of same-sex sexual practices, non-Western practices are marginalized and cast as 'premodern' or unliberated" (1997: 486). The traditional/ modern dichotomy of Western thought perpetuates the assumption that individuals who do not reflect "modern" identities are somehow marginalized, left behind, or beyond the reach of transnational lesbian and gay discourse (Grewal and Kaplan 2001).

Transnational lesbian and gay discourse contains within it the expectation of a new subjectivity or new self-consciousness or awareness of sexual identity. How do we theorize individuals who do not fit that expectation? In this chapter I use a theoretical approach to transnational studies of sexualities that takes into account particular locales within the global movements of queer identities and discourses. I examine the way individuals in a specific locality in West Sumatra, Indonesia, come to see themselves in relation to the queer discourses that circulate in that location. I resist placing these individuals outside global queer discourses by looking at the intersections of national and transnational discourses in their lives. I show that *lesbi* subjectivities are a product of modern state, Islamic, and queer discourses refracted through class location. In the following sections I map out the dominant and alternative discourses that circulate in Indonesia. For lesbi in Padang, West Sumatra, the circulation of queer knowledge helps to create, not a "modern" lesbian identity, but an imagined space of "like-minded" individuals situated within a larger global community.

I use the terms that individuals in Padang use to make sense of their lives, *lesbi* and *tomboi*. Despite being cognates of English terms (lesbi/lesbian, tomboi/tomboy), these two Indonesian terms do not share the same meanings and resonances as their English counterparts. The English word "lesbian" calls up Eurocentric notions of a sexual orientation or identity that is a core aspect of one's self, while the term "lesbi" is used more as an umbrella term for a range of sexualities and gender practices, as will become clear in the section that follows.[1] The history of colonization by the West, including its social scientists, has been the history of imposing categories and meanings on others. By using the Indonesian terms (with their own ambiguities), I want to leave open the meanings contained in those terms. Further, because tombois and their girlfriends position themselves differently in terms of gender, I distinguish between the two throughout this chapter where relevant.

Lesbi Lives and Connections

The city of Padang, in Indonesia, is a sprawling metropolis of over 700,000 people. Cosmopolitan and globally connected, Padang has been a major trading port in Southeast Asia for hundreds of years.[2] Located near the equator, this sultry city is currently the provincial capital of West Sumatra and a province of the state of Indonesia. Most of its inhabitants identify as Minangkabau, an ethnic group that is known for being Islamic and matrilineal.

Padang is typically viewed by others outside West Sumatra as devoutly Islamic and therefore conservative. Because of this impression, lesbi that I met in Jakarta assumed I would be unable to find any lesbi living in West

Sumatra. My earlier fieldwork in West Sumatra had already proven that to be false (see Blackwood 1995a, 1998). I first met a tomboi in 1989 while conducting anthropological fieldwork on women, kinship, and community in rural Sumatra, but it was not until 2001 that I was able to conduct extensive research devoted to the topic of lesbi in Indonesia. It remains true that those who identify as lesbi guard their lives and relationships very carefully. Consequently, my research in Padang, which was carried out in 2001 and 2004 with the same individuals, had to be conducted with extreme care. Few places were safe for open conversations. Despite the limitations, I met 28 individuals who were either tombois or involved with tombois. I spent time with them in the spaces that they inhabited, usually their work spaces but in some cases their living spaces. Of those 28, I formally interviewed 16 individuals with the assistance of my research associate.[3] I collected detailed life histories and asked questions that addressed their understanding of themselves and of their world.

The lesbi individuals that I met came from a range of socioeconomic backgrounds, from quite poor to well-to-do, but because I had to rely on friendship networks to locate contacts, the majority of the individuals I interviewed came from roughly the same class location.[4] Educational levels of the lesbi in this group ranged from middle school to high school, with one woman holding a college degree. Most, but not all, were Muslim. Their ages ranged from late teens to 30s; the average age was close to 30.[5] Almost all the individuals were unmarried, and, as is typical of unmarried individuals throughout Indonesia, were living with their natal families or close relatives. Most of these lesbi worked to support themselves and provide money to their natal families, although some were without work and were supported by their families.

Within Indonesia, their class is identified as "middle class" (*kelas menengah*) and includes families whose members work as petty traders, small business owners, and wage laborers. Class is a vexed concept that does not translate well across nations, but I use it here to signify primarily differences in income and ownership of property. Most of the families of these lesbi have limited income and little surplus for leisure activities or family ceremonies. This class location is an important factor in constituting the particular readings that lesbi make of gendered and queer discourses in West Sumatra.

Lesbi Gender

Being lesbi in Padang is generally understood as an expression of gender rather than a form of sexuality engaged in by two women. Tombois consider themselves masculine, like men, not women at all. One tomboi said,

"Tombois are pretty tough. They don't talk a lot, unless it's important, and they like to wear simple, practical clothes." All the tombois agreed that wearing short hair and smoking was typical of tombois. They describe their girlfriends as normal women: polite, quiet and considerate. Tombois comment on how feminine their girlfriends are and how they dress in the same style as other women. One of the tombois described tomboi girlfriends as "feminine and maternal," but then added, "they like lots of attention and like to be spoiled." On social occasions a girlfriend is expected to do "feminine" things, such as preparing tea and serving guests. This expectation became very clear when I visited Robi and Noni, h/er girlfriend.[6] This couple, both in their early 30s, were the only ones who had an apartment together. My research associate and I had been chatting with them for a few minutes, when suddenly Robi said, "Non, go make some tea for them!" Noni jumped up apologetically and went into the kitchen to prepare tea. Their interaction reflected gender expectations for women and men in social settings in West Sumatra.

Tombois' girlfriends see themselves as normative women who happen to be lesbi at this point because their boyfriends are female. Jeni, who was 23 at the time, explained to me, "I am the same as other women. I wear feminine clothes, sometimes even skirts, and put on make-up." She defined women as "neat, polite and warm-hearted." Asked what kinds of things she liked to do, Jeni replied, "I like to cook." When asked to describe tombois, girlfriends attribute to them the same traits they do to men. Jeni said, "They're just like guys. They can be very crude and egotistical." What girlfriends like about being in a relationship is how they are taken care of. Jeni said, "With Andri [her tomboi partner], I feel safe and protected."

With regard to sexuality, for women, it is proper and permissible only within marriage and under the control of a husband. Young women are expected to be chaste and lacking in sexual desire. Tomboi girlfriends did not speak of desiring their partners' bodies, and not surprisingly, given heteronormative expectations, were generally silent about their sexual desires. Tombois in contrast are quite interested in their girlfriends' bodies, as is considered "natural" to their gender. When I asked Tommi, a tomboi in h/er late 20s, what made her like a man, s/he said, "Well, first, because I love women and second because I do the things guys do." To h/er it was obvious that loving women made h/er a man. Within a system of gender duality, loving women is an attribute of masculinity. All the comments underscore the reality for these individuals of binary gender and the importance of maintaining difference. Lesbi in Padang envision themselves as either masculine or feminine. Although they identify with the label "lesbi," which both tombois and their partners use for themselves, their subjectivities coalesce around the heteronormative pair, masculine/feminine.

Discourses of Gender and Sexuality

The dominant discourses of gender and sexuality in Indonesia are produced by the state, by Islamic clerics, and by regional ethnic leaders. State, Islamic, and ethnic discourses are by no means insulated from each other, nor from global discourses, and in many ways work together to represent a normative view of gender and sexuality that explicitly limits women's sexuality within notions of proper femininity and motherhood. Their "transnational hegemonic 'borrowings' " underscore Grewal and Kaplan's point that "patriarchies collaborate and borrow from each other in order to reinforce specific practices that are oppressive to women" (1994: 24). I examine these hegemonic practices to show the particularities of each discourse as well as the collaborations among them.

The state discourse on sexuality in Indonesia is not directed at "homosexuality" per se but at the creation of normalized, reproductive citizens. The Indonesian state has maintained a benign legal stance toward homosexuality. Since the beginning of its existence in 1945 the state has passed no laws proscribing transgender behavior or sex acts between individuals of the same sex (Oetomo 2001). This is at odds with the history of other postcolonial states that have embraced the moral codes of the colonizers. (See, for example, Alexander 1991; Alexander and Mohanty 1997.) Dutch laws treated homosexuality and transgender behavior severely, but these laws were not imposed on the indigenous populations during the colonial period, due to the Dutch policy of noninterference in local customs and laws (*adat*).[7] The absence of explicit laws regarding same-sex practices does not mean, however, that the state condones such practices. As Foucault (1980) pointed out, the deployment of sexuality in the modern era is not juridico-discursive but operates through a multiplicity of mechanisms to create a knowledge of sex. Rather than addressing "homosexuality" directly or through legal means, the state relies on a gendered discourse as the primary vehicle for conveying normalizing messages about sexuality (see also Mohanty 1991). State gender discourse serves to marginalize and stigmatize practices that fall outside reproductive citizenship.

Laws against "homosexuality" are unnecessary because gender discourse encapsulates sexuality as the "natural" expression of one's sex/gender. As lesbians and gay men became more visible on the international stage in the 1990s, this gender formula was called upon by nationally recognized clerics and state officials to explicitly disconnect lesbianism from normal womanhood. Directly addressing the issue of lesbianism in a paper on Islam and women's rights, Abdurrahman Wahid (1994), a highly respected Muslim cleric who was the third president of Indonesia (1999–2001), declared that lesbianism was deviant and should not be condoned because women have a duty to be mothers and wives. That same year the minister for women's affairs was quoted in a national newspaper stating that "lesbianism is not part of Indonesia culture or state ideology" (Murray 1999: 142). While falling short of legal injunctions, these statements shore up normative gender within the nation by declaring lesbianism deviant, antiwoman and foreign (see also Bacchetta 1999).

Gender discourse produced by the postcolonial Indonesian state creates an image of "natural" binary gender that orients women to wifely tasks and men to leadership positions in the household and "public" domains (see Wieringa 1992; Sears 1996; Suryakusuma 1996). This new woman is encouraged to be an active citizen of the nation, but her status is dependent first on her ability to succeed as a wife and mother, thus effectively tying women's bodies as reproductive vehicles to their gender performance. Although the Indonesian state claims to have emancipated women, giving them greater access to education and some occupations, under Suharto's New Order the state enshrined mother and wife as women's primary role and duty.[8] Following the inception of the New Order in 1965, the Indonesian state avidly pursued a policy promoting nuclear families and motherhood through its health and welfare programs. State programs and policies were broadcast through the state-run school system, as well as television, which was state-run up until the early 1990s.

The gendered descriptions of tombois and their girlfriends mentioned in the previous section dovetail closely with the limited versions of men and women articulated through state policies and educational practices. In line with state expectations of womanhood, the girlfriends I interviewed expressed interest in feminine tasks and occupations, such as cooking and handicrafts; they wore clothes and makeup that were indistinguishable from the clothes and makeup of other women. In contrast, tombois had almost never worn makeup or skirts when they were growing up, except when at school. One tomboi said when s/he was young, s/he was nicknamed "Bujuang" (young man) by h/er family and was called Uncle by one of h/er nieces. The stories I was told about tomboi childhoods were consistent: they always played with the boys, liked boys' games and sports, and never liked wearing girls' clothes. As adults tombois usually worked in occupations that were specific to men, such as driver, parking attendant, and furniture maker. Tombois and their girlfriends were very comfortable in their gender differences.

The contrast between tombois and their girlfriends was brought home to me clearly one evening as I was returning home from a café run by one of the tombois. Noni and another one of the girlfriends rode in the car with me and my research associate, while Noni's partner Robi and another tomboi doubled up on the motorcycle for the ride home. The motorcycle swooped past us on a narrow dark road, the two tombois on it grinning broadly at us as they went by. In the back seat Noni made an exasperated noise and then commented, "Those boys! They go out late at night and they're not even afraid. They look just like guys so people don't know if they are men or not. Sometimes other guys are afraid of them because they act so tough. I would be so afraid to go out alone at night, for fear of being attacked and raped, but not them." Girlfriends felt they had to be careful to protect themselves and avoid being in unsafe situations, a practice that their tomboi partners supported, by escorting them home in the evening or refusing to let them go out at night unaccompanied.

The pervasiveness of the hegemonic ideology of the state is reflected in the fact that these lesbi in Padang offer no critique of gender differences between girlfriends and tombois. As Grewal and Kaplan assert, "We cannot think of sexual subjects as purely oppositional or resistant to dominant institutions that produce heteronormativity" (2001: 670). In contrast to a universalized model of gay resistance to hegemonic norms, lesbi subjectivity in West Sumatra reflects and participates in heteronormative ideals of gender. Gender difference is seen as a natural part of who they are, women are women and tombois are men. Noni commented that it is important to know what gender a person is, tomboi or woman, because then she knows how to respond to and interact with them. She said, "If the person is a woman, then we can sit together and be close physically, but if the person is a tomboi, then I won't allow h/er to sit near me or touch me." Such closeness with a tomboi would be construed as flirting. The physical separation between women and men in public spaces is preserved between tombois and women.

Despite restrictions imposed on women by gender discourse, tombois are allowed to slip through the net of womanhood because of their relative invisibility within communities and the historical tolerance of various forms of masculinity and femininity (tomboi, *waria*) in the islands of Indonesia (see Blackwood 2005).[9] Tombois are and are not seen by others as female. Growing up they were given permission by their families to act just like boys. Because they behave like men, they are allowed the privileges that men have. For tombois the gender binary is enacted in a contradictory way that serves to maintain the differences between the genders. Behavior that muddles a clear binary would not be tolerated by others. As Noni recognized, a *woman* who exceeds the bounds of femininity by going out alone at night risks social retribution, but a tomboi does not.

Permission for tomboi masculinity comes in part from their participation in and maintenance of the dominant gender binary. Tombois adhere to norms of masculinity and by so doing participate in the gendered practices that define and constrain women. Andri viewed women in the following way: "Women should be feminine, wear their hair long, and wear skirts. I told Jeni to grow her hair long because I don't like women with short hair." By encouraging proper femininity, tombois police the boundaries of femininity of their girlfriends. A properly feminine girlfriend also works in turn to consolidate and reinforce tombois' own masculinity.

I am not suggesting, however, that tombois consciously accommodate the gender binary because for them the binary is a natural and unquestioned fact of life.

Islamic and Ethnic Discourses

The terms of gendered subjectivities do not come only from the state. An intense web of discourses coalesces to produce and reproduce a binary gender that includes the discourses of Islamic clerics and Minangkabau leaders. In fact, the state and its regulatory practices were rarely mentioned as a factor in the everyday lives of these lesbi. The greatest difficulties in being lesbi arise from "religion and adat," according to the individuals I interviewed, "religion" here referring to Islamic beliefs and "adat," or local customs, referring to the discourses associated with Minangkabau ethnic identity. Religion and adat were problematic because of the gendered discourse of marriage, as well as the proscriptions against transgender or same-sex relationships, a point I return to later. Lesbi remained uncritical of the way these discourses reinforced ideas of binary gender, holding to the belief that the binary is the natural expression of gender.

As with the state, Islamicist discourses rely on gendered notions of human behavior to create a knowledge of sexualities. Contemporary Islamic doctrine in Indonesia draws strict boundaries between men and women. Although there are many threads of Islam in Indonesia, most sects uphold the idea of "natural" gender difference (see Bowen 1993; Hefner 2000). Women are idealized as mothers and wives under the supervision of husbands and encouraged to take only auxiliary roles in modernist Islamic institutions (see Blackwood 1995b, 2001). Even Islamic groups in Indonesia that have accepted the modernist idea of men's and women's equality, insist that men and women by nature are different. It is this difference, it is said, that makes women's realm the family and household, whereas men's realm is the nation and religious community (Wahid 1994; Hefner 2000). The failure to fulfill one's duty as a woman is seen as contrary to one's god-given nature. The close fit between state and Islamic gender discourses reinforces the normalcy of women's gender.

Ethnic identity is firmly embedded in notions of heterosexually productive marriage and family as well. Failure to marry and reproduce as a Minangkabau woman means failure to continue important kinship relationships that are the cement of family life and communities. Although the age at first marriage for women in West Sumatra has increased as women put off marriage to finish an education or start a business, it is considered shameful for both the family and the woman if she remains unmarried (see Blackwood 2000).

The normalizing discourse of womanhood and motherhood ensures negative repercussions for those who fall outside the norms. Sexual relationships for women outside of marriage are frowned upon. While I would argue that Indonesia is not quite the oppressive, patriarchal state that some feminists have claimed it is, the deployment of gender works to stabilize a limited heterosexuality for *women*, that is, sexuality is proper and permissible only within marriage and under the control of a husband. This intersection of normative prescriptions means that a woman continues to face strong pressure from family to get married to a man and have children.

In line with this discourse, the unmarried girlfriends I interviewed all averred that they expected they would get married at some point to a man, especially if their current relationships fell apart. In some cases marriage is a result of the pressure put on the woman by her family, in others it is the desire of the woman to have a "normal" relationship and have children. Noni, who has a child from her previous marriage, said, "To me it was important to have a child and I'm glad I did it." Tombois participated in this normalizing discourse of heterosexual marriage and motherhood. Dedi said, "If my girlfriend wants to get married, I'll let her. I won't prevent it." Tombois expected that their girlfriends would want children, which was one thing, Dedi noted, that s/he couldn't give h/er girlfriend.

Tombois hold a somewhat contradictory position as men. Despite the privileges allowed tombois as men, they too face certain pressures to marry because they are female. This is the point at which their female bodies drag them back into the cultural dictates of womanhood. Families want their tomboi daughters to marry men. But tombois are more successful in avoiding or ignoring those pressures than are their girlfriends. Here the bravado of tombois comes to their rescue in fending off marriage arrangements and sustaining their position within the masculine gender.

Despite efforts by family members to insert tombois in heterosexual marriage, tombois claim men's prerogatives sexually. Normative expectations of fidelity that attach to women are not enjoined on men, who are said to have greater sexual desires. Men's greater rights in sexuality find support in the Qur'an, which allows Muslim men to have up to four wives. The 1974 Indonesian marriage law made it more difficult for men to be polygamous, but the right to and desirability of having more than one wife or concubine continues to be a staple feature within the state bureaucracy for husbands, whereas women are expected to be faithful (Suryakusuma 1996). As do men, tombois see their own sexuality differently than their girlfriends. Tommi's girlfriend often complained to me that Tommi is not very faithful; she was not the only one to mention this particular "failing" of tombois. Andri admitted with characteristic nonchalance that when h/er girlfriend went away for two months, s/he started seeing another girl because s/he couldn't stand being left alone. The greater sexual privilege of tombois is written in the code of masculinity that attributes more desire to men and also gives them greater privilege in expressing that desire through having multiple partners over time.

Space and Gendered Discourse

The effects of the dominant gender ideology are apparent in the material constraints on and contours of lesbi space in Padang. Tombois and their girlfriends have distinctly different relations to public space, reflecting the gendered discourses circulating within the nation. Tombois move quite easily in public places and spaces, even in locations normally dominated by men, such as pool halls. They have an easy congeniality with men and are often in the company of other men, both tombois and male-bodied men, especially younger, unmarried men. On one bus trip I took with Robi across town, I tried to look invisible while s/he yelled out the bus window to young men s/he knew on the street. When we got off the bus, s/he started rough-housing with one man, playfully hitting him and thumping him on the chest, behavior that a woman would not engage in with a man on the street.

In contrast, the girlfriends of tombois move quietly through public spaces, taking care not to bring unwanted attention to themselves. As Noni noted above, she is fearful of men getting the wrong message and trying to take advantage of her. Nor are women as free to hang out with friends on the street in the way tombois are. Young unmarried women go out less often than tombois, and almost never alone; they go out only with a sister or close woman friend or two, and only for specific reasons. One of the girlfriends in her mid-20s almost never socialized casually with her lesbi friends who lived and worked nearby because she was afraid a neighbor or relative would notice her there. Young unmarried women have to inform their parents of their destination; consequently, unmarried girlfriends could only manage time away from home when they had legitimate excuses, such as going to the market or to a public event like a fair.

Because of the restrictions on women's movements, lesbi create and maintain social networks in Padang within public spaces. Lesbi networks depend primarily on tombois' ability to move more freely. Alison Murray (1999) notes a similar phenomenon among lower-class Jakarta lesbians, who do not have specifically lesbian spaces, but move in heterogeneous spaces shared with waria, street toughs, and others. Other spaces are created in the interstices of domestic life. Due to their class location both tombois and their girlfriends have similar domestic arrangements; they usually live with their natal families. However, because tombois have access to the privileges of men, they are not under as much surveillance and are not expected to sleep at home every night or even most nights.

Their greater mobility means they can surreptitiously stay at their girlfriends' houses, leaving early in the morning to avoid detection. Tombois' ability to move about with little surveillance provides the primary opportunities for intimacy in lesbi relationships, which are carefully hidden from relatives and even friends.

The normative expectations of heterosexual marriage and masculine sexual privilege are located in a dense knot of ethnic kin ties, state pronouncements regarding women's duty to marry, and Islamic beliefs about women's and men's natures. These various discourses combine to produce a gender binary that is unquestioned by tombois and their girlfriends. It also produces restrictions on lesbi space. In this locality state practices do not produce a queer subjectivity that resists the dominant discourse, pointing to the importance of refusing universalized models of gay subjectivities in the transnational era. Tombois and their girlfriends reproduce the gender ideologies of the modern state. They accept the material realities of gender difference and manipulate it to create space for themselves within the context of everyday life.

Translocal Queer Connections

As members of Indonesia's middle class in a small metropole outside Java, tombois and their girlfriends participate in the dominant understanding of gender and sexual norms. However, hegemonic state and Islamic gender discourses are interrupted by national and transnational queer discourses.[10] Queer discourse in Indonesia is produced in and through the intersections of three overlapping communities—lesbi, gay and waria—and their different connections with global queer discourses. "Waria" is one of the Indonesian terms for male-bodied individuals who act like women and take men as lover.

Transnational and national queer discourses circulate unevenly through rural and cosmopolitan spaces in Indonesia primarily through small urban-based activist organizations. Starting in the early 1980s several small organizations have appeared (and disappeared), primarily on the island of Java, to support the interests of gay men, and to a much lesser extent, lesbians and transgendered (waria) individuals (see Howard 1996; Wieringa 1999; Oetomo 2001; Boellstorff 2005). These organizations, which were usually spearheaded by well-educated, well-traveled, English-speaking activists, include the gay men's group (GAYa Nusantara) since the mid-1980s and, since 1998, two activist lesbian organizations, the Internet-based lesbian group in Jakarta, Swara Srikandi, and Sektor 15 of the Indonesian Women's Coalition (KPI).

These organizations have looked to the lesbian and gay movements of Europe and the United States as models and resources. The primary means of communication is through newsletters, and, since the early 1990s, the Internet. Their newsletters and websites contain translations or English text articles of the major academic and political treatises on sexual orientation and sexual rights, as well as reviews of gay literature, international conferences, gay rights marches, and American or European movies with gay or lesbian content. Sporadic conferences bring in Western activists and help to create global networks of organizations funded primarily by international Western-based lesbian and gay organizations.

Lesbi in West Sumatra intercept the circuits of queer knowledge in class-delimited ways. For lesbi in Padang, their class position directly impacts access to national gay activist discourse. Lacking the training or income to be able to access the Internet, and fearful of receiving or possessing written publications that might identify them as lesbi, most lesbi in Padang have no connection with activist organizations. Their sexual subjectivities are not directly informed by the growing gay movement in Indonesia or by the Internet, which has been viewed as one of the primary vehicles producing new sexual subjectivities. For them, access to queer discourses comes primarily through their interactions with waria individuals and organizations and the travel of tombois between Padang and metropolitan communities of Indonesia, primarily Jakarta and Medan.

Grewal and Kaplan note the importance of "power relations of travel . . . that are part of the knowledge production through which subjects are constituted" (2001: 671). The contours of lesbi travel are limited by available income and resources. The primary means of travel for lesbi consist of the small and large public buses and ferries that travel across and between the islands of Indonesia. Viable destinations are only those places where relatives can be found to provide a place to sleep; hotels and even hostels are unaffordable. Although most lesbi I interviewed have traveled within Sumatra and beyond, they travel in decidedly gendered ways. Women's travels are more closely monitored by family. I asked Danny's girlfriend, Epi, who has been to Jakarta on trips with family members, if she had ever been to a gay space or bar in Jakarta. She responded in the negative. She is unable to move outside the circle of family, relatives, or business contacts in Jakarta without raising suspicion or censure for her actions. She maintains her respectability by remaining within proper spaces. Tombois, in contrast, tend to travel more widely and stay away from home for longer periods of time than their girlfriends. Because tombois travel more widely and freely than their girlfriends, much of the information that comes to Padang is from tombois' interactions with lesbi and waria in other cities. Tombois' movements between urban areas and other locales in Indonesia expose them to urban queer discourses that they bring back "home" to be remarked on with others, reworked, and then updated with each new trip to the metropolis (Oetomo 1996).

Lesbi interactions with waria individuals and organizations in Padang are another source of queer information and discourse. Although waria "are denigrated" [by the larger society], they are accepted in certain feminine roles as regarded as experts on proper femininity (Oetomo 1996: 262). Throughout Indonesia waria work as entertainers, hairdressers, wedding planners, dancers, and dance instructors. They have also established their own organizations that put on costume balls, drag shows, and beauty contests. In Padang these shows are open to all members of the community, waria or not. Waria, like tombois and their girlfriends, do not challenge the gender binary, nor do they participate to any extent in activist circles. Yet by organizing and holding events, waria assert their right to public space and public tolerance, creating a community that connects with tombois and their girlfriends.

Tombois in particular feel a certain affinity with waria because waria, like tombois, express a gender that is at odds with the gender socially ascribed to their bodies. Several of the tombois are close friends with waria and frequently hang out with them or attend their functions, including costume balls, birthday parties, and drag shows. I attended one birthday party thrown by waria that included a small drag revue. Tombois sat with their girlfriends on the edges of the room, watching and laughing with everyone else. Tommi said, "I like to hang out with waria. We are one people (*satu bangsa*), after all. They are a different sex, but the same as us otherwise."

Through their conversations with waria, lesbi have access to waria experiences and views of the world, including most conspicuously waria language (see Koeswinarno 1999). Lesbi in Padang have readily appropriated waria vernacular language, using it in public spaces as a code to keep naïve bystanders unawares. It is also a way of signifying one's insider status. To create their language (*prokem*) waria typically add "bong" or "es" to word stems, such as the following: *laki-laki* (man) becomes *lekong* or *lekes*. The slang term for lesbi, *lesbong* comes from using the stem from "lesbi" (les) and adding "bong." The terms lesbi in Padang prefer are words that describe themselves and their partners in specifically gendered terms, reflecting and maintaining their gendered sense of identity as well as the difference between the two partners. Tombois have taken *lekong*, which uses the masculine stem from *laki-laki*, for their own term, and *mawar* (rose), *peré* (from English "paradise") for girlfriends. *Peré* is also the term that waria use for their boyfriends, thus the term signifies the gender normative partner for both waria and tombois.

The queer discourses accessed by lesbi in Padang, rather than creating a shared sexual identity as lesbi, have created a sense of a larger community of like-minded individuals. When I asked Danny how s/he felt toward waria, s/he explained that they "share the same spirit" (*sama jiwa*). *Jiwa* refers to one's soul or spirit, or one's spiritual or psychological being, thus suggesting that s/he sees waria as having the same being, or of being one with tombois in their hearts. This term expresses a sense of commonality between waria and tombois because their being is different from that normatively associated with their bodies. I use the term "like-minded" as a gloss for "sama jiwa" to avoid eliding their sense of community with an identitarian community such as those in Europe and America. Their sense of community is not based on a shared sexuality that is perceived as an identity but on a shared sense of being the same sort of person. This sense of community crosscuts genders by incorporating both tombois and waria.

Other idioms that circulate in lesbi circles in Jakarta as well as West Sumatra help to create a sense of imaginary space belonging specifically to lesbi people. Phrases such as "our lesbians" and "the lesbian world" appeared in *GAYa Lestari*, a section of the GAYa Nusantara newsletter that was put out by Chandra Kirana, a short-lived Jakarta lesbian organization. I heard both tombois and their girlfriends in Padang use the phrase "falling into the lesbian world" (*terjun ke dunia lesbi*) to describe a woman who had her first lesbi experience. This phraseology signifies movement from the everyday world of family and kin into a new world populated by others like themselves, lesbi. "Dunia lesbi" helps to create an imagined community of lesbi who occupy a space distinct from the rest of the world. Those who use it are indicating their familiarity with and membership in such a world. This world does not include waria and gays but draws a circle around those who are lesbi, those who are normatively and/or physically female.

Other terms that circulate among tombois and their girlfriends are indicative of specifically lesbi circuits of knowledge. These include a set of terms originating in lesbian circles in Medan, Sumatra: *sentul* (for tomboi) and *kantil* (for the femme), which are slang words for the masculine and feminine partners (see also Gayatri 1993). Lesbi in Padang were also familiar with the Anglo-American words "butch" and "femme" for the masculine and feminine partners in a lesbian couple. These words are recognized in the community as cognates for the Indonesian words for "guy" and "girl" (*cowok* and *cewek*), though they are not identical in meaning. The association between these two set of terms creates a sense of connection for lesbi with English-speaking lesbian communities.

The linguistic markers lesbi in Padang use to describe themselves do not serve as sexual identity labels. Although these words circulate nationally and internationally, they operate more as in-group words used by lesbi to identify themselves to each other and to signify belonging to the group. Rather than helping to create a modern lesbian identity as expected by the transnational lesbian and gay discourse, queer discourse in Indonesia creates an imagined community for lesbi in Padang based on a sense of shared spirit and shared world. This sense of belonging to a shared community of like-minded individuals encompasses not just lesbi in Padang but extends throughout the islands of Indonesia as well as globally through such internationally known queer figures, such as Martina Navratilova and Melissa Etheridge, both of whom are well known to Padang lesbi. Circuits of queer knowledge in Indonesia have not interpellated lesbi into a homogeneous international lesbian identity but rather have helped to create a sense of shared community among lesbi, waria, and gay in Indonesia, as individuals of like mind.

Conclusion

Queer discourses are accessed by lesbi in Padang in particular ways circumscribed by their class location. Because their location limits access to certain circuits of knowledge, their lesbi subjectivities reflect the particularities of place. The normative view of gender and sexuality upheld and enforced by state and Islamic pronouncements enforces a level of secrecy on lesbi lives that acts as a barrier to greater networking or communication. Despite their lack of access to new technologies and print media publications by national queer activist organizations, they do not experience it as a lack or hindrance. Tombois access social networks and waria circuits that accord with and reinforce their sense of gendered subjectivity. At the same time this queer knowledge conveys a sense of community of like-minded individuals, sama jiwa, that includes lesbi, waria, and gays in Indonesia and beyond. These sexual subjectivities encode differences that cannot be plotted on a developmental path toward a "modern" progressive sexual identity. Tombois and their girlfriends should not be seen as existing on the backward edge of a social movement whose full weight is yet to be felt. Their subjectivities reflect the particular class location, locality, and experiences that mark their lives with its own particular reading of modern, national and transnational discourses.

Under the terms of Western defined gayness, gendered models of sexuality appear backward and nonprogressive. While incorporating a transnational perspective, I found it difficult to resist the writing of "identities" onto the lives of the individuals I interviewed, or of creating a history or developmental teleology that would place them at the tail end of a progressive movement to a new queer identity. Lesbi subjectivities in Padang, however, are neither traditional nor backward but a product of modern, national, and transnational processes. As these stories reveal, lesbi in Padang reproduce the dominant modern gender binary in defining their own lives. But the apparently seamless flow of state and Islamic discourses is interrupted by queer knowledges that circulate indirectly through the movement of tombois and their connections with waria communities. These knowledges have not interpellated lesbi into a homogeneous national or international lesbian identity but rather have the effect of creating a sense of shared community and solidarity among lesbi as well as waria and gay in Indonesia, as individuals of like mind.

Notes

This is a slightly revised and shortened version of an article that was published in *Gender & Society* 19(2): 221–242, 2005. Research for this chapter was supported by a Fulbright Grant for Senior Scholars, the American Psychological Foundation Wayne F. Placek Investigator Development Award, and several small grants from Purdue University. I would like to thank Saskia Wieringa, Deborah Elliston, Jeffrey Dickemann, Jyoti Puri, and Christine Williams for their generous and thoughtful comments on earlier versions of this chapter.

1. For more discussion of the problem of terminology in sexuality studies, see Mohanty 1991; Elliston 1995; Wieringa and Blackwood 1999.
2. For a detailed history of the region, see Abdullah 1972; Dobbin 1983; Drakard 1990; Kahn 1993.
3. Most people in West Sumatra speak two languages, the national language Indonesian and Minangkabau, the language of the home and the region of West Sumatra. Indonesian is their second language, the language they learn in school. Interviews were generally carried out in the national language of Indonesian, but also in Minangkabau. My Minangkabau research associate handled the conversation in Minangkabau and provided translations for me.
4. To protect their identities, I use fictitious names for all the individuals that I describe in this article. Specific life history details are also left out or intentionally disguised so that individuals cannot be identified from the stories.
5. The bias in age range was due to a number of factors. Older (married) women were less accessible because they had an established family life or professional reputation to protect and were unwilling to even meet me. Even older tombois were more hesitant to discuss their lives with me, partly in fear of exposing their girlfriends to unwanted scrutiny. Using friendship networks to make contacts meant that most of the individuals I eventually met were of the same age cohort.
6. When referring to tombois (and waria), I use the pronominal constructions "s/he" and "h/er" (h/is) as a way to disrupt the binary genders of the English language. No English pronouns adequately convey the Indonesian usage, in which the third person pronoun is gender neutral.
7. Re Dutch treatment of homosexuality and transgender behavior historically, see Crompton 1981; Dekker and van der Pol 1989; and van der Meer 1991.
8. The New Order refers to the postwar regime of General Suharto, who became acting head of state in 1966 and remained President up until 1998.
9. Waria are male transgendered individuals who act like women and take men as lovers.
10. I do not have the space here to discuss mainstream Indonesian media representations of lesbi in Indonesia and beyond or their influence on lesbi subjectivities, but see Blackwood 1998.

References Cited

Abdullah, Taufik. 1972. Modernization in the Minangkabau world: West Sumatra in the early decades of the twentieth century. In *Culture and politics in Indonesia*. Claire Holt, ed. Pp. 179–245. Ithaca: Cornell University Press.

Alexander, M. Jacqui. 1991. Redrafting morality: The postcolonial state and the sexual offences bill of Trinidad and Tobago. In *Third World women and the politics of feminism*. Chandra Talpade Mohanty, Ann Russo, and Lourdes Torres, eds. Pp. 133–152. Bloomington: Indiana University Press.

Alexander, M. Jacqui and Chandra Talpade Mohanty. 1997. *Feminist genealogies, colonial legacies, democratic futures*. New York: Routledge.

Bacchetta, Paola. 1999. When the (Hindu) nation exiles its queers. *Social Text* 61 (Winter): 141–166.

———. 2002. Rescaling transnational "queerdom": Lesbian and "lesbian" identitary-positionalities in Delhi in the 1980s. *Antipode: A Radical Journal of Geography* 34 (5): 947–973.

Blackwood, Evelyn. 1995a. Falling in love with an-other lesbian: Reflections on identity in fieldwork. In *Taboo: Sex, identity and erotic subjectivity in anthropological fieldwork*. Don Kulick and Margaret Willson, eds. Pp. 51–75. New York: Routledge Press.

———. 1995b. Senior women, model mothers and dutiful wives: Managing gender contradictions in a Minangkabau village. In *Bewitching women, pious men: Gender and body politics in Southeast Asia*. Aihwa Ong and Michael Peletz, eds. Pp. 124–158. Berkeley: University of California Press.

———. 1998. *Tombois* in West Sumatra: Constructing masculinity and erotic desire. *Cultural Anthropology* 13 (4): 491–521.

———. 2001. Representing women: The politics of Minangkabau adat writing. *Journal of Asian Studies* 60 (1): 125–149.

———. 2005. Gender transgression in colonial and post-colonial Indonesia. *Journal of Asian Studies* 64 (4): 849–879.

Boellstorff, Thomas. 2005. *The gay archipelago: Sexuality and nation in Indonesia*. Princeton: Princeton University Press.

Bornstein, Kate. 1995. *Gender outlaw: On men, women, and the rest of us*. New York: Vintage Books.

Bourdieu, Pierre. 1977. *Outline of a theory of practice*. Cambridge: Cambridge University Press.

Bowen, John R. 1993. *Muslims through discourse: Religion and ritual in Gayo society*. Princeton: Princeton University Press.

Crompton, Louis. 1981. The myth of lesbian impunity: Capital laws from 1270 to 1791. *Journal of Homosexuality* 6 (1/2): 11–25.

Dekker, Rudolf M. and Lotte C. van de Pol. 1989. *The tradition of female transvestism in early modern Europe*. New York: St. Martin's Press.

Dobbin, Christine. 1983. *Islamic revivalism in a changing peasant economy: Central Sumatra, 1784–1847*. Scandinavian Institute of Asian Studies Monograph Series no. 47. London: Curzon Press.

Drakard, Jane. 1990. *A Malay frontier: Unity and duality in a Sumatran kingdom*. Southeast Asia Program. Ithaca: Cornell University Press.

Elliston, Deborah. 1995. Erotic anthropology: "Ritualized homosexuality" in Melanesia and beyond. *American Ethnologist* 22 (4): 848–867.

Foucault, Michel. 1980. *The history of sexuality, vol. 1: An introduction*. New York: Vintage.

Gayatri, B.J.D. 1993. Coming out but remaining hidden: A portrait of lesbians in Java. Paper presented at the International Congress of Anthropological and Ethnological Sciences, Mexico City, Mexico.

Grewal, Inderpal and Caren Kaplan. 1994. Introduction: Transnational feminist practices and questions of postmodernity. In *Scattered hegemonies: Postmodernity and transnational feminist practices*. Inderpal Grewal and Caren Kaplan, eds. Pp. 1–33. Minneapolis: University of Minnesota Press.

———. 2001. Global identities: Theorizing transnational studies of sexuality. *GLQ: Journal of Gay and Lesbian Studies* 7 (4): 663–679.

Hannerz, Ulf. 1996. *Transnational connections: Culture, people, places*. New York: Routledge.

Hefner, Robert W. 2000. *Civil Islam: Muslims and democratization in Indonesia*. Princeton: Princeton University Press.

Hefner, Robert W. and Patricia Horvatich, eds. 1997. *Islam in an era of nation-states: Politics and religious renewal in Muslim Southeast Asia*. Honolulu: University of Hawaii Press.

Howard, Richard Stephen. 1996. Falling into the gay world: Manhood, marriage, and family in Indonesia. Ph.D. dissertation, University of Illinois, Urbana.

Kahn, Joel S. 1993. *Constituting the Minangkabau: Peasants, culture and modernity in colonial Indonesia*. Providence, RI: Berg Publishers.

Koeswinarno. 1999. Sex, language and identity: A study about "being *waria*" in the Yogyakarta world of *waria*. *Jurnal Antropologi* 2 (3): 83–111.

Manalansan, Martin F. IV. 1997. In the shadows of Stonewall: Examining gay transnational politics and the diasporic dilemma. In *The politics of culture in the shadow of capital*. Lisa Lowe and David Lloyd, eds. Pp. 485–505. Durham, NC: Duke University Press.

———. 2003. *Global divas: Filipino gay men in the diaspora*. Durham: Duke University Press.

Mohanty, Chandra Talpade. 1991. Cartographies of struggle: Third world women and the politics of feminism. In *Third world women and the politics of feminism*. Chandra Talpade Mohanty, Ann Russo, and Lourdes Torres, eds. Pp. 1–47. Bloomington: Indiana University Press.

Murray, Alison J. 1999. Let them take ecstasy: Class and Jakarta lesbians. In *Female desires: Same-sex relations and transgender practices across cultures*. Evelyn Blackwood and Saskia E. Wieringa, eds. Pp. 139–156. New York: Columbia University Press.

Naim, Mochtar. 1971. *Merantau*: Minangkabau voluntary migration. Ph.D. dissertation, Australian National University.

Oetomo, Dédé. 1996. Gender and sexual orientation in Indonesia. In *Fantasizing the feminine in Indonesia*. Laurie Sears, ed. Pp. 259–269. Durham: Duke University Press.

———. 2001. *Memberi Suara pada yang Bisu*. Yogyakarta: Galang Press.

Peletz, Michael G. 1996. *Reason and passion: Representations of gender in a Malay society*. Berkeley: University of California Press.

———. 2002. *Islamic modern: Religious courts and cultural politics in Malaysia.* Princeton: Princeton University Press.

Sears, Laurie, ed. 1996. *Fantasizing the feminine in Indonesia.* Durham: Duke University Press.

Suryakusuma, Julia. 1996. The state and sexuality in new order Indonesia. In *Fantasizing the feminine in Indonesia.* Laurie Sears, ed. Pp. 92–119. Durham: Duke University Press.

van der Meer, Theo. 1991. Tribades on trial: Female same-sex offenders in late eighteenth-century Amsterdam. *Journal of the History of Sexuality* 1(3): 424–445.

Wahid, Abdurrahman. 1994. Islam and women's rights. Lily Munir, trans. In *Islam and the advancement of women.* Lily Zakiyah Munir, Abdul Mun'im, and Nani Soraya, eds. Pp. 32–47. Jakarta: The Forum for Islam and the Advancement of Women.

Whalley, Lucy A. 1998. Urban Minangkabau Muslim women: Modern choices, traditional concerns in Indonesia. In *Women in Muslim societies: Diversity within unity.* Herbert L. Bodman and Nayereh Tohidi, eds. Pp. 229–249. Boulder: Lynne Reiner Publishers.

Wieringa, Saskia E. 1992. Ibu or the beast: Gender interests, ideology and practice in two Indonesian women's organizations. *Feminist Review* 41: 98–114.

———. 1999. Desiring bodies or defiant cultures: Butch-femme lesbians in Jakarta and Lima. In *Female desires: Same-sex relations and transgender practices across cultures.* Evelyn Blackwood and Saskia E. Wieringa, eds. Pp. 206–229. New York: Columbia University Press.

Wieringa, Saskia E. and Evelyn Blackwood. 1999. Introduction. In *Female desires: Same-sex relations and transgender practices Across cultures.* Evelyn Blackwood and Saskia E. Wieringa, eds. Pp. 1–38. New York: Columbia University Press.

Part IV

Silencing and Modes of Invisibility

Chapter Eleven

Flames of Fire: Expressions and Denial of Female Sexuality

Abha Bhaiya

> The dominant culture defines the notions of sex and sexuality, of desire and desirability, senses and sensuality. Other cultural configurations will not only be subordinate to this dominant order, they enter into struggle with it, seek to modify, negotiate, resist or even overthrow its reign, its hegemony.
>
> —*Brah 1996*

The film "Fire" by Deepa Mehta, primarily described as a film on female sexuality, bagged as many as 14 international awards and simultaneously raised violent controversies in India. The film was caught in the crossfire between Hindu fundamentalists and lesbians—and an array of actors in between. The media presented the audience and the readers with a range of responses that often did not provide a neat picture with defined frames. While fundamentalists' outrage condemned the film as anti-Indian and an assault on Indian culture, human rights groups, a section of the women's movement, artists, and the film industry as well as members of civil society saw it as an issue of freedom of speech and expression. However, among all those protesting, the voice of a small number of lesbian women was particularly outstanding. These women made two significant claims: first, that the film was an explicit statement about lesbianism and second, that lesbians are Indian.

This chapter is an attempt to assemble the conflicting voices surrounding the film and suggest yet another frame, the vantage point of which is located within women's movements in India. The chapter not only reviews these diverse claims, but also interrogates expressions and denial of female sexuality, notions of citizenship, and the definition of culture expressed by each constituency. My voice resides as much in the feminist sensibility as any other. I, therefore, explore the meaning and the content of what is popularly (and universally) known and labeled as lesbianism.

That I have a different position is evident from my critique of the content of the film as well as of the various protesters who vociferously spoke in favor or against the validity of the film and its central theme. It is my contention that "Fire" is a homophobic film in as much as it trivializes and depoliticizes the issue of women-centered relationships. In fact, the film has pushed women-loving-women to explain and justify their sexual identities.

The Story Line

For those who have not seen the film, I provide a brief outline: "Fire" tells the story of two women—Radha and Neeta (called "Seeta," a mythological figure, in the first version of the film)—who are married to two brothers. The two women suffer almost complete neglect by their respective husbands; one has taken the vow of celibacy that he keeps testing by lying next to his wife lie without experiencing desire; the other brother spends his evenings with a Chinese woman, with whom he has been involved even prior to his marriage. However, when he is with his wife, he desires sexual gratification from her as his right, even if it is against her will.

This is the background against which Radha and Neeta's attraction for each other and their growing physical and emotional relationship are depicted. Near the end of the film, they are caught in the act of sexual intimacy and are condemned, at which point they choose to leave the house, Neeta first and Radha later.

The film ran uneventfully for three to four weeks in big cities and smaller towns; women and college students formed the majority of audiences until a fundamentalist Hindu organization, the Shiv Sena, began violent attacks on theaters screening the film, demanding its immediate ban. As a response, various women's groups, human rights organizations, as well as artists and film personalities held nationwide protests and demonstrations in Delhi and Mumbai, demanding the continuation of the screening of the film and appropriate action against the miscreants.

The Cultural Tyranny

It is not difficult to imagine why the film provoked such strong and diverse responses. Fundamentalist voices expressed outrage and condemned the film as anti-Indian and an insult to "Indian culture." It is significant that organizations such as the Shiv Sena used their women's wing—the Mahila Aghadi Sena—to mount an aggressive assault on the film by coming out onto the streets to attack and picket cinema halls, demanding its immediate ban. According to them, the lesbian relationship portrayed in the film was vulgar and a distortion of the culture and ethos of India. The Shiv Sena's objections were many: "It goes against our culture," "it hurts the religious sentiments of Hindus, particularly since the main character is called Seeta," and "if physical needs are shown to be satisfied through lesbianism, the institution of marriage will collapse and reproduction will stop."

Here, it is worthwhile to quote from the text of the application seeking court intervention, which was filed by a member of a Hindu fundamentalist organization, S.C. Sharma:

> The film and the scenes within it go against the established family norms of Indian society and vitiate the minds of the younger generation by showing vulgar scenes . . . That the unnatural acts depicted in the movie may kindly be taken care of by the honorable Supreme Court; that the screening of the said controversial film "Fire" among the citizens of our ancient country will be highly immoral; anti faith [of course, he means, the Hindu faith!], anti culture—absolutely perverse. The screening of this film has injured the religious sentiments of millions of our countrymen. These women want to vitiate the whole fabric of the Indian society. I seek apologies from the makers of this film.[1]

A state minister supported this petition with the statement that "though lesbianism is one of the older forms of sexual activity and it is also depicted in the architecture of the abandoned temple of Khajuraho, these things are not in the open. People do not know about it. So we must make sure that such films do not insult the public."[2]

The Shiv Sena's talk of "our culture" begs several questions: Which culture? Whose culture? Who defines what culture is? This is not the first time that Hindu fundamentalists have made an exclusive claim to a monolithic ideal of Indian culture, representing it as the natural, universal, and all-encompassing form of culture for India. This vision of Indian culture has always been regarded and used by fascists as an instrument of social control and cultural terrorism. Indian culture has been invoked to justify the ban on Salman Rushdie, to deny the Pakistani cricket team entry into the country, to stop a Muslim painter from painting a Hindu mythological figure, and to violently disrupt an exhibition by a secular organization depicting multiple versions of the Hindu epic the Ramayana. The long arm of the Sena has a terrifying sweep. Its ultimate target is the culture of dissent. In fact, by using the term "culture" as a monolith, they rob the term of its plurality, historicity, and its evolutionary dynamism.

However, to give the devil its due, the Sena outrage does get the point—the family and heterosexual marriage are in crisis. As one of the Sena members said, "Why do you want to destroy this structure? What do you gain by showing lesbianism? As it is, the institution of marriage is breaking down. This will make it worse."[3] In order to save this institution from moral corruption, the Shiv Sena pushed "their women" into the streets as vanguards in defense of Hindu morality and culture, thus pitting women against women—a familiar ploy to destroy women's solidarity. On behalf of the patriarchal fundamentalist institution, women were appointed as guardians of morality against other women who were supporters of the film. The assumption was clear—these women who supported the film were without men, without homes, without culture. In fact, the Shiv Sena went so far as to declare Shabana Azmi, the actor who played Radha on the screen and a member of parliament in real life, as antinational. She was castigated as a betrayer for acting as a lesbian on the screen. Her citizenship was rendered suspect.

Some also believed that the reason Shiv Sainiks panicked over "Fire" was that many housewives who saw the film found in it an imaginary release from their own tensions, as it depicts women exercising sexual choice. To a large extent, it is true that the film appealed to the women's constituency. This perhaps is the subversive possibility of the film, as it tries to legitimize women's desire.

Freedom of Expression: Tentative to Strident

On December 7, 1998, many organizations, including human rights groups, women's organizations, lesbian and gay rights groups, film personalities, artists, and representatives of grassroots organizations came together at a day's notice, both in Delhi and Mumbai, to hold peaceful demonstrations in support of the film. The quality and collective strength of support was crystal clear. The fundamental right to freedom of expression became a melting pot in which multiple voices converged. The incident brought together people who believed in an open democratic society that does not stifle creativity and free expression. The spontaneous mobilization of ordinary citizens, where, unlike in other campaigns, activists found support from onlookers, emerged as a new political formation.

The constitutional framework of fundamental rights was an uncontested territory for civil society and activists alike. According to them, by disrupting the film "Fire" and forcing the withdrawal of the film, the fundamentalists violated the fundamental right of freedom of speech and expression, thus making a mockery of democracy.

The defenders of democracy were strident in stating that the film was about tolerance and choice, as well as about freedom of artistic expression. For women's movements, a historical alliance with civil society emerged to build a larger consensus on what constituted freedom of expression and on whether expression of women's sexuality is integral to this freedom. In spite of the solidarity on the streets, the unease in response to the issue of women's sexuality was palpable. In their public posture, representatives of democracy showed reluctance to include expression of female sexuality as a component of the freedoms they sought to defend. Even prior to the demonstrations, differences on this issue had emerged among different groups supporting the screening of the film and opposing its ban.

While the film viewers' responses displayed a certain maturity because they found the expression of sexuality as natural and given, the liberal democratic group was still reluctant to see expressions of women's sexuality constituting freedom of expression, particularly if it was about women's relationships with women. As John and Nair (1998) acknowledge, the emergence of feminist groups in the 1960s, for the first time, transformed the debates on sex by politicizing the issue. The groups argued that the subject of sex as a political institution involves questions of power and patriarchy. While democratic solidarity can be a starting point for protest, until and unless the link between democracy and feminist politics challenging patriarchy is established, the democratic agenda remains unfaithful to women's total liberation. Within social movements and in academic pursuits, unless the dominant structures of patriarchy and heterosexuality are challenged, the struggle to expand democracy remains incomplete. If equality in all spheres of public and private life is nonnegotiable, equality for women in negotiating their sexuality is a hallmark of democracy. In fact, both those who swore by their commitment to freedom of expression and those who were obsessed with what constituted cultural correctness missed the point that women's sexuality is more than an issue of civil rights versus culture. To that extent, the search for a concept that dissolves these contradictions must continue.

One of the strategies used to strengthen the campaign was to establish the legitimacy of the Censor Board, which, rather ironically, was in favor of screening the film despite many of its earlier stands that were far from progressive. Women's groups had frequently engaged in blackening film hoardings, demonstrating outside movie theaters, raising dissent against the objectification of women's bodies, the use of brutal violence, and depiction of outrageous rape scenes, all of which had passed the Censor Board. Their opposition reflected the ambiguous and contradictory relationship of the women's movements with the state. If the role of the Censor Board is legitimized, by implication its authority is also established. Such a result may hurt the long-term objective of doing away with a body such as the Censor Board, which is itself an arm of the "thought police," an institution that has repeatedly demonstrated its lack of artistic and intellectual credentials as well as its lack of concern for the dignity and status of women and other marginalized, oppressed groups.

Lesbians and Indians

According to some lesbian groups in India, such as Sangini and Prism, based in Delhi, "Fire" is the first Indian film that explicitly acknowledges the existence of lesbianism. This claim is contentious as, apart from feminist literature, there have been a number of films in the past, such as "Subah," "Umbartha," "Daira," and "Tamanna," that were seen as "respectable" and alternative cinema. In their eagerness to claim primacy of public expression, some lesbian groups appear to fall prey to a tendency to obliterate the past and short-circuit the future.

Before I proceed to anchor the past, I would like to emphasize that politically and personally, I resist the label "lesbian" as a conceptual and defining category for women-centered intimacies—sexual, sensuous, or otherwise. In various cultural contexts, women's experiences with women are plurally named and defined. Labeling is a political act. This monolithic category, "lesbian," and the universal institution "lesbianism" have increasingly alienated those political women-centered women who dare to reject submission to this all-pervasive "label." Further, there is no such thing as a single lesbian movement. However, because within this marginalized political mobilization, women who are "out" define the content and form of the dominant discourses and practices regarding what it is to be a "lesbian," it should not be assumed that other voices do not exist.

With the increasing visibility of the "lesbian movement," these other voices may be stifled. This is the difficulty and the dilemma of many women-centered women who are located within women's movements. hooks brings out the subtle differences by emphasizing the need for voicing women's concerns in a patriarchal society that socializes women to repress and contain; what women say, how they say it, and what their politics are—all are crucial (hooks 1992). It is prudent for any movement to ensure that the spirit of subversion and rebellion from within is not relegated to the margins—even within the alternative discourse that challenges the dominant voice—and to make certain that certain voices are not advantaged against others. Women who do not identify with heterosexuality and yet refuse to be labeled as "lesbian" have felt the pressure to assume politically correct postures in a space already frozen by public sloganeering. I will come back to this later in the chapter.

In addition, relegating women-centered relationships to the realm of alternative sexuality is equally problematic because it leaves the institution of heterosexuality unchallenged. Parallel and plural sexualities are the heritage of human civilization as much as the plurality of our languages, fields and foods, rites and rituals, cultures, and religions. We need a rigorous and radical interrogation of "heterosexuality," and "heteronormativity," not a relegation of the alternatives to the realm of the exotic.

Having stated my position, there is still no denying that the public presence of women's and men's parallel sexualities has resulted in legitimization of marginalized groups of people, such as gay men and lesbian women, hijras, transvestites, transgender males, and male sex workers. With an evolving mobilization of women sex workers, the mainstream is forced to engage with issues of "abnormal and dangerous sexualities." These new sites for sociopolitical mobilization have enlarged the canvas for the "deviant" to destabilize the "decent." As Sherry Joseph mentions, "[T]he emerging gay and lesbian movement offers not just alternate identities but prospects for social reconstruction. In spite of its marginality, the movement rejects the monolith and the mass. It is a reminder that if forced conformity is to be resisted, it must be by representing human lives as multiple; selfhood as several; communities as voluntary and various" (Joseph 1996:2228).

In fact, as early as 1942, Chugtai published a short story "Lihaaf" on the issue of female same-sex exploration, which was later translated and published (1990). The story is about a frustrated housewife whose rich feudal husband does not have time for her and so she finds emotional and sexual solace in the companionship of a female servant. Charged with obscenity, the writer was submitted to trial in Lahore. The trial lasted for two years till she was acquitted.

If we were to look for any historical moment when women-centered relationships became the center of public debate, inside as well as outside women's movements in India, it is in the newspaper reporting of two policewomen in the state of Madhya Pradesh (*Times of India*, December 1987). These women were married in a temple in front of a number of witnesses. It seems their families had consented to the marriage. As a consequence of what they had thought was an innocent act of love, they were punished with dismissal from their jobs. As in the case of "Fire," the responses to the report were varied. The inspector general of police clearly stated his concern that "others could learn from their example." Not surprisingly, men's fear about women's sexuality has similar overtones, whether it is the fundamentalists (the guardians of morality) or the police (the custodian of criminality), as their tasks often overlap.

While the response of the media was confused and often homophobic, a few women's groups and feminist human rights activists made a concerted effort to support the choice of the two women as legitimate, while condemning their termination from jobs as unconstitutional. Since both women came from the lower rank of the police and the class hierarchy, their declaration could not be dismissed as a Western, middle-class aberration. On hindsight, it seems there was a larger public space for silent tolerance at that time than was evidenced when the "Fire" controversy arose ten years after the reported marriage of the two policewomen.

Subsequent to this, a number of instances of women's relationships with women have been brought to public or private notice. As the growing issue of women's sexual choices began to crystallize, women's movements have, on several occasions, been pushed from within to take sides. Responses range from outright hostility and a blanket denial of women-centered relationships, naming them as "abnormal," to internal reflections, debates, and new positioning on the issue of women's sexuality.

New stirrings, formations, and subgroups have begun to emerge. From whisperings to screams, a range of articulations have occurred. Initially, the strident middle-class gay movement formulated the discourse on desire and on male homosexuality in India. By and large, political, women-centered women found little space or voice on these male platforms, such as "Less Than Gay," a citizens' report on the status of homosexuality in India that was published in 1991. This historical document did not include women's experiences. It has taken a long time for feminists to publish their research on women-centered sexualities and physioemotional bonding (see Thadani 1996; Sukthankar 1999).

Ideological tension and posturing on various issues related to sexuality have been part of women's movements as women continue to take polarized positions. The challenge is to make it a creative and reflective surface, acknowledging the presence of diverse strands within the counterdiscourse. A small but significant group of feminist activists, lawyers, and others argued that expression of women's plural sexualities is an integral part of the agenda of women's movements for liberation. In the National Activists Conference at Calicut in 1990, the first large national level meeting of single women, the dominance and oppression of heterosexual marriage came under collective scrutiny. Women's choice to stand outside the institution of marriage was seen as legitimate and viable. Defining sexuality on their own terms was seen as a political act. These views led to an increased tension within women's movements. "The fear of losing power, status, or political, academic reputation . . . lead women to a strategy of postponing public claims about their bodies, sexualities and pleasure to an indefinite point in time, while focusing on power in other areas" (Ilkaracan 2000: 3).

Yet Another Site for Struggle

One of the recent films on a lesbian relationship, titled "Girl Friend," has drawn women's and lesbian and gay movements into another arena of struggle. The story line of the film "Girl Friend" is simple in its construction: the film starts with two women (and not girls) living together. Their relationship dates back to the boarding school where the heroine of the film becomes obsessed with another girl. They have a sexual encounter. Later, while they are living together, both go to a gay party where the second woman falls in love with a man and starts seeing him. The heroine from that moment onwards turns into a villain and becomes extremely violent, a love-triangle plot that is most familiar to Indian viewers in the context of heterosexual mainstream films. However, the director makes it very clear that the first woman is sexually abnormal and that she became so because she was sexually abused in her childhood and therefore hates men. The film, a product of the so-called modern mainstream Bollywood industry of India, is not about lesbian love but about lesbianism as an aberration; the plot churns out stereotypes of heterosexual sex, jealousy, and vengeance. No less than the film director Karan Razdar swears that the film is about lesbian love. However, unlike in the case of "Fire," in this instance, not only the fundamentalists, but also feminists pitched themselves against the film, although for entirely different reasons. The fundamentalists resorted to the same refrain, "[T]he film is anti-Indian culture." In an interview, the chief of the RSS (Rashtriya Swayamsevak Sangh), a hardcore fundamentalist group, said, "The film is to corrupt the society. It seeks to introduce 'such ideas' in society."[4] His statement proves the fundamentalists' longing to fashion themselves into thought police.

Feminists, lesbians, and other women's organizations are not convinced either of the film's lesbian content or its progressive posture. In fact, the film is outrageous in its content because it is nothing more than titillating in its intent. In the name of progressive cinema, the film is a severe blow to growing awareness around issues of women's sexualities and sexual choices outside normative marital heterosexuality. Replete with prejudice, the film "Girl Friend" in its very design is antiwoman and indeed anti–sexual freedom. In fact, the film is a reinforcement of an age-old refrain of the media and middle-class men's fear that "women are lesbians because they are sexually frustrated." One of the feminists, Anjoli Gopalan, cryptically commented that, "with the high rate of abuse in our country, most Indian women should become lesbians."[5]

As in the case of "Fire," in "Girl Friend" too, women's love for women is seen as an aberration and therefore must always be justified. It is invariably assumed that lesbian relationships are either a result of childhood abuse or neglect by men. Why should women otherwise turn to women for sexual gratification? In fact, the film pathologizes lesbian love, thus pushing it into the realm of perversion, abnormality, and obnoxiousness. It is a blatant misrepresentation of women who choose to be with other women. The Prism activists, a Delhi-based lesbian group, have clearly stated that "the filmmaker as well as the goons protesting against the film act from a place of homophobia." The film director's response is a testimony to this attitude: "[T]he theme is realistic. I am not saying we should *support* lesbians, but just that we should *accept* them" (emphasis mine)[6] Instead of raising the issue of same-sex love as natural and normal, the portrayal of lesbian women in the film is antilesbian. The central player is shown to be aggressive, a man hater, a local bully, at best, a mini-man. By reinforcing prejudice and a cloistered mind set, the film does disservice to the struggle of women-centered women.

As people belonging to sexual minorities organize themselves, expanding public spaces for their visibility, the media often trivializes the issue. Most newspaper reporting about the film, including interviews of women activists, sensationalizes issues of women's sexualities.

The Fourth View

> The object is to learn one's own history, free thought from what it silently thinks and so enable it to think differently.
>
> —Foucault 1985:9

It is my contention that not only "Girl Friend," but also the film "Fire" are homophobic undertakings that trivialize and depoliticize women-centered relationships. Is it not ironic that after every fundamentalist attack on its lesbian content, the filmmaker Deepa Mehta publicly denied its lesbian content? She insists that the film is not about lesbianism. In fact, she is being honest to the core about the film—fundamentally, between the frames, the film upholds heterosexuality as the norm. It is replete with heterosexual sex, either with the very act or with an obsessive reference to its pervasiveness. Lesbian love is cast against this failed heterosexuality—this context cannot be obliterated, hidden, or denied.

The film seems to suggest that the sexuality of women-loving-women is rooted primarily in the abuse and neglect of women by men, although their loving each other is shown to have its own strength. Women-loving-women have been presented as an outcome of a bad marriage, not as a possibility or a given where heterosexuality is simply irrelevant. In that sense, the depiction of lesbian desire seems more a gesture of powerlessness than a sign of active and critical resistance.

The film "Fire" in some ways tried to break new ground; it did make a very strong statement in the end (through Radha) for the autonomous existence of women-centered love relationships. Still, in the larger context of the film, women turning to one another are shown in the context of men's failure to satisfy women, thus presenting women's relationship to each other as derivative from heterosexuality. The attempt to draw women characters who are strong and capable remains hasty and superficial.

Emotional upheaval can destroy a person's sensibilities but to try and resolve the upheaval through lesbianism stemming from male rejection, as "Fire" does, can hardly be convincing or for that matter advantageous to counter the view that it is an aberration arising out of heterosexual frustration. In fact, the actress who played Neeta in the film, Nandita Das, who is a feminist activist, categorically says, "It is a love story. The emphasis is not on lesbianism, as most people are trying to portray . . . It is after all fiction. It does not mean that everybody who is in this situation has to get into a relationship like this . . . It appeared a justifiable fall out."[7]

In feminists' immense desire to end their marginalization, the entirety of the film, its construction, imagery, and the content escaped their feminist critical faculty. A film is often praised or decried by a viewer on the basis of what she or he is looking for. Some lesbian women waiting in the aisles seized this fragment of meaning and ignored the totality of the film; they decontextualized it from its larger premise, completely identifying with the depiction of the courage of two women to love each other on the screen. It is the same frame of meaning that the fundamentalists and lesbians alike saw.

Another issue of ideological discomfort arises for me in the responses to the film. During the activist demonstration in Delhi, among various placards stood out the slogan: "Indian and lesbian." This poster became a media icon in preference to many others. Most newspapers picked it up for large display. This lesbian posture was an ideological knee-jerk reaction that let them walk into the fundamentalists' trap as contestants for citizenship of this country named India. In response to the film, each struggling constituency tried to make a claim to this Indianness, whether in the name of culture, democracy, or sexuality; each held a share of it and claimed superiority for their brand of Indian heritage.

The film "Fire" also brings into play a range of family institutions. Radha, the wife of the elder son of the family, cannot have a child. She is not really a complete woman, as she cannot enter the glorified institution of biological motherhood. Her husband's rejection of her as a sexual partner and his vow of celibacy mount further insult on Radha who is depicted as a "barren woman" having no right to be loved. Yet she continues as a dutiful wife and daughter-in-law. It seems, perhaps not by intention, that as an outcast from both these institutions—motherhood and wifehood—she could seek gratification only with another woman. If she had a child, would the filmmaker have allowed her to fall in love with another woman and leave home? Similarly, if the two women had not been caught in the act, would they have left home? As one of the film critics has commented, "The lesbian factor is far too sudden and without any background whatsoever."

In fact, "Fire" lost a great opportunity to propagate the cause of true female bonding. In her desire to portray women's love as bold and beautiful, suddenly in the middle of the film, the filmmaker portrays women characters as radical. Men, however, appear as nothing more than cardboard cutouts; they are so stereotyped that they become predictable from the start and appear, at most, caricatured.

The film is extraordinarily far-fetched in that it shows both women leaving their dependent condition and middle-class family with absolutely nothing, lacking any support, and getting away without punishment. How Radha survived "FIRE" is anybody's guess. In my musings over the film, I have wondered whether it is difficult for a heterosexual woman to make a bold, outrageous film and yet not to deny its lesbian content. No wonder the film has forced women-centered women to justify who they are and why they are what they are!

The film does deal with the hollowness of the traditional middle-class, patriarchal family. That perhaps is its strength because the institution of the traditional family in India is fraught with contradictions and double standards. Women's experiences of rejection, submission, pain, oppression, and sexual exploitation, all constitute the rubric of the "glorified Indian family." The film is a critique of this patriarchal institution. It is a source of strength for the filmmaker and a source of fear and anger for the fundamentalists.

In the end, my plea is to see "Fire" as a fresh beginning over many prior beginnings: not to claim it as the first explicit lesbian film but to see its place in a continuum of depictions of multiple expressions of women's desire and pleasure, practices of intimacies, and defiance of dominating heterosexuality, all forming their individual and collective heritage. The depth of the history and continuum of the feminist struggle should empower women to claim the centrality of sexuality in all their social and political structures and cultural explorations.

Notes

1. From the intervention application filed by S.C. Sharma in response to the appeal filed by Yusuf Khan alias Dilip Kumar, a film star known for his secular views who appealed for the free showing of the film, 1998.
2. Quoted in an English-language national newspaper.
3. *Hindustan Times*, December 4, 1998.
4. Quoted in a national newspaper, 2005.
5. Quoted in *Indian Express,* "This is the worst piece of drivel I have ever seen," page 6, June 17, 2004.
6. Quoted in *Times of India*.
7. Personal conversation with the actress.

References Cited

Brah, Avtar. 1996. *Cartographies of diaspora: Contesting identities*. London: Routledge.

Chugtai, Ismath. 1990. *Quilt and other stories*. New Delhi: Kali for Women.

Foucault, Michel. 1985. *The History of sexuality*, vol. 2: *The uses of pleasure*. New York: Pantheon Books.

hooks, bell. 1992. *Black looks: Race and representation*. Boston: South End Press.

Ilkaracan, Pinar, ed. 2000. *Women and sexuality in Muslim society.* WFWHR: Istanbul, Turkey.
John, Mary E. and Janaki Nair, eds. 1998. *A Question of silence? The sexual economies of modern India.* New Delhi: Kali for Women.
Joseph, Sherry. 1996. Gay and lesbian movement in India. *Economic and Political Weekly*, August 17: 2228–2233.
Sukthankar, Ashwini, ed. 1999. *Facing the mirror: Lesbian writings from India.* New Delhi: Penguin Books.
Thadani, Giti. 1996. *Sakhiyani: Lesbian desire in ancient and modern India.* London: Cassel.

Chapter Twelve

Dying to Tell: Sexuality and Suicide in Imperial Japan

Jennifer Robertson

Introduction: "Homosexual Elegy"

On February 17, 1935, the humor column of the *Asahi Shinbun*, a nationally distributed daily newspaper, was devoted to spoofing an attempted lesbian double suicide that had taken place about three weeks earlier. The "feminine" partner was Saijô Eriko, a 23-year-old "woman's role-player" (*musumeyaku*) in a popular all-female revue, and the "masculine" partner, 27-year old Masuda Yasumare, an affluent and zealous fan of the actress (figure12.1).[1] (Yasumare was a masculine name that she chose for herself; her parents had named her Fumiko.)

The daily carried a ballad titled "Homosexual Elegy" (Dôseiai Hikaa) by an amateur songwriter. The following is the translated version:

Her love for a woman
Was greater than her parent's love for her;
And her older sister was cold-hearted.
She blushed and her heart danced when first they met.
But because they are two women together,
The fan's life is short.

Dashing from east to west,
Theirs was a passionate love
In a baneful world
Only to succumb to nihilism.
When will it fade, the anger in her heart?
For lesbians, the answer is suicide.
Because they are not man and woman,
The fan's grief is deep.

Figure 12.1 The all-female Takarazuka Revue, founded in 1913, in a scene from *Rosarita*.

As the masculine partner, Masuda was singled out as aggressive and deviant and cast as the more pathetic of the two, owing to her "unladylike" appearance and behavior. She belonged to the urban upper class whose female constituents were expected to epitomize the "Good Wife, Wise Mother" gender role sanctioned by the Meiji Civil Code that was based on the German model and operative from 1898 to 1947. Moreover, as a "masculinized" (*danseika*) female, Masuda was one of the "problem women" associated with the so-called Woman Problem (*fujin mondai*), a term coined around 1900 as a euphemism for issues related to females' civil rights and the struggle of the New Woman (*atarashii onna*) for full citizenship and equality, including voting rights and autonomy (or agency) (see Koyama 1982, 1986; Sievers 1983; Nolte and Hastings 1991). Obviously, not all New Women were lesbians, but all were castigated by conservative pundits as problematic and "masculine" females in contrast to the codified model of femaleness.

In addition to these verses, readers submitted different genres of satirical commentary on the incident, including ballad dramas and comic dialogues (Modan otona tôsei manga yose 1935). A pun-filled ballad titled "Suicide Journey of a Flapper and a Mannish Woman" (Datemusume Dansô Michiyuki), referred to the feminine partner as a "flapper" and a "revue girl" whose last dance (*dansu*) was with a female cross-dresser (*dansô*). The couple's suicide attempt was sensationalized widely in the mass media, including in *Fujin Kôron* (Women's Review) and *Chûô Kôron* (Central Review), two of the most prominent mainstream magazines in which articles addressing the intersection of sexuality, sexology, and modernity appeared on a regular basis.[2]

Three years before Masuda and Saijô tempted fate, the successful double suicide of a heterosexual couple, a Keio University student and the daughter of a wealthy (Christian) household, was similarly sensationalized, and elegies were published in the mass media memorializing the exquisite purity of their love—needless to say, the poems were not submitted to humor columns. The two had decided to commit suicide together by drowning (in a mountain lake southwest of Tokyo) after the woman's parents took steps to force her into an arranged marriage. Arranged marriage preparations motivated many women (and men) to commit, or attempt to commit suicide regardless of their sexual orientation. A comparison of "Homosexual Elegy" with a poem on the heterosexual couple's suicide, titled "A Love Consummated in Heaven" (Tengoku ni musubareru koi),[3] suggests the different narrative treatment of the psychological circumstances and, at least initial public reception of homosexual (*dôseiai*) and heterosexual (*iseiai*) double suicides. (The differential treatment was also apparent in the Japanese social-scientific literature on double suicide, as I discuss below.) The poem introduces the atmosphere defining the incident, followed by first the man's lament, and second the woman's, and ends in a joint declaration by the couple.

> This evening's farewell, the moon also
> Dims with grief; in Sagami Bay
> The fire lures of fishermen are damp with tears.
> So fleeting is love in this life.
>
> With you the bride of another,
> How will I live? How can I live?
> I too will go. There where Mother is,
> There beside her,
> I will take your hand.
>
> God alone knows
> That our love has been pure.
> We die, and in [Heaven],
> I will be your bride.
>
> Soon, we will fade away happily:
> Spring flowers on Mount Sakada.[4]

It is quite clear this poem was not intended as a spoof or critique of the practice of double suicide, and the incident inspired a popular movie of the same title (Seidensticker 1990:35). The pristine love of the couple is celebrated, and all of nature, from the moon to the fishermen, weeps with grief tinged with bittersweet joy for their union in heaven. The lesbian couple, on the other hand, and specifically the "masculine" partner, is portrayed as a casualty of, to use today's jargon, a dysfunctional family, represented by insufficient parental love and a cold-hearted older sister. Their attempted suicide is characterized as an act provoked by nihilistic anger, as opposed to visions of conjugal bliss in another life.

Masculinized Females as Social Disorder

Juxtaposed, these two cases underscore the common sense or dominant notion in Japan past and present about the dichotomous constructions of sex, gender, and sexuality. In modern Japan, as in the United States, a person's gender is assigned, and heterosexuality assumed, at birth on the initial basis of genital type, but this is neither an immutable assignment nor an unproblematic assumption.[5] Although, in the case of Japan, the existence of two sexes and two genders is taken for granted, "female" gender (femininity) and "male" gender (masculinity) are not ultimately regarded as the exclusive province of female- and male-sexed bodies, respectively.

Sex, gender, and sexuality may be popularly perceived as irreducibly joined, but this remains a situational, and not a permanently fixed, condition.

The introduction and coinage in the late nineteenth century of the new social scientific terms "homosexual" (*homosekushuaru*, also *dôseiai*) and "heterosexual" (*heterosekushuaru*, also *iseiai*) obfuscated actual sexual practices that were far more complex and boundary-blurring than the models of and for them. "Homosexual" and "heterosexual" were conveniently superimposed on the existing dominant dichotomous construction of sex, gender, and sexuality and stimulated a new, psychoanalytic exploration of their relationship. However, these terms, especially in their official Japanese translations of *dôseiai* and *iseiai*, were not used consistently and were qualified on the basis of extenuating circumstances and definition-stretching practices. For example, depending on the context, *dôseiai* was used to described either a relationship that involved a same-gender, same-sex couple (for example, two feminine females or two masculine males) or a same-sex, different-gender couple (for example, a "butch-femme"-type female couple, or a "butch-nellie"-type male couple). Masuda and Saijô clearly were constructed in the mass media as an *ome* or "butch-femme"-type couple—that is, a couple consisting of what was perceived as a masculine woman and a feminine woman.[6] Initially, they were ridiculed openly—as in the instance of the humor column—not for the simple fact of their unconventional relationship, but for other reasons, including their public and publicized conduct, their celebrity and affluence, and, most importantly, their apparent eschewal of heterosexual marriage and motherhood.

Japanese pundits have been adept at selectively adapting for domestic and often dominant purposes institutions and terminologies that were first established and coined outside of Japan. One of the earliest such sources was China, and since the sixteenth century, Europe has served as an important source. It was in the late nineteenth century that Euro-American loan words and Japanese neologisms in the new field of sexology rapidly made their way into professional and lay parlance alike, evidenced not only in a wide range of printed media, including translations of foreign texts, but also by the many dictionaries devoted to introducing and defining such words. Among the loan words and Japanese social scientific neologisms that were household words by the early 1900s were, in addition to "homosexual" and "heterosexual," "fan" (*fuan*), "love letter" (*rabu retâ*), "lesbian" (*rezubian*), and garçon (*gyaruson*), in reference to a mannish woman. Other somewhat less conspicuous loan-words referring to same-sex sexual practices were "sapphism" (*saffuo*), "tribadism" (*tsuribadeizumu*), and "uranism" (*uranizumu*), among others (Hayashi 1926; Ôzumi 1931).

Obviously, social and sexual practices labeled and categorized in the "feudal" Edo period (1603–1867) were undertaken and perceived differently in the succeeding Meiji period (1868–1911) and onward, when the country was embarked on a course of modernization, industrialization, and selective Westernization. In fact, a growing if grudging acknowledgment and new interpretation of sexual relations between females prompted the introduction of the term *dôseiai* to distinguish their activities from those of males, although before long the neologism became a standard word for homosexuality in general, regardless of the sex of the individuals involved (Furukawa 1994:115). Among the "indigenous" terms for lesbians and lesbianism are *aniki* (older brother), *dansô no reijin* (beautiful person [female] in men's clothes), *gôin* (joint licentiousness), *imoto* (younger sister), *join* (female licentiousness), *joshoku* (female eroticism), *kaiawase* (matching shells), *mesu* (female [animal]), *musumeyaku* (woman's role-player), *neko* (pussy[cat], similar in meaning to "femme"), *onêsama* (older sister), *osu* (male [animal]), *otokoyaku* (man's role-player), *shirojiro* (pure white, with etymological implications of falseness and feigned ignorance), *tachi* (an abbreviation of *tachiyaku*, or "leading man," similar in meaning to "butch"), and *tomogui* ("eat each other") (Sugahara 1971:4–5; Robertson 2001 [1998]:19–20). Japanese lesbian feminists today translate butch and femme as *tachi* and *neko* and often use the loan words *butchi* and *fuemu* (Minakawa 1987:23). Another Japanese term for "butch" often encountered today is *onabe*, or shallow pot, a play on *okama*, or deep pot, a slang word for a "feminine" homosexual male (that is, a "bottom"). In short, indigenous and foreign-derived words alike were and are historically and culturally specific to the Japanese discourse of sexuality.

The works of Freud, Krafft-Ebing, Carpenter, Ellis, Hirschfeld, Weininger, and others were imported directly to Japan where they were translated, often by Japanese scholars who had studied abroad, and employed immediately in the identification of social problems and their analysis and resolution, exercises in which the state became increasingly invested (see Furukawa 1994; Frühstück 1998, 2003). For Japanese social scientists and critics, the loan words "homosexual" and "heterosexual" helped to explain historical phenomena in a new way and to devise new categories of pathological phenomena, such as "female" psychology, neurasthenia, and fandom. Like all other methods of classification and analysis, these terms and their definitions both opened up new insights and closed off others.

For many critics, "moral depravity" accompanying the growth of the modernizing (or Westernizing) city seemed to be the only viable "explanation" for *ome* or "butch-femme" relationships among bourgeois urban women, at least until the advent of all-female revues, whose men's role-players (*otokoyaku*) inspired new ideas to account for the increasingly visible masculinized female (Robertson 1992). Whereas the Japanese "Good Wife, Wise Mother" was praised by conservatives as the embodiment of social stability and cultural integrity, her alter ego, the "Western" masculinized female—and New Woman in general—was perceived as the embodiment of social instability. As Sharon Sievers has shown, national cultural identity in Imperial Japan was premised on a sexual division of symbolic labor, where crew-cut males in dark suits evinced the nation's modernization program and kimono-clad females with chignons represented the longevity and continuity of Japanese "tradition," itself a modern product. (In fact, short hair for women was made illegal in 1872, although this law was routinely flouted and rarely enforced [Sievers 1983:14–15].)

The place of class in the overlapping discourses of sex, gender, and nationality cannot be underestimated. Some females, in the first half of the twentieth century at least, "passed" as men in order to secure employment as rickshaw drivers, construction superviors and laborers, fishers, department store managers, grocers, and so on (Tomioka 1938:103). "Passing" was associated unequivocally with sexual deviancy in the case of urban middle- and upper-class girls and women who, it was argued, wore masculine attire not to secure a livelihood but as an outward expression of their "moral depravity." As privileged and educated—in short, bourgeois—girls and women, they were supposed to fulfill the state-sanctioned "Good Wife, Wise Mother" gender role. Consequently, those who resisted were vilified in journal and newspaper articles on mannish women and roundly critiqued in texts and treatises on "female" psychology (Sakabe 1924; Sugita 1929, 1935; Yasuda 1935; Ushijima 1943).

The modern(izing) state discouraged gender ambivalence and sexual confusion, which were associated with social disorder (Watanabe and Iwata 1989:127), and the steady militarization of the society heightened the delineation of sex and gender. Whereas Donald Roden (1990) claims that debates about gender and sexual ambivalence were directed at males and females equally, my extensive perusal of hundreds of contemporary newspaper, magazine, and journal articles leads me to different conclusions: females almost exclusively were singled out as the source of sexual deviance and social disorder and as the targets of acrimonious debates about the relationship among sex, gender, and sexuality. If the sexes were converging, as some pundits argued (for example, Nogami 1920), it was because the masculinization of females was compromising the masculinity of males, who appeared more feminine in contrast; that is, the markers distinguishing male from female, masculine from feminine were losing their polarity. The dialectical dynamics of sex-and-gender were experienced as a zero-sum game. Because the nation itself was personified in contrastive gendered terms, it would not do to have androgynous females (and males) wreaking symbolic havoc. Gendering New Japan, as the imperial nation was called, was an ongoing project that was constantly adapted to extenuating circumstances. As I have illustrated in an article on the culture of Japanese imperialism, when the martial spirit of the

Japanese was at issue, the West and Euro-American cultural productions were cast as feminine and feminizing, in the "bad" sense of unmanly and emasculating. Contrarily, the nation was personified as feminine, in the "good" sense of traditional, when the superior cultural sensibility and artistic achievements of the Japanese were publicized (Robertson 1995). Mannish girls and women were therefore deemed un-Japanese (see Robertson 1998). Moreover, the "feminization of males" (*danshi no joseika*) was a consequence of the "masculinization of females" (*joshi no danseika*), and while the former was worrisome, it was the latter condition at which critics directed their fearful anger (see Roden 1990).

Siting Double Suicide

Suicide is a key component of a Japanese national allegory, as Alan Wolfe argues in his exploration of the relation between the concept of "national suicide" and autobiographical writing (Wolfe 1990:14–15, 215–217). "Problem women," who in the 1930s chose suicide, were squarely situated within this allegory. For female couples to commit or attempt double suicide was tantamount to their making a public(ized) claim for sexual citizenship and subjectivity through an act of ultimate resolve valorized for centuries in literature and reified as a quintessentially "Japanese" expression of sincerity and purity of intention. The suicide and parasuicide attempts, as well as notes and letters of lesbians constituted an important voice in contested debates about the relationship between sexuality and nationality in a modern (izing) Japan. Responding to the preponderance of such attempts reported in the press, one prominent sexologist, Yasuda Tokutarô, wondered, "Why are there so many lesbian double suicides reported in the society column of the daily newspapers? One can only infer that females these days are monopolizing homosexuality"(Yasuda 1935:150). Moreover, lesbian suicide attempts effectively highlighted the connection between self/social destruction and self/social reconstruction.

The several Anglophone works that deal analytically with "Japanese suicide" avoid mention of "homosexual double suicide" even though this particular category figures, quite prominently in some cases, in the Japanese social scientific literature on suicide. Likewise, whereas the long history in Japan of same-sex sexual relations between males (specifically Buddhist priests, samurai, and Kabuki actors) is well accounted for, if largely descriptively (for example, Leupp 1995), until very recently, sexual relations between females in general have remained largely unrecognized, unacknowledged, invisible, and inaccessible in the postwar scholarly literature in and on Japan.[7]

However, unlike the bridled Japanese and Anglophone scholarship of today, various types of lesbian practice, including double suicide, were widely and openly highlighted, discussed, sensationalized, and analyzed in the scholarly and popular media of early twentieth-century Japan. The involuted complexities of sexual practices and the instability of categories thereof, together with a perceived and internalized stigma on lesbian subjects, jointly have induced Japan scholars to disregard even what captivated the Japanese public and scholarly community at a given historical moment. Ironically, the space of sociosexual (in)difference is evident *not* in the popular cultural discourse shaping a specific period, but in the academic scholarship on Japan. The persistence of the dominant sex-gender ideology that females are objects of male desire and not the subjects of their own desire, effectively inhibits both naming that desire and identifying multiple modes of female *and* male sexualities in Japan. Attending to the early debates on sexuality, and conveying a sense of the contested rhetorical climate in which they took place, are a necessary beginning for a more complete (and more responsible) anthropology of sexuality, gender ideology, and associated practices today.

Double suicide is often translated as "love suicide" in keeping with the nuances of the Japanese terms *shinjû* ("hearts contained") and *jôshi* ("love death"). As Takie Lebra notes, the "theme of inseparability stands out not only in the motivation or goal, but also in the method [of suicide]" (Lebra 1976:195–196). Whereas prior to the seventeenth century *shinjû* denoted "milder pledges of love, such as exchanging oaths or tearing out a fingernail," it has since meant both a double suicide by lovers and any suicide involving the death of more than one person, such as *oyako shinjû* (parent[mother]-child suicide) (Keene 1976:253; Lebra 1976:195). Since the early twentieth century, *dôseiai shinjû* and *dôseiai jôshi* have been the most common terms used for homosexual double suicide.

Lesbian Double Suicide: The Practice

In his book on Tokyo since the great earthquake of 1923, Edward Seidensticker makes note of the "high" incidence of suicides and double suicides in the 1930s, and connects these acts to the "nervous and jumpy" national and international climate. The Japanese government withdrew from the League of Nations in 1933 after rejecting a demand for the Kwantung Army to withdraw from Manchuria, where they had established the puppet ("The Last Emperor") state of Manchukuo in 1932. Parts of Manchuria had been under Japanese control since 1906; the Kwantung Army plotted to occupy that country in 1931, which led to the outbreak of a full-scale war with China in 1937, a development marked as the "beginning" of World War II for Japan. Seidensticker suggests that the Japanese government's withdrawal from the League provoked feelings of isolation and apprehension among ordinary citizens which, with the economic depression, exacerbated the despondency, illness, and family difficulties that motivate suicidal acts (Seidensticker 1990:35, 37).

One might productively interpret lesbian double suicides as both signifying and symptomatic of another dimension of national isolation and apprehension, not only on the part of the females involved, but also on the part of culture critics obsessed with the figure of the masculinized female, and especially the mannish lesbian (compare Smith-Rosenberg 1985: 245–296). Yasuda Tokutarô's rhetorical question noted above about females' monopoly on suicide and homosexuality points to this other dimension. Unlike the majority of his contemporaries, Yasuda was unusual in looking favorably upon Japanese lesbian practices as representing female and ultimately cultural emancipation, in that mutual cooperation between females and males would insure that neither would be reduced to servile status (Yasuda 1935:152; see Roden 1990:54). His interest, in his words, in the "widespread phenomenon of same-sex love among females" was provoked by press coverage of Masuda Yasumare and Saijô Eriko's attempted double suicide, to which I now return (Yasuda 1935:146).

What were the circumstances of the female couple's attempted "love suicide"? The media focused mostly on Masuda, whose masculine appearance was perceived not only as a marker of aggression, but also as subversive and dangerous. Saijô, in contrast, was treated more leniently for the likely reason that her comparatively feminine, if problematically "modern," appearance was perceived as less threatening than Masuda's blatantly maverick aspect. It is also likely that as a "revue girl" (*rebyû gâru*), a vocation associated with wanton women, Saijô's conduct was already marked as beyond the pale (compare Asagawa 1921; Ozaki 1986). Masuda, though, was singled out as proof of the "recent, disturbing increase in the 1920s and 1930s in lesbian affairs between upper class girls and women"; affairs that presumably "in the past, were associated with lower class status" (Kore mo jidaisô ka 1935).

Saijô, the feminine partner, published an autobiographical account of the suicide attempt two months after the event in *Fujin Kôron*.[8] I recount most of Saijô's story to provide readers with a sense of its tone and colorful characterizations. Saijô begins by recalling how she first met Masuda backstage after a show in May, 1934 at an Osaka theater: the actress was stepping out of her bath wrapped in a towel when Masuda approached and struck up a short conversation. The cross-dressed fan's physical beauty, especially her straight, white teeth, round "Lloyd" spectacles, and "Eton crop" (a short hairstyle) impressed Saijô, and the visits became a daily affair. Come autumn, after half a year of constant contact at different venues in eastern and western Japan, Saijô reports that Masuda's letters to her grew intensely passionate; the handsome fan would write such things as, "I can't bear to be apart from you for even a moment." "Although these letters could be interpreted as expressions of lesbian love," the actress explains, "I viewed them as the confessions of a sincere fan" (Saijô 1935:170).

Saijô's admission of the fuzzy boundary between fandom and lesbian desire played into the dominant perception of female fans of the all-female revue as pathological and socially problematic. "Fan" was often used as a euphemism for lesbian (or for a girl or woman with lesbian proclivities) and fandom was identified as a serious illness marked by an inability to distinguish between sexual fantasies (themselves problematic phenomena in women) and actual lesbian practices (Hogosha wa kokoro seyo 1935; Kore mo jidaisô ka 1935; Robertson 2001 [1998], chaps. 4 and 5).

In her account, Saijô refers to herself by her first name, Eriko, and characterizes herself as a gullible actress—as highly impressionable and thus "naturally inclined" to become absorbed into Masuda's charismatic aura. She waxes nostalgic about their walks, hand in hand, along the bay: "[F]or those who didn't know us, we probably looked just like [heterosexual] lovers" (Saijô 1935:171). The couple traveled widely in the Kansai area; New Year's Day 1935 found them together in bed in a Kyoto hotel. Saijô claims that by that point she had wearied of the intensity of their relationship and wanted to return to Tokyo, where she had a photo shoot scheduled for the first week of January. But whenever she mentioned the word "return home" (*kaeru*), Masuda became deathly pale and stern, and Saijô would lose the courage to insist.

They spent the next several days on a ferryboat to Beppu on the island of Kyushu—a "gateway to death," as Saijô describes the experience (Saijô 1935:172). Travel provided this and other same-sex couples an opportunity for extra-ordinary activities and practices that could not be practically sustained in the more mundane realm of everyday life (compare Ôhara 1973:244–245). A couple would often travel for several days to a particular suicide site, enjoying each other's intimate company to an unprecedented degree. It was on the trip to Beppu that Masuda first recited to Saijô the sad story about her sterile, dysfunctional, and fatherless family. Masuda's father had separated from his wife shortly after his brokerage firm went bankrupt and set up housekeeping with a mistress with whom he eventually produced six children (Dansô reijô no kashutsu jiken 1935).

Much to her apparent chagrin, Saijô's chronic appendicitis flared up shortly after they arrived in Beppu and the actress was hospitalized for three days. The doctor encouraged her to return to Kyoto by train, which was faster and more comfortable than a ferryboat. Back in Kyoto, the tension between the two women escalated, although they "fought silently." When Saijô insisted on returning to Tokyo, Masuda threatened to commit suicide.

Meanwhile, Masuda's mother had hired a private investigator to locate the itinerant couple, at which point the press, alerted and ready to exploit the splashy story, filed daily reports on the couple's saga, noting that their real "suicide journey" (*michiyuki*) began on the night of January 23

(Dansô no reijin 1935), when, after a "storybook-like" chase involving trains and cars, the couple was apprehended in Nagoya by the private investigator. Masuda's mother and sister blamed the revue actress for the love-struck fan's transgressions, including the theft of money and stock certificates out of which their travels were paid and fancy gifts bought. Masuda was sent back to her mother's house in Osaka and Saijô retired to her parents' home in Tokyo.

That was not the end of their relationship, however. Late at night on January 27, Saijô received a telephone call from Masuda, who had fled to Tokyo the previous night and was staying at a city hotel. (The press described her escape as a matter of "re-entering the fickle world of sexual desire" [Dansô no reijin 1935].) Saijô went immediately to the hotel, her father in tow. Feeling sorry for her "special friend," Saijô, "at [her] father's urging," prepared to spend the night with Masuda, who recounted her escape. Apparently Masuda had fooled her mother into thinking that she was asleep in bed by stuffing cushions under her blankets. Breaking open the terrace door, she climbed over a tall wall to freedom, cutting her hands badly in the process. Borrowing money from a neighbor, she made her way to Tokyo, vowing never to return to her family from hell. Before leaving, she left a note on her bed instructing her mother and sister not to pursue her—advice they ignored.

Masuda and Saijô conspired to move secretly to another city hotel in order to avoid the droves of pesky newspaper reporters who had tracked the handsome fan to Tokyo. At around midnight, they pushed their beds together and "went to sleep." No mention is made in Saijô's account of a double suicide pact or the ingestion of tranquilizers and sleeping pills. The narrative as a whole is crafted defensively, with the actress represented as a victim of her fan's willful passion. Acknowledging the widespread press coverage of the attempted double suicide, Saijô allows the reader to supply the missing details and notes simply that she was shocked to find herself awake in the morning.[9] Looking at Masuda's "peacefully sleeping form," Saijô read the masculine female's suicide note, which was reprinted in her *Fujin Kôron* article as follows:

> Eriko (Saijô's first name).
>
> Even though it seems as though we've known each other forever, ours was a very short-lived relationship. But you more than anyone have left a deep and everlasting impression on my heart. What this means not even I know for sure. What I do know is that I loved you (*suki deshita*) unconditionally. Now as I approach the end of my life, I can say that I never thought that I would become so profoundly indebted to you. In any case, thank you; thank you very very much. I don't know how I can thank you enough. No, it's not merely thanks, I will die indebted (*osewa*) to you and that is a happy thought. My incorrigibly selfish ways have caused you much grief. Please forgive me. Once I had made the decision to die, I cried and cried thinking

> of all that we've shared and how much I would miss you. And I realized how sad it is to die alone. To be perfectly honest, I wanted you to die with me. But I am aware of your circumstances, and you always assumed a rational stance in contrast to my emotional one. So, I'll go alone after all. Goodbye.
>
> Yasumare (Masuda's self-selected first name)
> January 28, evening (Saijô 1935:178)

Masuda's letter was likely edited by Saijô or someone else in a way that exonerated the revue actress from any complicity in a double suicide attempt. Saijô also appears as a rational counter to Masuda's emotional self. Perhaps this was a strategy designed to minimize the incident's damage to her acting and modeling career? In any case, shortly after her double suicide attempt, Saijô left the Shôchiku Revue to pursue a career in film. She all but disappeared from that revue's fan magazines, where she had been featured regularly before the incident.

In concluding her tale of love and suicide, Saijô reveals that she was able to deal influentially with the Masuda family lawyer, requesting that her masculine partner be allowed the unprecedented step of forming a branch household (*bunke*) and living independently, as if Masuda were, in fact, male. And when Masuda's estranged father visited his daughter in the hospital, Saijô criticized him for being an absentee father. Saijô herself vows henceforth to keep a close watch on Masuda's behavior. Self-interest aside, Saijô and others' accounts (see Tani 1935) of the couple's ordeal in prominent mainstream magazines effectively parried the earlier disparaging treatment of their double suicide attempt in the humor column of the *Asahi Shinbun*.

Lesbian Suicide: The Theories

Quite a few Japanese psychiatrists and social critics of the time assumed that females' "natural" passivity and hormone-provoked melancholia made them susceptible to neurasthenia (*shinkeishitsu*) that in turn occasioned a pessimism expressed in the form of homosexuality. Their melancholia was exacerbated, in turn, by homosexual practices that made them further susceptible to suicidal impulses (Tamura 1913; Shôjo no hi no sei mondai 1934; Fukushima [1935] 1984:562). Pundits and critics also asserted that all-female revues on the subject of romantic love and its ephemerality, together with certain European films, such as the antipatriarchal "Mädchen in Uniform," first shown in Japan in 1933 to sold-out audiences, valorized both lesbianism and suicide (Shôjo no hi no sei mondai 1934:9).

"Homosexual Elegy," quoted at the beginning of this chapter, parrots the various explanations for lesbian sexuality and double suicide popularized in the press. For example, a 1935 newspaper article on the fad at that time among girls and women of dressing as men included an interview with a physician, Saitô Shigeyoshi, who cited the theories of bisexuality proposed by Otto Weininger in explaining female transvestism in Japan (Kore mo jidaisô ka 1935). Weininger's formulations contributed to the "psychiatric style of reasoning" that emerged in the late nineteenth century in America, Europe, and Japan (see also Davidson 1987). Today, his *Sex and Character* (1906) is recognized as racism (anti-Semitism) and misogyny in the guise of scientific analysis.

Saitô acknowledges a long history of lesbian sexuality and mannish women in Japan, but claims that the permanent condition was "more prevalent in the West," implying, as did others, that an incorrigibly masculinized female (in this case, a mannish lesbian) was thoroughly Westernized and therefore un-Japanese (Kore mo jidaisô ka 1935). Doubtless Saitô was also familiar with the work of Weininger's contemporary, Richard von Krafft-Ebing, whose *Psychopathia Sexualis* (1886) was standard reading for Japanese psychologists and sexologists. It was even appropriated as a template for *Hentai seiyokuron* (The theory of deviant sexual desire), co-authored by Habuto Eiji and Sawada Junjirô in 1915 (and reprinted 18 times over the next decade) (Roden 1990:45). Krafft-Ebing created a new "medico-sexual category, the Mannish Lesbian," in which he linked "women's rejection of traditional gender roles and their demands for social and economic equality to cross-dressing..." (1985:272). What was a universal, if new, "medico-sexual" category for Krafft-Ebing was for Saitô a consequence of Westernization.

Masuda and Saijô were referred to disparagingly in the newspaper article as practicing a "deviant homosexual love" (*hentai dôseiai*). "Deviant," because same-sex, different-gender (for example, "butch-femme") relationships were regarded as abnormal, while same-sex, same-gender relationships, or passionate friendships among outwardly feminine couples, were and are regarded as part of a normal and self-limited stage in the female life cycle (Tamura 1913; Mochizuki 1959; Robertson 1989, 1992). Lesbianism, broadly defined as eroticized, intimate relations between two females, was not itself an issue so long as it was self-limited and unmarked by the presence of a masculine partner. Provided sexual practices neither interfered with nor challenged the legitimacy of the twinned institutions of marriage and household, nor competed with heterosexist conventions in the public sphere, Japanese society accommodated (and still does) a diversity of sexual behaviors. To wit, social reproduction need not be synonymous with human reproduction (as in the case of adopted sons *cum* sons-in-law, a common strategy of household succession in Japan in the absence of a male heir), but the former must not be compromised by a politicized sexual identity that interferes with the latter.

Following their European and American counterparts, such as Havelock Ellis, some Japanese psychologists active in the early twentieth century drew a distinction between "real" or "permanent" (*shin*), and "provisional" or "transient" (*kari*) homosexuality in females. Unlike their European and American counterparts, they sometimes referred to the former condition as "Western" and the latter as "Japanese." Whereas the former condition, embodied by the masculine woman, was deemed "incurable," the latter condition, embodied by the feminine woman, supposedly resolved itself quickly once she married. Parents were reassured that "provisional lesbianism" was not the result of "mental insufficiency or illness," but rather should be perceived as a short-lived "spiritual hedonism" (*seishinteki kyôraku*) (Kore mo jidaisô ka 1935).

The works of the European and American sexologists named earlier "quickly captured the imagination of Japan's earliest students of psychology," amateurs and professionals alike (see Hirschfeld 1935:7–39; Roden 1990:45). The application of these theories by Japanese scholars and clinicians was informed by an apparent contradiction: a subscription (sometimes on the level of academic lip-service) to the universality of Euro-American psychological theories and a belief in Japanese uniqueness that in turn was typified by a lack of both awareness and theoretical engagement with everyday sexual and gendered practices in Japan (see Yasuda 1935; Yoshimoto 1989:25). In this connection, the German sexologist and advocate of homosexual rights, Magnus Hirschfeld, reported that during his lecture tour of Japan in the spring of 1931 he encountered among his Japanese colleagues, many of whom had studied in Europe, an apparently "widespread ignorance of intersexual male and female types off the stage, and especially of the extent of homosexuality in general" (Hirschfeld 1935:30). He recorded the following illuminating account of his conversation with Miyake Kôichi, a professor of psychiatry:

> Professor M[i]yaki . . . said when we first met: "Tell me, my dear Hirschfeld, how is it that one hears so much about homosexuality in Germany, England and Italy and nothing of it among us?"
>
> I answered: "That, my dear colleague, is because it is permitted by you and forbidden by us."
>
> "But it seems to be more prevalent in Europe," he continued. "In all my long practice I have never yet seen one single case."
>
> "I can scarcely believe that the phenomenon is rarer among you than among us," I replied, "but I shall be able to tell you better in a few weeks when I have done some investigating among specialists in the subject."
>
> I gave him my opinion shortly before I left, after I had had a chance to find out, from letters written to me by Japanese and particularly from people who came to see me after my presence was known, that every form of homosexuality, in tendency as well as in expression, is precisely the same in Japan as in Europe. My old observation was again completely confirmed: the

individual sex type is a far more important factor than the *racial type*. (Hirschfeld 1935:30–31)

Despite a cultural history of same-sex sexual practices among males, not to mention the sensationalized coverage of homosexual love and its social implications, some of Hirschfeld's Japanese colleagues claimed to be unaware of the history and present situation of same-sex or homosexual practices in Japan—or they at least maintained a public posture of ignorance—as is obvious from their published works. In an article on "deviant sexual desire," for example, Ôzumi Narumitsu focuses on homosexual practices *outside* of Japan, providing Japanese translations for English, French, and Latin terms (Ôzumi 1931). Roden suggests that Japanese sexologists writing for an educated but popular audience were obliged to grace their articles and books "with just enough pseudo-scientific information and prescriptive advice to limit government censorship without dampening the curiosity of their middle-class audience" (Roden 1990:46). The use of Euro-American examples to illustrate allegedly universal (homo)sexual practices may have been, in part, a strategy to avoid official censure, which was considerable by the late 1930s. But what could account for earlier self-censoring practices?

Sabine Frühstück (1998) suggests that some German- and Austrian-trained sexologists, like Miyake, willfully dismissed those sexual practices which they felt would compromise Japan's international image as a "civilized" country, while others used new sexological categories to isolate and rebuke all types of New Women, and particularly the Mannish Lesbian. It might also be the case that Miyake and others like him simply did not recognize certain historical same-sex sexual practices in Japan as categorizable under the new sexological terminology adopted from continental *Sexualwissenschaft*.

Dying to Tell

Suicides and attempted suicides generated a variety of narratives representing a spectrum of genres, including social scientific analyses, suicide notes, letters, wills, autobiographical accounts, magazine and newspaper articles, poems, dramatic chants, and so forth. Masuda's suicide note to Saijô apparently was one of five she had prepared for members of her family, a close friend, and for the public (Nakano 1935:164). Only the note to Saijô was made public, although it may have been doctored, as I have suggested. Significantly, the suicide and parasuicide narratives written by Japanese lesbians and published in the print media contradict the various dominant theories about both suicide and lesbianism such as those ventured by Komine Shigeyuki, a prominent sexologist. Komine draws distinctions between heterosexual and homosexual double suicides. He claims that whereas a heterosexual couple's double suicide was premeditated and often provoked by their inability to marry, a homosexual couple's decision to commit double suicide was spontaneous and carried out for apparently "trivial" reasons. While Komine does not discount entirely the possibility of sexual desire between females, he does insist that "empathy and commiseration" (*dôjô*) and not frustrated sexual desire (sometimes in the guise of resistance or opposition to an arranged marriage), was the catalyst for lesbian double suicides (Komine 1985:197–198).

The various narratives generated by the Masuda-Saijô attempted double suicide and others demonstrate that the women's decision to die was neither spontaneous nor motivated by petty concerns. Moreover, although a couple's frustration at the futility of maintaining their romantic relationship was underplayed, there seemed to be a public consensus about both the "causes" of lesbianism and the suicidal effects of melancholia, loneliness, a dysfunctional family, and/or parental efforts to force a woman into an arranged marriage—causes that were hardly trivial. This was a consensus that coexisted with attempts in the press to trivialize female couples and their tribulations.

Komine tabulates the numbers of "female same-sex double (or 'love' suicides" (*joshi dôseijôshi*) reported in the daily press between 1925 and 1935, acknowledging that the actual figures were probably much higher (Komine 1985:232).[10] The haphazard quality of suicide statistics in the early twentieth century, in terms of collection, categorization, and interpretation, make it difficult to determine accurately both the number of suicides per se and which of the double suicides actually involved lesbian couples. Clearly, a proportion significant enough to attract critical attention was committed by lesbians. Komine himself suggests this in his study of homosexual double suicide. He warns that not only are double suicides committed by female couples hidden in statistics for heterosexual suicides, such as in cases involving a man and two women, but also that not all female double suicides involved lesbians, as in some cases siblings were involved (Komine 1985:176). According to Komine's data, there were 342 incidents of "female same-sex double (or 'love') suicides" (totalling *at least* twice as many females) reported in the press between 1925 and 1935. His category *joshi dôseijôshi* is ambiguous; given the subject of his book, Komine most probably means "lesbian double suicides," although it is not entirely clear whether he adjusted his statistics for the possibility that some of these suicides (or attempts) involved female siblings or love triangles (for example, two women in love with the same man).

More than half of these acts occurred during the "nervous and jumpy" years of 1932 and 1935. Komine claims that confirmed lesbian double suicides amounted to about 31 percent of all categories of suicides

(1985:174–175). The average age of the women at the time of their resolve to die was between 20 and 25 years. The vast majority of lesbian double suicides involved factory workers, waitresses, and nurses, in that order; prostitutes constituted the majority of female actors in the case of heterosexual double suicides (Komine 1985:178, 174). Komine reports that whereas the actors in heterosexual double suicides tended to be of different social statuses and classes—for example, a male novelist and a prostitute, a wealthy housewife and a chauffeur—the vast majority (more than 80 per cent) of partners in homosexual double suicides were of the same social status, class, or occupation (Komine 1985:175).

As I have noted, one reason the Masuda-Saijô attempted suicide generated so much interest and attention was their social prominence: Masuda's upper-class status and Saijô's celebrity status. However, their statuses alone did not clinch their notoriety, for the newspapers and magazines of those and earlier years were filled with accounts and analyses of female homosexual practices and their consequences. Widespread press and magazine coverage facilitated the public intertextuality of lesbian practices and acts (both successful and unsuccessful) of double suicide, although the majority of actors in these incidents were but names and statistics without faces. Doubtless a widely publicized lesbian double suicide attempt on June 12, 1934, was familiar to Masuda and Saijô, just as the partners in that attempt were inspired to die after reading an article about a female student from Tokyo who jumped into the crater of Mount Mihara on the offshore island of Ôshima.

The June 1934 case concerned a love triangle involving a so-called masculinized female (age 23) to whom two feminine females (ages 18 and 23) were attracted. All three worked at a Tokyo coffee shop where the cross-dressed, mannish partner was a manager and the other two, waitresses.[11] The many newspaper articles on the case quoted the women as recognizing that in society at present a bonafide love relationship was only possible as a couple and not as a threesome. Acting upon that realization, the "kindhearted" older feminine partner decided to withdraw from the group to simplify matters. One morning in early June she left suicide notes at her sister's and brother's homes and proceeded to a park were she swallowed an overdose of tranquilizers. She later recovered (Dôseiai no onna san'nin shinjû 1934; Dôseiai no seisan 1934).

Meanwhile, the couple had resolved, independent of the third woman, to die together and set out on a two-day suicide journey to the offshore island of Ôshima where they planned to throw themselves into the volcanic crater. The masculine partner had chosen this particular mode of death inspired by the aforementioned student's suicide there the previous year (apparently most suicidal females elected either to drown themselves or to swallow either tranquilizers or sleeping pills [Komine 1985:183]). Alerted by the siblings of the estranged partner, the press trailed the couple

Figure 12.2 The lesbian couple dejected at the failure of their suicide mission.

to Ôshima, updating readers on their whereabouts and activities. The masculine partner was described as sporting short hair and dressed like a man's role-player in the all-female revue theater. She cut a dapper figure in her white knickerbockers, red jacket, two-tone shoes, and Panama hat. The feminine partner wore a "Western-style" dress, short socks, and straw thongs. Guided by the island's residents, who had easily spotted the two climbers, the paparazzi caught up with the couple shortly after the proprietor of a summit teahouse, sensing their melancholia, had grabbed them as they headed toward the crater (figure 12.2) (Watashi wa koi no shorisha 1934).

Two months later, Sakuma Hideka, the masculine partner, published an autobiographical account of the incident in *Fujin Gahô* (Women's Illustrated News), a mainstream women's magazine. After asking for everyone's forgiveness, Sakuma dismisses categorically the rumors that were spread like wildfire through the press of her "father's alcoholism," her grandmother's "geisha past," her impoverished, dysfunctional family, and her alleged "biological maleness" and "ability to impregnate women." She also criticizes sharply the newspapers' role in trivializing her ordeal by inviting readers to submit satirical songs about the incident (as the press did a year later in the Masuda-Saijô case) (Sakuma 1934:82).

It is clear that Sakuma understood the link between economic autonomy and self-representation and subjectivity, for she makes the radical argument that, provided they could support themselves, why shouldn't two women (much less three) in love with each other be able to live together in the same way that heterosexual couples can and do? "I don't hate men, I've just felt closer to women since graduating from girl's high school," she declares.[12] As for her so-called masculine appearance, Sakuma explains that "although I may have assumed a man's role, I am neither physically nor mentally malelike." And she stresses that by wearing trousers, she is not impersonating males but rather wearing what is most convenient and comfortable given the demands of her managerial job. Sakuma closes her narrative by lamenting her loneliness (1934:83). Meanwhile, notoriety was good for business, and large, expensive ads for the coffee shop where Sakuma worked began appearing in the press (e.g., Yaesuen 1934:3).

More vividly than the actress Saijô's autobiographical account, the manager Sakuma's account suggests an apparently ironic connection between the resolve to commit suicide and the resolve to challenge on some level a family-state system that rendered women docile and subservient. Historically in Japan, suicide or attempted suicide was recognized, and to some extent valorized, as an empowering act that illuminated the purity and sincerity of one's position and intentions. A suicide letter corroborated these virtues by documenting one's motives. In other words, suicide was a culturally intelligible act that turned a private condition into a public matter.

Obviously, attempted (or unsuccessful) suicides have more direct political capital for, as in this case, the women live to talk in greater complexity about the circumstances informing their resolve to die, and they live to act on their resolve and to encourage action on the sometimes radical vision articulated in their suicide notes. Saijô, for example, claims in her account that she was able to deal influentially with the Masuda family lawyer regarding the unprecedented establishment of a branch household for her masculine partner. And Sakuma's article about her attempted double suicide introduces to mainstream audiences ideas and arguments about self-representation and the connection between economics and gender ideology that were (and still are) quite radical.

Lesbian suicide and parasuicide letters and accounts collectively constituted another voice, whether explicitly controversial or defensive, or both, in heated public debates about the articulation of sexuality, gender ideology, cultural identity, and (inter)national image. Moreover, like acts and attempts of suicide themselves, these texts, including those that doubled as love letters, were both private explorations and public proclamations—"public" because the art of writing letters consists in making one's views known to a correspondent, whether that person be a lover, parent, sibling, or anonymous reader. Suicide notes in this sense were an extension of, and not a substitute for, lesbian practices. Largely as a result of the cultural intelligibility of suicide in Japan, stories of suicide and attempted suicide seem to have served as an effective way to get controversial ideas into print and integrated with the popular discourse of sexuality. I have reviewed the circumstances of only some of the hundreds of cases of lesbian suicide and parasuicide reported, yet these cases generated a significant number of newspaper and magazine articles and analyses, whether sympathetic or hostile.

Clearly there is more to suicide than simply the "cultural appeal [in Japan] of masochistic behavior" (Lebra 1976:200). Lesbian double suicides and attempted suicides were predicated on—and both used and criticized as a trope for—a revolt against the normalizing functions of "tradition" (*qua* the "Good Wife, Wise Mother") as sanctioned by the civil code. Double suicide itself was a mode of death eulogized and allegorized in literature, particularly since the late seventeenth century, but when linked with women's unconventional sexual affinities and practices, lesbian suicide and parasuicide accounts drew attention to the symbolic death of the traditional Japanese Woman and the emergence on the public stage of new and more complex female actors.

Notes

This paper is a abridged version of my article, "Dying to Tell: Sexuality and Suicide in Imperial Japan," *Signs: Journal of Women in Culture and Society* 25, no. 1 (1999):1–36, parts of which appear in my book, *Takarazuka: Sexual Politics and Popular Culture in Modern Japan* (2001). Many thanks to Evelyn Blackwood for including it in this volume. All translations from Japanese to English are mine except when noted otherwise. Japanese names and authors published in Japanese are presented with the family name followed by the given name.

1. Saijô was a member of the all-female Shôchiku Revue founded in Tokyo in 1928, 15 years after its arch rival, the Takarazuka Revue, was established in the city of Takarazuka near Osaka (see Robertson 2001 [1998]).
2. By the 1930s, the population of 65 million purchased 10 million copies of daily newspapers, and the number of registered magazines and journals was 11,118. Print culture was available to all classes of consumers (Silverberg 1993:123–124) and the Masuda-Saijô "love story" was circulated countrywide.
3. The poem was subtitled, "The Philosophy of Suicide" (Shinjû no fuirosofui).

4. The Japanese text is in Ôhara (1965:210). Verses two and three appear in English in Seidensticker (1990:35) and I have deferred to his translation with one exception: I changed the original *tengoku* in the third verse from "paradise" to "Heaven" to underscore the woman's Christian faith. The remaining verses are my translations.
5. While this method of gender assignment is most typical of but not limited to Anglo-Americans, the lack of specific information on the assignment and assumption of "female" or "male" gender among non-Anglos makes me reluctant to generalize for all Americans. To generalize a "Japanese" notion of gender admittedly is problematic, given the various ethnic groups comprising that superficially "homogenous" society, although "Japanese" arguably is a more inclusive signifier than is "American."
6. *Ome* or *ome no kankei* ("male-female relations") were the expressions often used to identify lesbian couples. *Ome* is an abbreviation of *osu* and *mesu*, terms reserved to distinguish between male and female animals. They become pejorative when used to label humans, as in this case.
7. Recent works addressing lesbian practices include the "lesbian special issues" of the "alternative" journals *Bessatsu Takarajima* (1987) and *Imago* (1994), apart from authors Yoshitake 1986; Roden 1990; and Furukawa 1994. Privately circulated newsletters (printed by women's, feminist, and lesbian groups, for example) are another source of information about Japanese female sexualities.
8. The details of this incident are drawn from Saijô's account unless otherwise indicated (Saijô 1935).
9. If the story filed by a veteran reporter for the *Fujin Kôron* and friend of Saijô's father is accurate, then the actress' account is disingenuous. Apparently, the reporter interviewed a woozy Saijô after she had swallowed an overdose of sleeping pills. Following her back to her room, he found Masuda in a near coma and called for medical help (Nakano 1935).
10. Komine also tabulates the number of male homosexual double suicides (Komine 1985:202–232). I have focused exclusively on lesbian double suicides.
11. The press noted that the fact that all three lived with 17 others in an attached dorm increased the likelihood of their lesbianism—an argument premised on a type of demographic determinism (Dôseiai no onna san'nin shinjû 1934).
12. Girls' schools and the all-female revues, along with their (unmarried) teachers and members, were singled out by sexologists and social critics as the sites and agents of homosexuality among females (Tamura 1913; Sugita 1935; Ushijima 1943; compare Smith-Rosenberg 1985:266; and Vicinus 1989)—thus, the critics' perception of the deleterious effects of the German film, *Mädchen in Uniform*, on girls and women.

References Cited

Asagawa Kiyo. 1921. Joyû to onnayakusha (Actresses and women's role players). *Josei Nihonjin* 4:112–113.

Bessatsu Takarajima. 1987. [Special issue] Onna o aisuru onnatachi no monogatari (A tale of women who love women) 64. Dansô no reijin (Cross-dressed beauty). 1935. *Asahi Shinbun*, Osaka morn. ed., January 28:11.

Dansô no reijô no kashutsu jiken (The cross-dressed beauty's escape from her home). 1935. *Fujô Shinbun*, February 3:3.

Davidson, Arnold. 1987. Sex and the emergence of sexuality. *Critical Inquiry* 14(1):16–48.

Dôseiai no onna san'nin shinjû (The suicide of three lesbians). 1934. *Asahi Shinbun*, Tokyo eve. ed., June 13:2.

Dôseiai no seisan (Settlement of differences among lesbians). 1934. *Asahi Shinbun*, Tokyo morning ed., June 13:11.

Frühstück, Sabine. 1998. Then science took over: Sex, leisure and medicine at the beginning of the twentieth century. In *The culture of Japan as seen through its leisure*. Sepp Linhart and Sabine Frühstück, eds. Pp. 59–79. Albany: State University of New York Press.

———. 2003 *Colonizing sex: Sexology and social control in modern Japan.* Berkeley: University of California Press.

Fukushima Shirô. 1984. [1935]. *Fujinkai sanjûgonen* (Thirty-five years of women's world). Tokyo: Fuji Shuppansha.

Furukawa Makoto. 1994. The changing nature of sexuality: The three codes framing homosexuality in modern Japan. Alice Lockyer, trans. *U.S.-Japan Women's Journal* (English supplement) 7:98–127.

Habuto Eiji and Sawada Junjirô. 1925 [1915]. *Hentai seiyokuron* (Treatise on deviant sexual desire). 18th ed. Tokyo: Sun'yôdô.

Hayashi Misao. 1926. Danjo to shiyû (Man and woman, male and female). *Nihon Hyôron* 3:319–325.

Hirschfeld, Magnus. 1935. *Women east and west: Impressions of a sex expert.* London: William Heinemann (Medical Books) Ltd.

Hogosha wa kokoro seyo—byôteki na fuan buri (Guardians, beware of pathological fandom). 1935. *Asahi Shinbun*, Tokyo morn. ed., January 31:8.

Imago. 1991. Tokushû: Rezubian (Special issue: Lesbian) 2(8).

Keene, Donald. 1976. *World within walls: Japanese literature of the pre-modern era 1600–1867*. New York: Grove Press.

Komine Shigeyuki. 1985. *Dôseiai to dôseiai shinjû no kenkyû* (A study of homosexuality and homosexual double suicide). Tokyo: Komine Kenkyûjo.

Kore mo jidaisô ka (Is this too the shape of the times?). 1935. *Asahi Shinbun*, Tokyo morn. ed., January 30:7.

Koyama Shizuko. 1982. Kindaiteki joseikan to shite no rôsaikenbo shisô (The good wife, wise mother as a modern idea about women). *Joseigaku Nenpô* 3:1–8.

———. 1986 Rôsaikenboshugi no reimei (The dawn of good wife, wise motherism). *Joseigaku Nenpô* 7:11–20.

Krafft-Ebing, Richard von. 1893. *Psychopathia Sexualis*. Stuttgart: F. Enke.

Lebra, Takie. 1976. *Japanese patterns of behavior*. Honolulu: University of Hawaii Press.

Leupp, Gary. 1995. *Male colors: The construction of homosexuality in Tokugawa Japan (1603–1868)*. Berkeley: University of California Press.

Minakawa Yôko. 1987. Tachi: Kono Kodokuna ikimono (Butch: This lonely creature). *Bessatsu Takarajima* 64:18–23.

Mochizuki, Mamor[u]. 1959. Cultural aspects of Japanese girl's opera. In *Japanese popular culture*. Hidetoshi Kato, ed. Pp. 165–174. Tokyo: Charles E. Tuttle.

Modan otona tôsei manga yose (The latest variety comics for modern adults). 1935. *Asahi Shinbun*, Osaka eve. ed., February 17:4.

Nakano Eitarô. 1935. Dansô no reijin to Saijô Eriko: dôseiaishi misui no ikisatsu (The cross-dressed beauty and Saijô Eriko: The circumstances of their double suicide attempt). *Fujin Kôron* 3:161–167.

Nogami Toshio. 1920. Gendai seikatsu to danjo ryôsei no sekkin (The association of modern life and androgyny). *Kaizô* 2(4):185–204.

Nolte, Sharon and Sally Hastings. 1991. The Meiji state's policy towards women, 1890–1910. In *Recreating Japanese women, 1600–1945*. Gail Bernstein, ed. Pp. 151–174. Berkeley: University of California Press.

Ôhara Kenshirô. 1973. *Shinjûkô: Ai to shi no byôri* (A treatise on double suicide: The pathology of love and death). Tokyo: Rogosu Sensho.

Ozaki Hirotsugi. 1986. San'nin no joyû o chûshin ni (Focusing on three actresses). In *Meiji no joyûten* (Exhibition of Meiji-period actresses). Meiji-mura Hakubutsukan, ed. Pp. 10–16. Nagoya: Nagoya Tetsudô.

Ôzumi Narumitsu. 1931. Hentai seiyoku (Deviant sexual desire). *Hanzai Kagaku* 4:75–83.

Robertson, Jennifer. 1989. Gender-bending in paradise: Doing "female" and "male" in Japan. *Genders* 5:48–69.

——— 1992. The politics of androgyny in Japan: Sexuality and subversion in the theater and beyond. *American Ethnologist* 19(3): 419–442.

———. 1995. Mon Japan: Theater as a technology of Japanese imperialism. *American Ethnologist* 22(4):970–996.

———. 1998. "It takes a village: Internationalization and nostalgia in postwar Japan." In *Mirror of modernity: Invented traditions in modern Japan*. Stephen Vlastos, ed. Pp. 209–239. Berkeley: University of California Press.

———. 2001. [1998.] *Takarazuka: Sexual politics and popular culture in modern Japan*. Berkeley: University of California Press.

Roden, Donald. 1990. Taishô culture and the problem of gender ambivalence. In *Culture and identity: Japanese intellectuals during the interwar years*. J. Thomas Rimer, ed. Pp. 37–55. Princeton: Princeton University Press.

Saijô Eriko. 1935. Dansô no reijin Masuda Fumiko no shi o erabu made (Up until Masuda Fumiko, the cross-dressed beauty, chose death). *Fujin Kôron* 3:168–178.

Sakabe Kengi. 1924. *Fujin no shinri to futoku no kisô* (The foundation of women's psychology and morality). Tokyo: Hokubunkan.

Sakuma Hideka. 1934. Jôshi o ketsui suru made (Until [we] resolved to commit love suicide). *Fujin Gahô* 8:82–83.

Seidensticker, Edward. 1990. *Tokyo rising: The city since the great earthquake*. New York: Knopf.

Shôjo no hi no sei mondai: Haru no mezame (Girls' day and the problem of sex: Spring awakening). 1934. *Asahi Shinbun*, Tokyo morning ed., June 18: 9.

Sievers, Sharon. 1983. *Flowers in salt: The beginnings of feminist consciousness in modern Japan*. Stanford: Stanford University Press.

Silverberg, Miriam. 1993. Constructing a new cultural history of prewar Japan. In *Japan in the world*. Masao Miyoshi and H.D. Harootunian, eds. Pp. 115–143. Durham: Duke University Press.

Smith-Rosenberg, Carroll. 1985. *Disorderly conduct: Visions of gender in Victorian America*. New York: Oxford University Press.

Sugahara Tsûzai. 1971. *Dôseiai* (Homosexuality). Tokyo: San'aku Tsuihô Kyôkai.

Sugita Naoki. 1929. Seihonnô ni hisomu sangyakusei (Sado-masochistic qualities latent within sexual instinct). *Kaizô* 4:70–80.

———. 1935. Shôjo kageki netsu no shinden (All-female revue: A sanctuary for feverish infatuation). *Fujin Kôron* 4:274–278.

Tamura Toshiko. 1913. Dôseiai no koi (Same-sex love). *Chûô Kôron* 1:165–168.

Tani Kazue. 1935. "Dansô no reijin" no jogakusei jidai o kataru (On the girls' school years of the "cross-dressed beauty") *Hanashi* 4:250–256.

Tomioka Masakata. 1938. Dansei josô to josei dansô (Males in women's clothing, females in men's clothing). *Kaizô* 10:98–105.

Ushijima Yoshitomo. 1943. *Joshi no shinri* (Female psychology). Tokyo: Ganshodô.

Vicinus, Martha. 1989. Distance and desire: English boarding school friendships, 1870–1920. In *Hidden from history: Reclaiming the gay and lesbian past.* Martin Duberman, Martha Vicinus and George Chauncey, eds. Pp. 212–229. New York: New American Library.

Watanabe, Tsuneo and Jun'ichi Iwata. 1989. *The love of the samurai: A thousand years of Japanese homosexuality.* D.R. Roberts, trans. London: GMP.

Watashi wa koi no shorisha (I am a survivor of love). 1934. *Asahi Shinbun*, Tokyo morn. ed., June 14:11.

Weininger, Otto. 1906. *Sex and character*. New York: G.P. Putnam's Sons.

Wolfe, Alan. 1990. *Suicidal narrative in modern Japan.* Princeton: Princeton University Press.

Yaesuen (Advertisement for the Yaesuen coffeeshop). 1934. *Asahi Shinbun.* Tokyo morning ed., June 24:3.

Yasuda Tokutarô. 1935. Dôseiai no rekishikan (Historical perspectives on homosexuality). *Chûô Kôron* 3:146–152.

Yoshimoto, Mitsuhiro. 1989. The postmodern and mass images in Japan. *Public Culture* 1(2):8–25.

Yoshitake Teruko. 1986. *Nyonin Yoshiya Nobuko* (The woman Yoshiya Nobuko). Tokyo: Bunshun Bunkô.

Chapter Thirteen

"She Has Come from the World of the Spirits . . .": Life Stories of Working-Class Lesbian Women in Northern India

Maya Sharma

Introduction

Research documenting the life stories of working-class, lesbian women was undertaken on behalf of Vikalp and Maanjal, women's groups based in the north Indian states of Gujarat and Delhi respectively. It stems from a personal journey of emergence from a space of silences and half-truths and is committed to advocacy work for the rights of lesbian women. Its location is the contested sociocultural fissure between the private and the public domain as well as private and public discourses about alternative sexualities, choices, and practices. The context within which the project emerged is rooted in the women's movement in India.

Indian culture views the female body as a site for all kinds of action and reaction but not as a legitimate space for sexual autonomy or personal agency. Women's sexual experiences are generally understood solely within the established parameters of reproduction. Within this framework, the life experiences of lesbian women have been almost completely invalidated because sex and sexuality are generally understood only in relation to a heterosexual paradigm of oppositional duality that prescribes gender roles and gendered social codes; those who violate these roles and codes are seen as transgressive, condemned as obscene, and perceived as appropriate subjects for various forms of persecution and punishment.

Through the women's movement, it has become possible to bring into public discourse sexual and domestic violence and make laws for protection against such violations. The Indian women's movement, however, has adopted a policy of distancing itself from issues related to homosexual women. Though it has not extended public or political support, it has provided valuable support by taking up individual cases. This support is appreciated by its direct beneficiaries as well as activist groups, yet because it is private, it remains unknown to the general public and inaccessible to others who are urgently in need of it. This mode of support, which simultaneously involves mechanisms of denial operating under the larger umbrella of cultural silence around issues of alternative sexuality, enmeshes homoerotic desire and its practices in phobia and prejudice.

Scope of Project

For this project we mainly used in-depth interviews and one-on-one interactions with the subjects in their own contexts. Despite the overwhelming void in terms of available research material and statistical data, we focused on working-class women in same-sex relationships. We wanted to dispel the myth that lesbians in India are all urban, westernized, and from the upper and middle classes.

We soon realized, however, that not all the narratives would qualify as life stories. Some of them do not go beyond immediate fraught circumstances and the jagged time and space of a brief, intense exchange. When we made an attempt to access the subjects' personal histories or reestablish contact at a later time, we often failed for many different reasons. Sometimes others talked on behalf of the subjects. In at least two cases, our interaction with the subjects was minimal. Yet we continue to use the term "life story" and use it interchangeably with the word "profile." The reader will encounter both "I" and "we" in the text, as I collaborated with Shanti, my partner, who is from a working-class background. "We" is also indicative of the spirit of solidarity and identity with the subjects that emerged in the process of doing the research.

The category "woman" that we had used unquestioningly in an earlier narrative project documenting the life stories of working-class single women became problematic when the focus shifted to alternative sexuality. Some of our subjects did not identify as women and used masculine pronouns to define themselves. Most of our subjects had not heard of the word "lesbian" and asked what language it was from. They were uncomfortable with and unaccustomed to naming themselves.

We clearly found a single category restrictive and unrepresentative of the complexities of the same-sex relationships as well as of the realities that intersected with caste, class and other factors, which often included marriage, husband, and children. "The homosexual" as a category of sexual being and "homosexuality" as a sexual practice are generally rendered invisible by Indian culture. Modern activists have begun to use the word "sanglaingik" (same-sex) in Hindi contexts, but this remains an abstract term.

Most of our subjects did not speak English and were equally unfamiliar with the words "lesbian" and "sanglaingik." In their own contexts, the male form of address and gender-ambiguous plural forms in Hindi were used both by the masculinized subjects and by people around them. The words used were "Babu," "Bhai." Most often the same-sex partners referred to each other as *dost, saheli, sathin*, and *sakhi*, terms which, like the term "female friendship" itself, are general in nature, nonthreatening to the heterosexist paradigm and socioculturally acceptable. One same-sex couple we interviewed was uniformly referred to by their neighbors and colleagues as "miya-bibi jodi" (husband-wife pair).

For this project we made a conscious decision to use the word "lesbian" precisely because it was a word "so loaded with fear and embarrassment and prejudice, a word shrouded in silence, a whisper that spoke of an identity that must be hidden from others, that frightening word that dare not cross any threshold" (Caleri Report 1999:7). We use the word "lesbian" consciously as activists involved in the struggle for human rights. We are aware that the hegemonic use of one specific word can effectively silence a diverse and shifting range of sexual and social orientations, identities, and practices. Thus the word "lesbian" represents our continual efforts to build a politicized identity because we consider lesbians as valid political subjects, even though we live out the absurdity of having no status in the eyes of Indian law.

Influenced by society's denial of same-sex relationships, we choose to use the word "lesbian" to mean women who are sexually involved with one another. Yet our collection includes life stories of women who do not acknowledge a sexual relationship. While these stories continue to pose an ethical dilemma, we argue that one way to confront the socially imposed silence regarding issues of alternative sexuality as well as mechanisms of sexual policing and censorship was to "write in" these stories. And at the same time we demonstrate a diffused understanding of sexuality that exists in the sensuous and the notion of friendship/companionship played out in everyday exchanges in the life stories. Through them we attempt to critique a patriarchal system that reifies and perpetuates itself through coercing "other" sexualities into paradigms of conformity with ideologically driven heterosexuality.

I begin the chapter with my own life. I then go on to describe the specific sequence of events that catalyzed our wish to document the lives of working-class lesbian women. I also trace some earlier responses of the women's movement to lesbian visibility, as part of my intention to demonstrate the ideological shifts and conflicts within the movement. The third section describes our research methodology. The final section focuses on the narratives and presents our observations.

My Story

The three of us, my older brother, my younger sister, and me in the middle, often tiptoed out of a cool, dark room that occasionally sparkled with drops of sunlight that sieved through the moist *chiks* (window blinds woven from fiber). I was neither a real tailender like my younger sister, nor a real adult since I had three other older sisters. Each of my sisters' births had been announced by an earthen vessel being struck, so that its dull clap did not spread far and wide. But my only brother's birth was heralded by beating a steel plate so that the good news could resound in all directions.

I was in that indefinable position that was bent to fit whatever the occasion demanded—like that afternoon sun. Fleeing in the summer afternoons through the burning courtyard of the house, we passed the neem tree and ran up the incline to the railway tracks behind our house. We competed to see who could walk straight on the tracks for the longest time. When the adults caught us, I was chided the most. I was a girl, older than my younger sister. To make matters worse, I was slapping and kicking! Didn't I know that girls did not raise their hands against boys? Good grown-up girls did not venture into lonely places in lonely afternoons. No matter what I did, I ended up breaking some rule. I thought marriage would give me the maturity and the respect that had thus far eluded me. To the family's satisfaction, I "settled down." Even better, I soon had a son.

In the midst of the daily tasks of child-raising and cloistered domesticity, I happened to see women's groups on the television screen, demonstrating on the streets and demanding a stop to violence against women and women's rights. The boldness of these groups, bringing private issues into the public arena, initially shocked me. Yet I was drawn to them. Saheli, one of Delhi's earliest autonomous women's groups, was based in a locality adjoining the one I lived in. I joined them as a volunteer in 1983. In 1991 I joined the women's group Jagori as a full-time paid employee.

One of my first assignments involved working at a resettlement colony (slum) in Delhi. The work included local organizing and also documentation of the lives of single women. Women, who were technically considered illiterate and lived in poverty and at subsistence level, reeducated me in immeasurable ways on a daily basis. It was one of the most empowering periods of my life.

The first woman I wrote about was Bhavari, a widow in her 60s. Clad in the same colorless sari each day, she had come to the city from a rural area to find work. Her dark, deeply wrinkled, furrowed visage reflected the intensity of her struggle. When others would judge situations and individuals harshly, she would always retain a humane perspective and urge us to do the same. When I sat close to her, she held my chin in her hands and ran her work-worn fingers along my face and arms. "My husband never asked me how I am, what I drink, eat and wear, he never loved me like this . . ." (Bhaiya 1996:45). I became aware of something new, an unexpected sensation of pleasure at her touch. I recognized with a shock that I was experiencing arousal through the caress of a woman.

Later, in my meetings with more women, traces of what I had absorbed would return to me, like the weathered touch of Bhavari. Listening to the women, I began to see a larger pattern in our individual and varied lives, reflected in the identical words we used in the telling of our stories: "caged," "good woman," "bad woman." The daily presence of women who put at stake their precarious resources in order to change their lives inspired me to change mine. I gathered the courage to speak to my son and step out of my 16-year marriage.

The turning point came when I listened to Bhavari talk of a relationship between two women. Simply and without judgment, she said that these two women met one another in the fields away from their homes and families. "They loved one another dearly. They could not live without seeing one another . . ." (Bhaiya 1996:46). Even though I acknowledged my love for women, I was living in fear. I had only Bhavari to go to. It was only later, in private conversations and carefully coded disclosures that I learned there were many women like us in the movement. I slowly understood the connection of Bhavari's story to my own life—the fear and secrecy around lesbian relationships and the intolerable weight of living day after day in sheer invisibility and silence.

The Politics of Utterance

Caleri (Campaign for Lesbian Rights), a Delhi-based nonfunded autonomous umbrella organization of groups and individuals—lesbians, gays, bisexuals, and heterosexuals—was the first activist organization to consciously dedicate itself to foregrounding lesbian issues in the public domain. Caleri was formed in December 1998 following broad-based protests against the Shiv Sena's attacks on cinema halls screening Deepa Mehta's film "Fire" (see Bhaiya this volume). This right-wing political party demanded that the film be withdrawn because it contained explicit scenes of a physical relationship between two sisters-in-law living in a joint family under the same roof. Such depictions, according to the Shiv Sena and its supporters, were a manifestation of promiscuous Western morality that would corrupt Indian values and Indian women.

As activists in the women's movement, some of us initiated the process of organizing a public rally against the attacks on the film. In the planning meeting, however, we had differences with some individuals and women's groups. While we strongly advocated the mention of vandalism, attacks, and the ban on the film as a violation of the rights of lesbian women, others resisted such a direct mention. They argued for a protest under a "broader" rubric of the right to protect the democratic constitutional right to freedom of artistic expression. And instead of the word "lesbian" the words suggested were "woman-woman relationships" because, according to the logic of those who resisted the use of the word "lesbian," the people on the street were not ready to hear the term.

Consequently there were two sets of pamphlets distributed during the protest: one that talked of violations of freedom of artistic expression and another emphasizing the "need to break the silence around the fact that violent enforced closure of the film constitutes yet another violence against lesbians in particular and women in general" (Caleri Report 1999:22). After the "Fire" uproar, Caleri decided to make lesbian issues visible in the public domain of human rights in India and consciously strategize toward this within the larger frame of the women's movement. Since violence against women was one of the globally chosen themes for International Women's Day 2000, in the planning meetings for the public march, we brought up the need to include the demand for lesbian rights. But the left mass-based women's groups resisted the inclusion of the word "lesbian" in the literature to be distributed on March 8. The logic was that the name of the group, Campaign for Lesbian Rights, could not go on the pamphlets because those would be distributed in working-class localities where people were still not ready to openly discuss homosexuality. The press would pay attention only to the sexuality issues; the flaunting of sexual terminology would detract from important political issues that needed to be the focus of media attention.

At a subsequent meeting it was shared that the lack of information about lesbians and the absence of documentation of a sufficient and specific number of cases of lesbian life prevented women's groups from going against the majority voice in the Indian culture. In response, we made presentations of some cases that had already been reported in the press. We cited feature stories and reports published in a Malayalam fortnightly named *Sameeksha* entitled "Same Sex (Female) Lovers Commit Suicide" and "Lesbian Suicides Continue . . ."[1] The stories, however, lacked a face; women's own voices and the context within which they lived their daily lives was missing. We ourselves had no idea what happened to the women following the exposure and the outcry raised by public scandal.

The kind of distancing that takes place can be seen by comparing the movement's response with two instances of sexual and emotional violence against women. One case involved the fate of Mamta and Monalisa, two young women from Orissa (ABVA [AIDS Bhedbhav Virodhi Andolan]1999:15). Both women knew that their same-sex relationship was not acceptable to their families and had filed an affidavit for a partnership deed so that they could live together. The imminent job transfer of Monalisa's father, a government employee, led the women to attempt suicide because they knew they would be separated. They consumed insecticide and also slashed their wrists. Discovered while still alive, they were taken to the hospital. Monalisa died on the way, while Mamta survived and was later forced to undergo psychiatric treatment. While Mamta's father stated in a letter to ABVA, "For your information, this is not a case of homosexuality," Monalisa's grandfather stated, "It is a case of lesbianism." In their joint suicide note the women had expressed the wish to be cremated together on the same pyre.

The other case was also from Orissa. Anjana Mishra, the 30-year-old victim, was the estranged wife of an Indian Forest Service officer and the mother of his two sons. Mishra strongly resisted her husband's attempt to separate her from her two children and have her secured within a mental asylum. Mishra wrote, "Utkal Mahila Samiti, the leading women's organization in the state, actively took up the case and pressured the Human Rights Protection Cell (HRPC) to rescue me; I had spent nine months and ten days in the gloom and horror of the lunatic asylum" (Bhaiya 1996).

Later she bravely fought off the state Advocate-General Indrajeet Ray's attempts to rape her. When she did not compromise on or retract her charges of molestation and attempt to rape against Ray, she was brutally gang-raped by three men at Barang on January 9, 1999, while en route to Cuttack with a journalist friend to meet her lawyer.

The assault took place at the same time as the Mamta-Monalisa suicide attempt. Women's groups supported Mishra's struggle for justice within the state and organized a public demonstration at Orissa Bhavan in New Delhi protesting against the gang rape, but were totally silent about the Mamta-Monalisa case.

Historically the presence of lesbians and violence against them has found cautious acknowledgment within the women's movement mostly in the form of letters, personal comments, and private communication after meetings and conferences. For instance, in February 1992, a letter was drafted and signed by over three dozen women in response to a report that appeared on January 29, 1992, in the national daily *Indian Express* headlined "Lesbian Group in Kerala School." The letter stated that the suspension of these girls from school on the grounds of homosexuality was a violation of their fundamental rights. Some of these signatories were from the women's groups but they chose to sign as individuals.

Between 1989 and 1991 amongst the autonomous women's groups, a new articulation took shape: "single woman" was beginning to be recognized as a valid, self-chosen identity. Lesbians were seen as belonging to this category. At the Autonomous Women's Movement Conference held in Calicut in 1990, an informal session on single women was held; perhaps for the first time the word "lesbian" was used. A middle-class woman identified herself as a lesbian in that meeting. After the Calicut conference, the women's group Jagori began research on single women, but did not openly address lesbian issues within these parameters. Nor did the category "single women" accommodate more complex positions, such as those of married lesbians with or without children. Nor did it take into account that two women who lived with one another could not be seen as "single." The usage of the word derived its meaning only in the context of a heteronormative society.

The Northern Regional Conference of the Women's Movement held in Kanpur in 1993 had a session on sexuality, but women standing outside the room predicted dismissively that such a session would contain "nothing more than lesbianism." Anticipating such comments, we who were organizing the workshop on behalf of Jagori had committed to a strategy: to avoid a predominant focus on the lesbian issue and, in order not to distract from more general issues, we ordained that women who were not "out" but did self-identify as lesbians would keep a low profile during the discussions. Also, to ensure that this strategy was not interrogated, we excluded an out lesbian who we felt would not comply with our plan. Ironically, during the session someone asked about women who did not marry, "What about their sexual desire?" We had created a space where such issues could be interrogated, yet lesbian issues could not. Today in retrospect we are aghast at our response when we said that we would raise the issue of lesbian sexuality in the session on single women; we acknowledge the extent of internal and external homophobia that compelled us to strategize in this manner.

The Fifth Women's Movement Conference in Tirupati in 1994 was different. For the first time "sexuality" was a separate workshop theme with lesbianism as a subtheme. There was an open discussion led by a mother who fully supported her daughter's relationship with a woman. The session turned stormy when a resolution supporting lesbian rights was formulated. Inconclusive and acrimonious debate prevented this resolution from being passed. However a majority of attendees openly expressed support for lesbian women (Report 1994:58).

The 1997 National Conference of the Women's Movement held in Ranchi states in its declaration: "We support the empowerment of women who may be further marginalized by other facets of their identities: *adivasis* (tribals), *dalits* (oppressed caste), poor and working-class women, disabled women, religious minorities, lesbians, bisexuals" (Report 1997:6). And yet the Bihar State Coordinating Committee organizing the conference deleted the word "lesbian" from its invitation letter because the members felt strongly that the inclusion of this word and a specific session on lesbian sexuality would have alienated many women's groups and individual women who then would not attend the conference. They also felt that women would not want to work as volunteers at a conference that included a focus on homosexuality.

In contrast to the autonomous women's groups, the mass-based women's groups have had a different response to the issue of lesbian rights. Responding to a letter from Caleri in 2001, the National Federation of Indian Women (NFIW), expressed its reservations about including lesbian issues.[2]

In fact, when the state itself is an offender, the nature of such intervention is founded on a fundamental paradox that lesbians in India live without rights as legal subjects. Since they do not exist in the eyes of the law, they do not violate the law. But neither do they have any political or social rights. Section 377 of the Indian Penal Code criminalizing homosexuality states:

> Whoever voluntarily has carnal intercourse against the order of nature with any man, woman or animal shall be punished with imprisonment for life, or with punishment of either description for a term which may extend to ten years and shall also be liable to fine. Explanation: Penetration is sufficient to constitute the carnal intercourse necessary to the offense described in this section.

This muddy rhetoric criminalizes what is perceived to be male homosexual activity, that is, the act of sodomy and its sexual practitioners who are going "against the order of nature." Lesbianism is not specified as a criminal act but since it is perceived as "unnatural," it is illegal by analogy and association.

Methodology

We used various methods to approach our subjects, such as holding group meetings, conducting workshops following newspaper stories, going on fact-finding visits, and intervening in some cases. Word of mouth, personal networking and, to a large extent, intuition were some of the means by which we identified potential subjects. Our project, begun in June 2001, took over two years to complete. Documentation and fieldwork were done simultaneously, depending on what material we collected, in what form, and how much. We compiled 15 stories of working-class women. Each story we present in the sections that follow exemplifies one specific aspect of the research.

In eight stories, the subjects openly acknowledge their same-sex attraction, though they use varied terms to describe their homosexual relationships. Two stories focus on women who are in a same-sex relationship and who categorize their relationship as friendship. We recorded whatever was possible to record, the denials, the affirmations, and the circumstances as well as the contexts in which they were rooted, for it was the only way to give an authentic picture of the ground realities. Two stories emerged from fact-finding visits to the subjects' homes after the relationship had been exposed in the newspapers and had become a cause for public scandal.

Many women simply trusted us from the start and shared their stories verbally. However, when it came to allowing their life stories to be printed, they refused permission. How could they undertake the risk of disclosure and its repercussions without the assurance of external support, when there was no evidence that such support existed, no politicization of their issues, no collective demand that their needs be addressed? For others, the recognition of lesbian sexuality had been an impossibility until the actual moment of interview.

Of the 20 participants at a workshop that we conducted to identify lesbian women, 16 women admitted to having relationships with women. Some of them continued in these relationships in spite of their own marriages or the marriages of their lovers. Inadvertently, the workshop opened up a space for two women to address their anger. "In this very room," one of them said with sadness, "we had vowed to be together but you married . . ." In contrast, another woman shared how she had intercepted the prospective husband coming to see her and told him she would not marry him. Rather than directly say no to her family and thus risk losing their support, she took action on her own behalf. The man withdrew his proposal.

With some subjects we experienced an instant recognition and camaraderie, a sense of being on the same journey while on different paths. But we also faced instances when the subjects themselves denied or were silent about being in a same-sex relationship, yet a friend or an acquaintance explicitly disclosed this. The lack of words for lesbian relationships combined with the stigma attached to such relationships forced us to fall upon those words that derived meaning only in the context of heterosexuality. Often our sources were not aware of the real nature of our inquiry and we could not articulate openly what we were looking for. We usually phrased it as "single women," implying those women who had not married or having married, were now single. Though women rarely lived alone, it was a phrase that helped us to hide what we were actually seeking from the gaze of the others until we met with the women themselves. We often phrased our inquiry as "a woman who lives with another woman."

The silence around homosexuality is slowly being broken in the media. While we question the skewed and partial media representation, its dependence on stereotypes and its hesitant imaging, we simultaneously acknowledge its use and appreciate its existence, for it brings same-sex love into the public domain and the realm of public discourse. Critically, in more than one instance it enabled us to locate subjects and made fact-finding interventions possible. However, the media remain in general more committed to the sensational and catastrophic, and rarely do follow-up stories or in-depth investigations that might create more awareness in the readership or viewership with regard to homosexuality. After the disclosure and public scrutiny of lesbian scandal, the women simply cease to exist in mainstream consciousness, as the following story illustrates.

On September 8, 2001, the national Hindi daily *Navbharat Times* carried a front-page story about two women who ran away together from their homes in Indore on September 1. They went to a place called Dahod in Gujarat and got married to one another in a temple. From Dahod they went to Beas in Punjab and took shelter in a Radha Soami Satsang, a popular sect which accepts unmarried women as members. From here they were forcibly retrieved by the police after their families lodged a Missing Person's report. They were returned to their respective homes in Indore. After the shocking terrorist attacks on New York's World Trade Towers on September 11, the national media was fully occupied and lesbian elopement did not make the front pages.

We had to accept that frank, extended, and honest communication would not always be possible with our subjects for reasons other than cultural conditioning and self-censorship. Usually no space was made available for us to have any private conversations with the subjects, as family members were invariably present in the congested living spaces, participating in and often controlling the dialogue. We had to try as hard to win their trust as to win the trust of the subjects, simultaneously. When we did manage to talk to them privately, there were time constraints and various kinds of disruptions. The issues of sexual choice and the larger questions of sexuality often remained subtextual, tacit, and circuitous; we had to work intuitively, hoping and sometimes praying that our gestures and signals were being correctly decoded.

Negotiating the phobia of others as well as internal phobia catalyzed a certain courage and nerve within us. We attempted to silence the stares, sniggers, and comments of coworkers by confronting them directly. The confrontation helped to gradually create a tenuous space for further discussion. Risking censure by our bosses, colleagues brought reports from regional newspapers to our notice. They even gave us contact information that might help us in locating subjects. A colleague ensured that one of the "talked-about" women, Vimlesh, had been invited for a workshop we were organizing.

The first conversation that drew Vimlesh and me together was our love for Rajasthan. Then, when she said she was single, I felt a stir of recognition. One day I received a letter from her. I wrote back at once. She replied eagerly and after we had exchanged some more letters, I asked her if she would allow me to write her story. During this time, another friend of mine wanted to visit Rajasthan with me, so we decided to visit Vimlesh in her hometown during the Diwali holiday. I thought I would ask her the forbidden question then.

That day when we returned from Vimlesh's home, I realized that we often talk about other people's fear, their homophobia, but neglect to scrutinize our own. I could not bring myself to ask her "the question." I also saw that I would not be able to do the asking on my own. I asked Shanti to accompany me. Both of us acknowledged that we would have to talk about our own lives before we could ask Vimlesh about hers. On our next visit, the household members, as always, welcomed us affectionately. We were asked to have a meal. Almost the entire family dispersed to prepare the meal. We were in the room with Vimlesh for a moment. Shanti suggested that we go out. Vimlesh agreed. With a quiet simplicity Vimlesh affirmed her attraction for women without so much as looking away. And we had taken so long to ask her. The woman she loved lived in another town. All the women in the factory that Vimlesh worked with knew her sexual orientation. Later as we got to know Vimlesh better, we went to meet her girlfriend Kanak. When we asked Kanak how she would describe her relationship with Vimlesh, she replied without hesitation, "It is a love affair. I love her." Vimlesh's gender remained indeterminate in this form of address in Hindi. When Vimlesh referred to herself, she always used the masculine pronoun.

During a visit to Rajasthan my circuitous inquiries about single women caused one of the activists there to describe "Babubai," who lived in a village where this activist did her fieldwork. The name itself aroused my interest—"babu" is a generic term of address for men, "bai" is a generic term of address for women. The activist said that Babubai lived with another woman, wore her hair short, always dressed like a man, and used the masculine pronoun when referring to herself. The activist who gave me information about Babubai could not recall her address but gave me the contact number of another woman. This woman said she would get in touch with a woman in the village who knew Babubai. "She is generally known as Babu Maharaj. I warn you, she may not want to be contacted at all." I asked whether I could meet Babubai on my own, as I was leaving the next day. She said it would be all right and gave me directions. "Take a bus to the village, when you are there, ask anyone for the house of Babu Maharaj."

It was a typical village, slightly developed: dirt roads, a few small shops, a bus stand with food stalls playing film songs, and decrepit buses. I got off and asked someone for the house. I was eager, yet very anxious and uncertain. The second man I asked knew Babubai. The house was about ten minutes' walk from the bus stand. The man led me to the door and knocked. The person who opened the door looked about five feet four or five inches tall. Fair complexion, sturdy build. Very short hair. I guessed her age to be about 40. The man who had guided me said, "This is Babu Maharaj." She was wearing a white *banian* (undershirt) and *dhoti* (a lower garment worn by men). I noticed she had bound her breasts with a cloth. Quickly I introduced myself and gave the reference of the women's group and the specific coworker. Babubai put her hand forward. I cannot forget that handshake—strong, firm, warm.

She showed me very willingly into the courtyard. It was neat and clean, well-swept, with a tap and a platform where drinking water was stored in *matkas* (earthen vessels). A woman sat in the verandah outside the kitchen. The television was on. Babubai switched off the set. The handshake had put my fears to rest. I marveled at the perfection of the term of address as it signified a combination of male and female. "Maharaj" was also appropriate as she belonged to a devotional sect and the word has a religious connotation in Hinduism. The seated woman was slightly plump, wearing a dull green sari. She had a long plait and her head was covered. She was introduced as Sita. I had been told she was a widow by one of my informants.

They asked me to sit down. From my position I could see part of the kitchen. Sticks of firewood in the *chulha* (earthen stove) had just been extinguished with ashes. It was that languid time of the afternoon when the daily chores have been done. The guttural cooing of pigeons resonated in the still heat. The women asked me if I would have a cup of tea. I said, "Please don't bother, you will have to light the *chulha* again." They said, "We have a stove, also a gas cylinder but we use it sparingly as we have to get it from some other place." Sita went inside. I said to Babubai, "Basically I am collecting stories of women who have managed to stay single."

Sita brought tea. One cup, only for me. Babubai said, "We are Ramsnehi *bhakts* (followers of a religious sect). Our life revolves around worship and singing *kirtan-bhajan* (hymns)." I had learned that this sect was founded in the late sixteenth century and was rooted in the bhakti movement. It is not a form of institutionalized religion. It is non-Brahmanical and non-Vedic. I asked tentatively, "How do you support yourselves?" Babubai explained that they lived in one part of the house and the other part was rented to boys who came from villages in the interior to attend school in the village, which was more developed and had some educational facility. I asked why she did not attend the women's group. Babubai began to swear.

> At the meeting [on women's health] I went to, they showed dirty pictures, talked about sexual organs and having children. I hate these types of conversations. What have I to do with such matters? It was so disgusting, I wished the ceiling would collapse on us, maybe then everyone would be quiet. Earlier with a friend I have attended such meetings in other villages and it is always the same. I have had enough of such topics.

Listening to her derogatory language gave me a sense that she had a kind of hatred for women. She identified as male. And my inquiries into her personal life and the fact that I referred to her as a single woman might have aggravated the hostility. I asked Babubai,

> "Did you have a difficult time resisting marriage?"
> "I never wanted to marry. I joined the Ramsnehi sect, since then I have not had to face any further pressure."
> "How is it that you are dressed like this? How have you been allowed to?"
> "When I was small I used to wear shorts. When the *dukh* (menstruation, literally, sorrow or suffering) started, I began to wear pajamas. Near my house there was another Ramsnehi woman who always dressed like this, in *dhoti-banian*, so I decided to do the same."
> "I am very impressed by the fact that you have stayed single. How many years have you lived with Sita?"
> "Twenty years."
> "How is it that you were able to hold out against social pressure and live together?"
> "We have given ourselves to Him, the Lord. Our families also take care of us, to some extent."

I had been told by the women's group that Babubai's Ramsnehi guru, who lived to be 105, was also a woman who dressed like a man. Babubai had met Sita at this guru's house. I became aware of the couple's gaze, of how keenly they were scrutinizing me and observing my difference from them, of the unasked question as to why anyone would spend time, money, energy, to come all the way from Delhi to this village just to meet them. I also knew they would never admit to having a same-sex relationship because their mode of religion, which accommodates them as a unit, does so on condition of silence and denial.

My discomfort was increasing. All three of us were becoming very tense. I felt a kind of panic that I was not reaching them at all, that I was asking the wrong questions, that I was too abrupt and inappropriate. As long as I talked about religion and God, it was all right. But my focus on their single status made them distrustful. Babubai reacted by proceeding to guide the conversation in a way that made it impossible for me to stay longer. Something had changed; the warmth of that initial handshake had completely gone.

She said, "My chest is hurting, yesterday too at this time it began to hurt. It happens very often. I am feeling dizzy. Let's go outside for some fresh air."

Perhaps she was telling me that she suspected my motives and that I should stop my probing. But at that moment I was unaware of anything other than the frantic realization that she was terminating the interview. We got up and moved in the direction of the tenants' area.

Slightly dazed, I took leave. I stood at the bus stand in the midst of dogs and cows and *karhais* (cooking vessels) of samosas and *kachauris* (salty snacks) being refried in bubbling black oil. I was uneasy, having a premonition of something worse to come. I tried to push it aside, but I knew that

I had mishandled and probably lost the connection to Babubai. I had gone about interviewing Babubai in such a self-absorbed manner that I didn't realize I was disturbing something serious, something that was very strong and also very delicate.

Meanwhile the bus had arrived. I took a window seat and started writing as passengers got on and off and settled in the seats. Suddenly there was a tapping below my window. I looked up and saw Babubai, looking extremely handsome in a light mustard *khadi kurta* (a loose upper garment of handspun cloth) with a brown weave, *dhoti jootis* (traditional footwear). There was a pen in her breast pocket. She looked me in the eye and said, "This bus will take the *kuccha* route (unpaved road) and will take very long. Take the other bus."

I got up. Just then the driver climbed in. I said to him, "Is the bus leaving?" He said, "Yes, right now." Babubai had her eye fixed on me. Then some of the passengers said, "Don't be misled by Babu Maharaj's words. Go back to your seat." Confused, I went back. I understood that she was trying to lure me out of the bus. I noticed she had other people with her along with the young tenants. I saw that I was in deep trouble. Through the open window she demanded, "Give me what you are writing."

I said, "Why? This is mine. Instead of creating a scene, come in and read it and satisfy yourself."

The whole bus was watching. My heart was thumping wildly but I stubbornly would not give up my papers. Babubai strode into the bus and one of the young students followed. She snatched the pad from me and gave it to the boy, commanding, "Read!"

However the boy could not decipher my handwriting. In a shaky voice he tried to mumble something. Babubai snapped, "What! Are you illiterate? I thought you could read English!"

I said, "It is not his fault, my handwriting is terrible. Give me the papers and I will read them out."

To cover up my fear, I too was talking aggressively. She stood over me, glaring. I patted the seat next to me and said, "Why make such an issue out of this, sit down and I will read it."

She sat down. I took the pad and began to translate into Hindi what I had written—impressions, scraps of feelings, descriptions. As I read, she tried to snatch the pad from me again. I pulled it back. I said, "If you want these pages, take them, not the whole pad." She tore the pages off and strode out of the bus through the staring passengers, the boy in tow. I was totally speechless and very relieved. All the while we were arguing, I had been having visions of her beating me up.

The ethical dilemma of consciously writing about someone who absolutely does not want to be written about is a primary consideration here. However, I choose to narrate what took place because I can see no other way to break the cultural silence that frames, yet resists, the inscription of women like Babubai. Such stories are also a way of honoring personal courage that enables such women to live their lives in the way they choose.

On my next visit to the area I came to know from a coworker that Babubai had actually been engaged once but had run away from her village to avoid marriage. I also learned that there was another woman like her, who wore men's clothes and was a follower of another religious sect; she lived as a wandering mendicant.

The Stories

It is ironic that while our political intent was that of disclosure and revealing the intricacies of actual lives, we ended up having to consistently conceal the faces and identities of our subjects. In the overall consciousness of the family, community, society or state, the (homo)sexualized subject has no name, no face, no location, no body, no voice. How could we demonstrate that "women like us" actually existed? We initially thought that women who had already been "outed" by the media would be willing to talk about themselves. We soon realized that it was impossible to talk to the women even when we were able to meet them. Often the families stood in the way like the walls of a fortress within which the women were confined. On one occasion we were able to meet one of the runaway women without family interference.

Following up a newspaper report about a case of alleged lesbian elopement in Rajasthan, we were able to see how the nexus of denial operates from within the family right up to the state. Our first source of information about where the two runaway schoolgirls, Mallika (age 16) and Payal (age 15), lived came from the police. We were told the girls had run away because of poor examination results. Now that they were home again, all was well. There was no reason for the police to give us their addresses. Finally, convinced that we were indeed genuine social workers, the police officer sent a constable to guide us to Mallika's house. The family said their daughter ran away with her friend because Payal felt unloved and uncared for by her stepmother. Anyone who tells Mallika a sad story steals her heart, insisted Mallika's family. Payal wanted to escape from her stepmother and all Mallika did was to go along in support of her friend. There was no elopement story here.

Payal gave us the real reason for the girls' running away from their homes: she categorically said they both loved one another and wanted to live together. When we reached Payal's house and knocked, she opened the door. Both her parents had gone to work and the other siblings had gone to school. She had been forbidden from going out. We could not believe that the chance to talk to her alone had thus unexpectedly materialized. We said we worked in women's groups that supported same-sex relationships and also included "women like us" among their members. She immediately wanted to know if there were any such groups in the city she lived in. We advised her to get in touch with local women's groups and gave her some contact information. We then left quickly as her mother was shortly due back from work.

During the next few weeks we only managed to talk to her twice on the phone; at other times family members answered the call and told us she was not at home. The two conversations we did manage to have were brief, tense, and noncommittal. Clearly she could not talk openly or for long. Ironically, while we kept asking about her, she kept asking about Mallika. It was clear that the families had succeeded in keeping the girls apart.

Finally, a letter from Mallika explained the situation: ". . . Didi (sister), you are a good friend of mine, that is why I wish to tell you that I do not want to keep any relationship with Payal. Because of her, I have been maligned by the whole world. But that apart, after I left school she said all kinds of things about me, because of which I lost all my friends. I do not want to talk to her any more. I request you to not talk about her to me, from today."

During the fact-finding activity the interiority of our subjects remained elusive. The subjects were either unable or unwilling to speak in the presence of family control. Paradoxically, our lack of success in this regard itself rendered the contours of our project more precisely visible. All the stories clearly indicate the control that family and state exercise over women's sexuality.

Manjula, a married subject with a small child, and her partner Meeta, a separated woman, met at their workplace in the city. Manjula's husband lived in the village. Meeta had come to the city from her village to earn a livelihood after terminating her marriage. They began living together. Their friend Shobha, who introduced us to the couple, says, "Manjula and Meeta had already been at the workplace I joined for two years. They were known as the 'miyan-bibi jodi' (husband-wife pair). They always reported for their duty together, Meeta riding a bicycle with Manjula sitting behind on the carrier." Their choice of garments—Meeta always dressed like a man in trousers and shirt, while Manjula wore women's clothes—seemed to replicate stereotypical male-female gender coding. However, Shobha, who knows the couple fairly well, recognizes that a same-sex couple cannot replicate heterosexual power equations. She commented, "In a relationship between two women, one will not eat after the other has eaten, or get up early to do chores and go to sleep late finishing chores, or meekly obey the other without question, as it is in man-woman relationships." Meeta says,

> A number of my friends, like Shobha, think that I do not teach Manjula how to do things for herself because I am afraid she may run off and become independent. But if this was true, would I have taught her whatever I have thus far? Going out of the house on her own, being on her own, talking to

> people confidently . . . When we met in the training camp, she was not as assertive as you see her today. She had lived within her family all her life, was accustomed to being sheltered and obedient, even though they were in the city. She was not given the chance to learn a simple thing like cycling.

Manjula nodded her head in agreement. "Yes, I have learnt a lot being with Meeta, but it is also because I began to work."

Using the term "husband-wife" to describe homosexual partnership can be deceptive because in practice these relationships are often egalitarian. Unlike a traditional heterosexual couple Manjula and Meeta, for instance, talk openly about the frictions in their relationship. In choosing the extent and the manner of their telling, easy and almost casual, they project an apparent transparency that skillfully deflects further interrogation. In the village they will not be allowed to live together as "friends" but in the relative anonymity of a smaller city the partial visibility of their "friendship" has protected them from social judgment and punishment.

Same-sex partners, whether living separately or together, have different notions of family, but more than one subject felt that good relationships were based on a sense of friendship. Mary, a single woman involved with a married woman, said, "I think we make a good couple. We have the same expectations of each other. Even though we live in separate houses we live like a family. Sometimes she comes to stay with me and sometimes I go over. It takes about an hour-and-a-half to reach the other's house. Recently, when she had a fight with her husband, she came over to my house and stayed with me for a month." A little later during the interview she added,

> When we had a misunderstanding we talked with one another and cleared the misunderstanding and we were together again, our friendship stronger. We became such friends . . . how do I describe our friendship? We did not even have to talk to one another. We looked into each other's eyes and understood. It is something very deep, as if we always knew one another. It feels like coming home at last, I found myself. All I can say is that we are crazy about one another.

Some subjects had resisted the almost intolerable pressures of an arranged marriage. At other times this resulted in the relationship being sustained alongside of or despite the complexities of marriage and motherhood. Razia and Sabo, from a village in Uttar Pradesh, had loved one another from childhood. Razia said,

> As children we girls lived, slept, ate, worked together. We had dreams of remaining single, being together. But fate was against it . . . As we grew up together we came close to one another . . . what followed was bound to be. We touched each other, feeling, and enjoying the other's touch all over the body . . . We found on our bodies the special places which gave us pleasure

> and we sought each other out for the giving and taking of that pleasure. We love each other. It is simply so comforting to be with her . . . Sleeping with a man is not enjoyable, nothing like what we enjoyed with each other.

Culturally sanctioned spaces for the expression of female friendships and bonding rituals have always existed in India and have a long history of being aesthetically imaged within the approved canon (see Bhaiya, Spring, this volume). Mythology, miniature paintings, temple carvings, lyrics of classical poetry and music, folk songs, stories, ceremonials, all provide rich variations of the figure of the *sakhi* or best friend, the *dasi* or faithful maidservant or confidante who carries messages, brings good and bad news, arranges (strictly heterosexual) trysts, testifies to partings and unions, and shoulders the weight of the heroine's sorrow if love is unrequited, and rapture if the love is returned. The ordered symbolic world of connotation and aesthetic ideology socially translates itself in sanctioning gynocentric spaces that permit the articulation of nonsexualized female friendships, or rituals and celebrations, such as fasts and festivals, that sometimes privilege married women. Such spaces, however, do not accommodate the articulation of sexualized female friendships that are perceived as threatening, deviant, obscene, corrupt, and sinful.

For instance, the relationship of Manjula and Meeta was described by the subjects themselves as a friendship, while on the contrary, people in their context called them "miya-bibi jodi" (husband-wife pair) with a slight note of contempt. Meeta insisted, "We are only friends. It is not what you understand it to be." When I asked Meeta what it was she thought I had understood, she dug her hands deeper into her trouser pocket and looked away.

The gendered spaces and codes prescribed for women in the sociology of daily life exclude the visually more masculine or androgynous subjects or renders them an ever-problematic and often shocking exception to the rule. From early childhood our subject Vimlesh had refused to feminize her boyish appearance. "She would cut the frock with scissors whenever I made her wear one," her mother had told us. All her life Vimlesh kept very short hair and dressed only in men's clothes. When we asked her how she dealt with phobic stares and derogatory comments in public, she bravely said, "I am not bothered by other people's opinions . . ." Vimlesh was initially aloof even when she talked to us. Later it became apparent to us that her reserve was a habit, developed in response to the pressures of having to negotiate her complex situation completely on her own.

Hasina, another subject who denies being in a same-sex relationship, describes her first meeting with her "friend" thus:

> I was standing by the well in the *kachehri* (local court) compound one day, all dressed up in red. At that time he emerged from the well and told me,

> "I love you." He came for me disguised as a woman and cast on me a magical spell. I cannot explain it. I cannot live without her. She has not come from your and my world; she has come from the world of the spirits.

Hasina's story, based on the logic of supernaturalism, radically decenters the heterosexist paradigm and the dichotomous rationale of male-female duality, which in patriarchal societies silences homoeroticism, legitimizes male exclusivity over the female body, and confines female sexual agency to reproductive processes.

Vimlesh resists the binary division of male-female. She asks,

> Do bodies alone make us men and women? First, we are not all that different when we are young . . . when my body began to change like all men and women's bodies do . . . I felt strange. Besides, no one had prepared me for these changes. But I had to accept the law of nature. I thought, because of these changes I cannot stop living. I had to overcome the shock, adjust to these new developments in my body. But I hate the life of a girl. If I could, I would ask Brahma [the Creator of the universe in the Hindu pantheon], why did he make me a girl, a woman? If it was within my control, I would change my body. But the truth is that I can change my clothes but not what is within the clothes. I say I am a man. I choose to be one.

Any implicit suggestion, or explicit proof, that the homosocial space of female friendship is also potentially or in actuality homoerotic, is countered with immediate punishment. When we heard about Sheila, one of our subjects, we were told that she was well-liked in her village. We were given various descriptions of her. She "was not a bad woman." She was not linked to any man, so her character was without a blemish until "it was found out that her job was to sell women." She had a close relationship with a Muslim woman. They were inseparable. Their friendship was highly visible. When the family found out that their daughter was not prepared to marry because of her bond with Sheila, they plotted to have Sheila thrown out of the village. Sheila had to leave, but she returned quietly on the day her friend was to be married and eloped with her. By making off with "*hamari beti*" (our daughter), she had challenged the honor of the entire village. A week later they were sighted in a nearby village and were forcibly brought back. Sheila was locked up for two days, beaten, and stripped to verify that she was indeed a woman. Before being released, her face was blackened and she was paraded around the village with a garland of shoes around her neck. A man who took part in this proudly declared, "We did not report the incident to the police because 'our daughter' would also have been dragged into the mess. Besides, the whole affair of two women developing such relations would have brought shame upon our village. We settled things amongst ourselves."

Conclusion

The mainstream insistence on slotting the marginalized as a problematic "other" (not an "other" with problems but an "other" who *is* in and of itself, existentially, a problem) is exemplified by the persistent political and sociocultural silence, invisibility, and absence conferred on lesbians in India. There are few autonomous, nonheterosexist relationship models and little or no thoughtful media coverage of homosexual issues. The heterosexual paradigm firmly denies that noninstitutionalized relationships may in fact offer valuable alternative models of sexuality, family, and community within the all-pervading culture of heterosexuality and its prescribed, gender-specific regime centering on marriage.

We have come to a tentative understanding of some ways in which our subjects resisted this patriarchal regime. There were obvious contradictions in rhetoric and behavior, for in some cases subjects denied that they were in a same-sex relationship, but at the same time they refused to marry, or if they were married, refused to make the marriage work. In most of the stories we documented, the subjects have had to separate from their lovers due to family pressures, lack of support and support structures, compulsory marriage, or other obligations and coercions.

Our subjects skillfully used the patriarchally sanctioned space of "female friendship" since it was seen as nonsexual and therefore nonthreatening. Often, socioeconomic necessity was in fact used as the rationale to live together, with both partners working—they shared living space, rent, finances, and domestic responsibilities. Subjects also used traditional family structures to participate in one another's lives, sometimes to the extent of supporting each other's dependents and relatives. The more masculine subjects tended to consistently adopt male modes in order to create a space for themselves in a society where men are more privileged (see also Minturn and Kapoor 1993).

In the face of overwhelming opposition and intractable circumstances, our subjects have tried to realize their dreams. It is humbling to interact with such heroism that will never be celebrated. Instead the women battle daily with the constant threat of being disgraced, ostracized, or even killed. These so-called ordinary, obscure, and anonymous lives are in fact quite extraordinary.

Notes

Thanks to Astraea (National Lesbian Action Foundation), New York, for their financial support, patience, and constant encouragement. I thank Rohit and Reenu Sharma, Indira Pathak, Nighat Gandhi, Shernaz Italia, Freny Khodaji, Padma Singh, Ashley Trellis, Arunesh Mayyar, Ranjana Padhi, Ashwini Sukthankar,

SatyaNagpaul, Kanchana Natarajan, Julia Dutta, and other friends who supported me in many, many ways. I am indebted to all the women who agreed to be my subjects, who opened their lives and their homes to me. I am equally indebted to women who shared their life experiences with me, but did not wish to be written about. A very special thanks to SV who patiently did the editing and whose faith in the project never faltered

1. The reports, written by K.C. Sebastian, were published in June 28–July 11, 1998 and June 1–15, 1999.
2. Letter dated February 20, 2001, signed by Sehba Farooqui on behalf of the State Council of Delhi State Committee of NFIW.

References Cited

ABVA (AIDS Bhedbhav Virodhi Andolan). 1999. *People like us*. New Delhi: Imprint.

Bhaiya, Abha, ed. 1996. *Kinaron Pe Ugti Pehchan* (Identities Growing on the Margins). New Delhi: Raj Kamal Prakashan.

Caleri, Campaign for Lesbian Rights. 1999. *Khamosh! Emergency Jari Hai!* (Lesbian Emergence: A Citizens' Report). New Delhi.

Minturn, Leigh and Swaran Kapoor. 1993. *Sita's daughters: Coming out of purdah*. New York: Oxford University Press.

Report: Fifth National Conference of Women's Movements, 1994. Tirupati, January 23–26.

Report: Sixth National Conference of Women's Movements, 1996. Ranchi, December 28–30.

Index